PEN
THE TR

A. Revathi is a writer, actor and activist based in Bangalore. She works with Sangama, a sexuality minorities human rights organization for individuals oppressed due to their sexual preference. She is the author of *Unarvum Uruvamum*; and her autobiography, *The Truth about Me*, is the first of its kind in English from a member of the hijra community.

V. Geetha is a writer, translator, social historian and activist. She has been active in the Indian women's movement since 1988, and has written widely, both in Tamil and English, on gender, popular culture, caste and politics of Tamil Nadu.

The Truth about Me

A Hijra Life Story

A. Revathi

Translated from Tamil by V. Geetha

PENGUIN BOOKS

PENGUIN BOOKS
Published by the Penguin Group
Penguin Books India Pvt. Ltd, 11 Community Centre, Panchsheel Park, New Delhi 110 017, India
Penguin Group (USA) Inc., 375 Hudson Street, New York, New York 10014, USA
Penguin Group (Canada), 90 Eglinton Avenue East, Suite 700, Toronto, Ontario, M4P 2Y3, Canada (a division of Pearson Penguin Canada Inc.)
Penguin Books Ltd, 80 Strand, London WC2R 0RL, England
Penguin Ireland, 25 St Stephen's Green, Dublin 2, Ireland (a division of Penguin Books Ltd)
Penguin Group (Australia), 250 Camberwell Road, Camberwell, Victoria 3124, Australia (a division of Pearson Australia Group Pty Ltd)
Penguin Group (NZ), 67 Apollo Drive, Rosedale, North Shore 0632, New Zealand (a division of Pearson New Zealand Ltd)
Penguin Group (South Africa) (Pty) Ltd, 24 Sturdee Avenue, Rosebank, Johannesburg 2196, South Africa

Penguin Books Ltd, Registered Offices: 80 Strand, London WC2R 0RL, England

First published by Penguin Books India 2010

10 9 8 7 6 5 4 3 2 1

ISBN 9780143068365

Typeset in *Bembo* by Mantra Virtual Services, New Delhi
Printed at Manipal Press Ltd, Manipal

preface

In our society we speak the language of rights loud and often. But do the marginalized really have access to these rights? Individuals are denied their rights in the name of sex, sexuality, caste and religion. They have to either arrive at a compromise or engage in a struggle. I am one such individual who has been marginalized because I was born a male and wanted to live my life as a woman. *The Truth about Me* is about my everyday experience of discrimination, ridicule and pain; it is also about my endurance and my joys.

As a hijra I get pushed to the fringes of society. Yet I have dared to share my innermost life with you—about being a hijra and also about doing sex work. My story is not meant to offend, accuse or hurt anyone's sentiments. My aim is to introduce to the readers the lives of hijras, their distict culture, and their dreams and desires.

I am proud of the results wrought in the state of Tamil Nadu by my book *Unarvum Uruvamum*. I hope now that by publishing my life story, larger changes can be achieved. I hope this book of mine will make people see that hijras are capable of more than just begging and sex work. I do not seek sympathy from society or the government. I seek to show that we hijras do have the right to live in this society.

I thank Ravi Singh at Penguin for publishing my story. I thank V. Geetha for translating my story and R. Sivapriya for editing it. I also thank Sudeshna Shome Ghosh for her support and help.

22 December 2009
Bangalore

one

I am from a small village in Namakkal taluk, Salem district. If I am to describe the village to you, I would start with the Mariamman and Vinayakar temples that are right in the middle of the village. Beyond the village boundary, skirting the cremation ground, is the Kaliamman temple. There's a school from half standard up to the fifth standard. You'll have to go to Namakkal town to study any further. The town is about three kilometres away and has the Namagiri Amman–Narasimha Perumal temple and the Hanuman temple. There is also the famous hill fort, which is really a temple carved out of a single rock. All around it runs a high wall built in the time of Tipu Sultan. Every year, in the month of Panguni (mid-March to mid-April), there is a ten-day-long temple festival.

If you want to know about the castes in the village, there are the upper castes and lower castes. The Gounders are upper caste. The lower castes do not live inside the village, but separately, in the fringes. They come into the village only to work in fields owned by the Gounders. Even when there is a temple festival, they do not enter the temple precincts, but stand outside and offer worship. When it comes to marriage, everyone marries within their own kind but only after the village panchayat has met and decided on the merits of the case.

Around the village are several rock formations. One of them is called the Sun Rock. If you are to see it at dawn, you'll find that it looks as if the sun is rising from behind it. It is a beautiful sight. The Sanyasi Rock is also well known. People say that a sanyasi once consecrated and worshipped a sivalingam on top of this rock.

Lorries, workshops that build 'bodies' for lorries, hatcheries for chickens and eggs—these are the things Namakkal is known for. Around the town are fields ripe with paddy, sugarcane, corn, tubers and flowers. And so I can go on about my hometown.

I WAS BORN last in a family of five with three brothers and a sister. My parents named me Doraisamy and since I was the youngest son, I got a lot of attention and affection from both my parents. We lived in an old double-storeyed pucca house in those days. It was limewashed and had a large frontyard. Facing the entrance was a cowshed. At that time, we owned two lorries and five acres of dry land. My father drove a lorry, with my eldest brother helping out as a cleaner.

My father had a difficult time with his milk-delivery business. He would leave home with my brothers at 5 o'clock in the morning and drive to the villages nearby, collect the waiting cans of milk and deliver these to the milk factory. He had to do this by 9.30. In the afternoon, he had to leave at 4 o'clock and do the same thing all over again. If the lorry broke down and we delivered the milk late, or if the milk turned rancid because of the delay, we earned that much less—they cut the costs of spoilt milk from the 'tender' money owed to us. But if the milk went bad much after it was delivered, then that was not our problem. The factory would have to deal with angry buyers.

For my father and brothers, the day ended at 10. They would eat their dinner only after their work is done. My mother stayed up every night waiting to serve them food. My sister and I were asleep by this time. My father would usually have rice with sambar, followed by a little rice with rasam. Then he would mix curd with rice and wake me up saying, 'Little one, my love, won't you wake up? Open your eyes and eat this ball of rice. I never quite woke up, but managed to swallow the food in a haze of sleep.

My sister and brothers went to the school in the town. I think I must have been around ten, studying in Class 5. I would go to the village school along with the girls from the neighbourhood and return with them. I played only girls' games. I loved to sweep the frontyard clean and draw the kolam every morning. I even helped my mother in the kitchen, sweeping and swabbing, washing vessels. My work was certainly not tidy, not like that of grown-up women. But all the same, I would do it with confidence. On days when the kolam outside the yard opposite ours was more beautiful, I would smudge the marks with my feet and flee before I was discovered.

As soon as I got home from school, I would wear my sister's long skirt and blouse, twist a long towel around my head and let it trail down my back like a braid. I would then walk as if I was a shy bride, my eyes to the ground, and everyone would laugh. No one thought much of it then, for I was little. They reasoned, 'He'll outgrow all this when he grows older,' and did not say much else. But boys at school, as well as men and women who saw me outside the house, would call out 'Hey, Number 9!', 'female thing', and 'female boy'. Some even teased me, saying, 'Aren't you a boy? Why do you walk like a girl? Why do you wear girls' clothes?' I understood that I was indeed like that. In fact, I wanted to be so.

A college student had rented the house opposite ours around that time. Whenever I needed help with my school lessons, I would go to him. Sometimes, I would end up staying there for long and even play with the man. He would pinch my cheeks, kiss me and hug me. I liked it when he did these things. But when he called me 'female thing', I felt painfully shy.

He once asked me, 'Why do you sweep the frontyard and draw the kolam, like a girl?' I replied, 'I've been drawing kolams since I was in Class 3. My mother would wake me up early even then. While she milked the cow, I swept the yard, splashed water mixed with cow dung and drew the kolam. My sister doesn't wake up in time to do these things. And when she does wake up, she jealously complains to my mother that the girl-boy has done the kolam all wrong and not swept the yard well.'

ON HOLIDAYS, CHILDREN whose families had land would bring their cows and goats to graze on the village pasture land. I was part of this group. We built temples, climbed palm trees and brought down juicy nuts. My family's field was about a mile's distance from the village and was known as karungadu. When the sun was high, we would switch on the water pump in the field, let the tank fill up and then dive in. When the field stood tall and gently green with crops, I walked and sang and danced to my heart's content, imagining myself to be a girl.

I remember the time when they had planted sweet potato in our field. Usually those who worked our field stayed with us. But this time around, more hands were needed and more men and women were brought in. The men dug and raised the bunds and watered the fields, whereas the women planted. I stood along with the women and helped with the planting. My mother shooed me away though, saying that I did not know how to plant.

I then teamed up with the son of one of the workers, and together we built a mud temple in the shade of a coconut tree. He offered to share a murukku with me. No sooner had I started munching, my mother came rushing at me. She grabbed the murukku from me and threw it down. I couldn't understand why my mother was scolding us. 'You must not accept food from that child. It'll pollute you!' she said. 'What does "pollute" mean?' I asked her. 'You won't understand, you are too young,' she retorted. 'At school we eat like this— we share sweets by biting off pieces. Is that polluting too?' I asked. 'If you accept food from Chakkili children, God will poke your eyes out,' said my mother. I was perplexed, for I did not know what a Chakkili child was or how he looked. But I made sure I never took food from anyone, for I was truly afraid of God poking my eyes out.

At school in the village, boys played at gilli–danda, robber–police, cricket and football. I played with the girls—we played five stones, hopscotch and hide-and-seek. On some days, one of the girls would ask me, 'Why do you play with us? Boys like you are playing there, go join them.' 'I don't wish to play with them,' I'd reply. I was teased often at school, for behaving like a girl, for doing women's work, and on the streets too, was bullied often. I had a stammer and would also get teased for that. I was thus a regular source of amusement and curiosity.

Since I wore the same uniform every day to school, frequent washing had worn down the seat of my shorts. My classmates used to stick a bit of rolled paper into the tear, clap their hands loudly and scream 'Post box!' I would go all hot and angry and hurl obscenities at them, as I have heard women do. This would set them off even more, and they would chant, 'Girl-boy!' 'Ali!' 'Number 9!' My heart would sink at these words, but I also felt faintly gratified and even happy that these boys actually conceded that I was somehow a woman.

In class, I would sit staring at the girls, taking note of the way their braids fell, the intricate knot of their colourful ribbons, the jasmine and kanakambaram they wore in their hair, and their skirts and blouses. I longed to be like them and suffered that I could not dress so. Since I was often inattentive, the teacher would pinch me on my thigh and make me stand on the bench. I remember having knelt down on the floor too. I think I was punished not just for being distracted, but also because I spoke like a girl, holding my body coyly like one. I remember being caned for 'not being brave like a boy'. And since I did not play boys' games, I got punished by the PT teacher too. He would box my ears and yell, 'Are you a girl or what? Pull your trousers down, let me check.' He would make as if he was going to strip me and I would start crying. The other boys laughed at this.

I did know that I behaved like a girl, it felt natural for me to do so. I did not know how to be like a boy. It was like eating for me—just as I would not stop eating because someone asked me not to eat, I felt I could not stop being a girl, because others told me I ought not to be so.

two

I passed my Class 5 exams and started going to school in the town. I wore khakhi shorts and a white shirt and was very happy going to the big town school. I felt scared walking on the big roads, especially when I saw lorries, buses, cars and bicycles rushing past me. And then I would remember my mother's anxious advice—that I ought to hold the hands of one of the bigger boys and learn to avoid going close to these speeding vehicles. I walked those three miles every day trailing behind older children.

On my way to school, I enjoyed looking at the tall houses that lined the roads. I loved the flowers peeping over high walls and often resolved that I would pluck them some day and store them in my tiffin-box. One day I managed to climb a wall when no one was looking and pluck a flower. I began to do that often and would pray to Vinayakar in my village and offer the stolen flowers in worship.

I think I was in Class 7 when I took part in the school annual day celebrations. There was to be dancing, singing and also a play. I played Chandramathi in *Harishchandra*. In the play, Chandramathi's child dies of a snake-bite and she has to bury the corpse. She takes it to the burial ground but is told that she has to make an offering of money to the grave-digger's master. The grave-digger is actually her husband, but he refuses to relent on the payment. She then returns to the village to beg for graveyard money. For this particular scene, I had to walk to a sad song, my false hair streaming about me, and the sari end held out like a begging bowl. I think I did this exceptionally well, because everyone praised me saying that I looked and acted like a real woman. This pleased me very much.

At school, I felt fear looking at the big boys, those in Classes 11 and 12. And they were always on the lookout for me. They had marked me out from the others. Whenever I walked past them on the school grounds, they would yell, 'Hey girl-boy' and hit me on the head with their balled-up fists. They would pinch me on my chest, and taunt me saying, 'When you played Chandramathi, what did you stuff your chest with?' On the days this happened, I did not want to sit next to the boys in my class, for I felt coy and shy. On the other hand, I felt drawn to the boys who did not tease me, and I imagined I was in love with them. This confused me—I was a boy and yet I felt I could love other boys. Was this right or wrong?

I could not talk to anyone about my confusions. Not to my brothers, or my parents. Nor could I stop my heart from wandering and so I went about as if crazed. I was fed up with being teased, and besides was not doing well in my English classes. I stopped going to school regularly. I began to cut classes and, stealing money from my father's shirt pocket, went to the cinema often. The films were in black and white then. I loved watching those starring MGR and Saroja Devi. I would buy a floor ticket for 75 paise and for the two and a half hours that I was in the cinema hall, I forgot my troubles. But when I came out, my confusions would flare up again. And so, after the morning show, I would go to faraway fields, bemoan my fate and sometimes sing the songs I had heard Saroja Devi sing earlier in the day. I even thought I was her, as I echoed her songs. Around evening, I would return home, just as if I had gone to school.

My family was rather keen that I study well. Even when it was clear I was not doing this, my mother would say, 'See, because they did not study, your brothers have to spend their time in greasy banians and shirts, working in the sun and rain. Do you want to suffer like them? No need for that if you study.' Since my father was busy with his lorry rides, he did not have time for me. My mother was busy too, with goats and cows, working in the fields and at home, and so could not worry about me beyond a point. Only my sister spent time with me and we often fought.

Somehow my family got to know that I was not going to school regularly. My mother complained to my brothers and thus earned me a thrashing.

They had a plan for me. 'You mother-fucking sissy! So young and yet you steal money to go to the cinema! Can't you see that we are working only to send you to school? Make sure that you go to school. From now on, first thing in the morning, you will gather all the buffalo dung there is, feed the animals, water them and then leave for school. You'll do this in the evening too, as soon as you return home. Only then you'll know what life is, how tough it is.'

How could I expect them to know what I was going through? I bundled my feelings and confusions into a tight roll, laid it aside, and, in spite of all the teasing and bullying, went about doing what I was asked to do. This lasted for some time.

THAT WAS THE year of the Mariamman festival in our village. It was a marvellous affair, with the entire village lit with lamps, the goddess, decorated and lovely, and the night sky lighted by fireworks. In every home, women pounded rice into flour and made a paste by mixing it with syrup. They placed a lit wick in the paste, thus getting ready a lamp offering, which would be ritually carried to the Mariamman temple. Girls of my age, in flowing silk skirts and half-saris, their oiled hair braided elegantly and adorned with flowers, carried these rice-flour lamps. I was envious and wished that I too could somehow be part of that procession.

In the night, after the rituals and the puja were done with, the boys in the village got ready to stage a play. They had hired actresses from outside for the occasion. An avid watcher of plays, I sat right in front on a sack laid out on the floor and kept staring at the women. When I got home, I stood in front of the mirror and examined myself.

Something came up, the day after, when the goats are sacrificed at the temple. That afternoon, a group of boys decided they would dress up as bears and tigers, policemen, gods and kurathis (female gypsies), and go around the neighbourhood, singing, dancing and collecting money. They asked me if I would like to dress up as a kurathi, since I appeared feminine anyway. I said that I would like to, but confessed that I was afraid of what my brothers would say. They laughed and said, 'Don't be silly. You'll be in disguise and you won't be found out.'

'But I need to wear false hair, earrings and a skirt. Where'll I find those?'

'Those can be hired. There are places in town that rent out clothes and jewellery. And no need to worry about costs. We will earn money from our performance and pay the hire for the costumes and jewels, and also the drummer—we need one for the music.'

I was excited, but again said that I was afraid of my brothers finding out. The others persuaded me saying, 'Look, we are dressing up and dancing for the goddess, and to make our village people happy. If your brothers ask, we'll explain.'

To the world, it appeared that I was dressing up and playing a woman, but inside, I felt I was a woman. I had to make my chest big, and wore a blouse stuffed with cloth balls. With the skirt, anklets, long false braid decorated with paper flowers, kohl-lined eyes and painted lips, I knew I looked beautiful. I looked at myself in the mirror several times, astonished at what I had become. The boy who had to play my partner muttered, 'Hey, Doraisamy, you look like a real woman. If you were one, I'd fall in love with you.' My face flushed with pride and I felt warm and bashful. The other boys sniggered and yet it all felt very good.

The drummer sounded his beat and we stepped out on to the streets. We decided that we would do our first dance in front of the temple. As we made our way to the temple, we found the streets full of people, trying to guess who was who. When the boy dressed as a bear took off his mask and waved it at the crowd, some yelled out, 'That's Karupannan, son of Munusamy.' Looking at the boy dressed as Vinayakar, a wag observed, 'Look at that balloon of a stomach. That must be Kanthayi's son. No one else has a stomach like that.'

Our party was accompanied by four men who would be in charge of the money that we would eventually collect. They were also meant to protect us from the watching crowd. As we walked past, a few people called out to these men, 'Who's this kurathi? From this village or from outside? Is she a real woman or a dressed-up one?'

'You all know this lad,' replied one of the men. 'But I won't tell you who he is. Find out for yourself.'

We began to dance as soon as we reached the temple. A few drunken men from the crowd of watchers joined us and began to dance too. It was a lot of fun and there was much excitement all around. One of the drunken men veered close to me, and touching my chest, muttered, 'What have you got there? Coconut shells?' Irritated, I pushed his hand away, and the crowd roared with laughter on seeing this. I felt dizzy with joy, though I continued to be afraid of my brothers finding out and beating me for dressing up as a woman.

That evening when everything was over, I got rid of my disguise and went home. By then, everyone knew that I was the kurathi at the temple. My sister hissed to my mother, 'Look Amma, he's back,' whereupon my mother snapped,

'Okay, so you dressed up, but why dress up as a girl? Don't you have any shame?'

I insisted that I had done this for the goddess and so got away with it. On that occasion, my family decided not to make much of my dressing up and dancing.

The entire village knew that I had been the kurathi, and so the day after several people called out to me, when I got out of the house. 'Hey, kurathi! Where's your kuravan?' 'You looked like a woman. Honestly, we couldn't make out that you were not one.' A few people even told me that I ought to have been born a woman and that it was unfortunate that I had been born a man. I felt elated from all this praise.

In my kurathi's garb, I could express all those female feelings that I usually have to suppress and so felt happy for days afterwards. But I felt troubled by the feelings that men incited in me. I felt horribly shy, and whenever I saw young men, I automatically lowered my head. I felt drawn to them, but wondered if I should not be drawn to women instead, since I was a man. Why did I love men? Was I mad? Was I the only one who felt this way? Or were there others like me, elsewhere in the world? Would I find them, if indeed they were there?

I lived with these questions and doubts, which lay buried deep inside me. Days passed and I wondered when and if I would find answers, and if indeed I would find someone who understood what I felt.

I SOMEHOW GOT to Class 10. I experienced changes in my body and in my being. I experienced a growing sense of irrepressible femaleness, which haunted me, day in and day out. A woman trapped in a man's body was how I thought of myself. But how could that be? Would the world accept me thus? I longed to be known as a woman and felt pain at being considered a man. I longed to be with men, but felt shamed by this feeling. I wondered why God had chosen to inflict this peculiar torture on me, and why He could not have created me wholly male or wholly female. Why am I a flawed being, I wondered often. I might as well die, I thought. I could not study, yet pretended to, and all the time I was obsessed, confused and anxious.

I did not pay attention to my school books, and since, anyway my English was poor, I failed my Class 10 English exam. I got only twenty-six marks. However, I had done well in other subjects. I would have to stay home for a year and take my English exam again. At that time, that was how it was. My father did not scold me, though. 'If you think you'll do well, I will send you to school again. Otherwise, come and help out with the lorry.'

My brothers were not so charitable. 'We knew it'd come to this. We knew this girl-boy would fail. We knew it even then, when he started to dress up as a girl, that he was up to no good. And now he has to stay at home and waste a year!'

But I worked hard that year, washing their clothes, gathering cowdung, keeping the cowshed clean, cutting grass for the cows... I did want to take my English exam again, and asked if I could go to a tuition class to help me pass it. My request was granted. I began to go for tuitions in the town from 6 to 8 in the evenings and was given a cycle to go up and down.

There was a Mariamman festival that year too, and as always

the village wore a joyous, festive look. Deep down, I was sad. I was called to dance once again, not to act though. I was to dance to a salutation to the gods just before the play for the year began. They wanted me because they thought I made a good woman, and that I looked beautiful. The spectators like you, they said. I requested the girl who lived in a neighbouring house to help me with my clothes and hair. When ready, I danced to the tune of two songs, 'Goddess of the arts, who bears a ruby veena in her hands' and 'She who is a golden peacock'. I must have danced competently, for as soon as I got off the stage, several people came forward to shake my hands. Others noted that I had danced well indeed, and yet others yelled, 'Damn good, son-in-law!' As I walked home, urchins followed me, chorusing, 'Disguise! Disguise! Female disguise!'

I finally reached my neighbour's house. I had not worn a disguise I said to myself; I had given form to my real feelings. I was unwilling to shed my female clothes and stood for several minutes in front of the mirror. My neighbour rushed in and whispered, 'Dorai! Take it all off! I don't want your brothers scolding me!' Reluctantly, I changed into my regular clothes. As I re-emerged in my man's garb, I felt that I was in disguise, and that I had left my real self behind.

three

I saw the fort looming over the town every evening when I cycled to Namakkal for my classes. One evening, I decided to climb up to the fort. Half way up the hill, I sat down to enjoy the view. I could see the town and the outlying villages, including my own. I could even spot the rocks that formed a ring around it. It was peaceful there and I was hardly aware of time passing. It must have been around 7 in the evening, when the twilight hour gives way to the gathering dark. I saw four men dressed in lungis climbing up. I noticed that they swung their hands as they walked and that one of them had grown his hair long. They stopped at a point below where I was sitting and I could hear them address each other as girls do. After some time, they began to dance a women's dance.

The man with long hair had spotted me and began to climb up. I was wondering whether these men were perhaps like me, female inside and male outside, when the man arrived and sat down beside me. 'Where're you from, lad?' I mentioned the name of my village and asked him where he was from. He gave his name and so we began to talk. It appeared to me that we were similar, that our voices and gestures were not very different. And as I continued to speak, I felt close to him, even affectionate, and my heart grew calm.

After I met these men, I started attending tuition classes only three times a week. On other evenings, I would go up the hill and spend time with my new friends. We talked, sang, danced. The oldest of them, he was probably thirty years old, knew Bharatanatyam and even taught me a few steps. From them, I learnt that there were people like us—who wore saris and had had an 'operation', and that they lived in Erode and Dindigul. I learnt too that some of them even went as far as Delhi and Mumbai. But here, in Namakkal, we could be women only on the hill. We could fold up our lungis and address each other as women. I guess these men were more my female comrades than mere friends; my *thozhi*s, in fact. On some evenings, we were there until it was 8 o'clock and it was time for me to go home. When my mother questioned me about coming home late every day, I told her that I stayed back to study with others in my tuition class.

Those who come to visit the hill-fort do so in the mornings and are all gone by sunset. We, on the other hand, went up the hill only after 6 o'clock and since there was no one around then, felt we could be women and do as we pleased. The odd rowdy did come up the hill and whenever we saw them come in a group, we fled. One evening, though, two rowdies caught hold of one of my thozhis and marched her off, further up the hill. We could not fight with them, but neither did we want to leave until she was back with us. After about half an hour, and much to our relief, she returned. She looked exhausted. Sweat ran down her face and she could barely walk.

I asked her what had happened, and she said that they had done *danda* on her. 'Danda? What is that?' I asked. She told me that they had forced her to have sex through her mouth and her backside, 'near where you shit,' she explained. I was horrified and wondered if such things were indeed possible. She looked so wan and tired and was in obvious pain. When I asked the others about this, they said that this is how we would have to have sex: 'If you are a girl-boy you have no choice. Don't you know this? Don't you want have sex this way?'

When I said that I did not want to have sex that way, and, above all, I desired to become a woman, marry an educated man and only then have sex, they laughed derisively. I was told that it was not all that easy to become a woman. Only if I went to Mumbai and Delhi and stayed for years with those who wore saris and had undergone 'operations', could I hope to become one.

SOME OF MY friends had grown their nails long, and wore nail polish. They stood at bus stands, their lungis folded above their knees, and even dared address each other as women. I liked their style, the way they spoke and gestured, but was afraid to be like them. I was scared that someone from my village would notice and report home that I was a girl-boy. Some men teased my friends, calling them Number 9. Some others would wink at them. While I felt jealous of them for being the way they were, I did not like the way they were stared at and the manner in which they were teased. And so I kept away from them in public.

I learnt from my friends that there was a woman, an 'amma', in Dindigul, who wore saris and had had an 'operation', and that she received other women like her from Mumbai and Delhi during the time of the Goddess festival. This was during the month of Aadi (mid-July to mid-August), when the Amman festival was celebrated there. I decided to go meet these women. Everyone at home was busy with the preparations for my sister's marriage in Aavani (mid-August to mid-September) and I thought I would be able to sneak away to Dindigul to see the sari-clad women. I used some of my tuition money to buy bangles, ribbons and earrings. I had also hidden away my sister's skirt, blouse and half-sari.

My friends and I boarded the bus to Dindigul on the morning of the temple festival. There were five of us. To everyone on the bus, we must have appeared to be boys and men. Only on the hill-fort did we address each other as women. But that morning, my friends began to address each other as women would. They cast blushing glances at men and from time to time dusted powder on their faces and applied lipstick. Some on the bus looked at us oddly and I heard them whisper 'Number 9'. Some even asked, 'Are you going to dance? Where's it happening?' This agitated me and I scolded my companions, 'Why behave like this on a bus? Why apply make-up here? Look at how they're talking about us.' To which they replied: 'Keep quiet! We can't be ourselves at home or do what we want to. There isn't anyone on this bus who knows us. It's only like this, without anyone at home knowing, that can we do what we wish to do—express our desire to be women. We can't ever live if we fear being teased. Or dare express our feelings. We must then reconcile ourselves to a life that is neither here nor there. Come on! Let's be happy at least for the time we're away.'

But I would not be placated. I was a boy, and if I behaved like a girl, obviously people would make fun of me. It felt wrong to me that we should behave thus. If we so wished, perhaps we ought to dress as women, wear women's clothes and jewellery, and appear modest in public. Then, we might not get teased. If we were heckled, we could always justly retort, 'How dare you tease a woman?' I wanted to live as a woman, at the same time I knew that I would have to live in fear of what people thought and said.

Soon we got off at Dindigul and found our way to Amma's place where we found at least ten other older people. If you looked at them you would not suspect that they were actually like us, for they looked like real women. Only their voices gave them away. As soon as they saw us, they knew what we were all about. 'Come, *bete*, where are you all from? Say *paampaduthi* to your elders,' they instructed us. I saw my friends touching the feet of each one of the sari-clad and saying, 'Paampaduthi amma.' I did the same, bent and touched their feet, all the while saying, 'Paampaduthi amma.' As soon as we did this, the sari-clad said, '*Jiyo, jiyo.*' I learnt that this was very important, that a feminine man offers respect to the sari-clad and earns their goodwill. This is our tradition, I discovered.

The sari-clad women asked us who we were, where we were from and what was it that we felt. We answered all their questions. An elder asked me my name. When I gave my name as Doraisamy, she said, 'I meant your female name.' I explained that I did not have one yet. We then asked if we could wear the saris we had brought with us and make ourselves up as women. They said yes, and so we changed into saris, wore wigs and also the jewels we had brought along. Thus arrayed, we came out and stood in front of the elders. One of them said to me, 'You look like the actress Revathi.' And in my heart, I imagined that was my name—Revathi. I looked at myself in the mirror and felt a glow of pride. I did look like a woman. It was at that moment that I was convinced I was indeed one.

I was around fourteen or fifteen years of age. I was tall and slim and had no facial hair, or even hair on my arms and legs. One of the elders exclaimed on seeing me, 'If this one were to undergo *nirvaanam*, she'd look like a real woman.' (To undergo nirvaanam is to submit to castration and turn into a full woman. This is what was meant by 'having an operation' I later found out.) I felt even more gratified on hearing this. My friends nodded and said, 'Yes, amma, she has no facial hair and is very beautiful.'

I asked one of the elders how she had become a woman. I said I too wanted to be like her and asked what I should do. She said that if I had to go and stay with others like me, have my ears and nose pierced, let my hair grow long and learn their ways. I would have to agree to be a *chela* to a guru and do whatever work I'm given. If I stayed for one or two years with a guru and earned for her, then she would agree to help me become a woman.

A guru was like a mother, she would allow her chelas to share her home, and would clothe and feed them. Like a daughter, the chela was adopted by a guru according to tradition. It turned out that the elder I spoke to was from near my village. This made me happy and I requested her to accept me as her chela. She said, 'Our *jamaat* meets tomorrow evening. I will accept you as a chela in front of the jamaat.'

A jamaat is a meeting of sari-clad elders. They discuss matters of importance to them and others like them, agree to take on chelas, and so on. On the evening of the jamaat in Dindigul, several sari-clad people arrived from towns like Erode and Madurai. There were some like me, who came and changed into saris. A huge pot of rice had been prepared for the group and we were asked to help with the serving of the food and other odd jobs.

I went along with others like me, young girl-boys in saris, to fetch water. I let my pot into the well, watched it fill, leaned over to haul it up, and then took the pot to my hips and began to walk, tucking my sari around my waist, just as I'd seen girls in my village do. We filled several vessels with water. After that, we washed the clothes of the elders. I was thrilled to be doing all this work in women's clothes.

I think of that day as very special, a day that would never happen again—the first time when I did a woman's work just as a woman would. Elated as I was, I did not feel tired. I knew my guru was watching me doing women's work. I felt her eyes on me and knew that she was waiting for me to be her chela, I, who was from the same neighbourhood as she. I felt an inexplicable love between us. It was as if God has created such hearts as these to protect and care for those like me, who had come there leaving their families and homes.

That night I slept next to my guru. Her affectionate embrace was comforting and brought tears to my eyes. At home, I usually slept in my half-pants, but that night I went to sleep as a woman. Whenever I felt that my sari was a bit awry or imagined a bit of leg showing, I drew my feet in, tucked my hands into the folds of my sari and felt all the more womanly. It was not so easy though to fall asleep wearing a wig, a bra, a blouse, a sari, and bangles and earrings. These things made me feel itchy and I wanted to scratch myself constantly. So this is what it is to be born a woman. I wondered how women manage to get any sleep with all this stuff on them.

The next morning when we left for the fields, our open-air bathroom, my guru told me that I ought to be careful and make sure that my penis was not visible when I peed. 'We are clad like women. And so people think we are rid of it. They see us as women, so make sure you don't let it dangle. Then they'll think you are a man in a woman's garb. Until you are operated upon, make sure that you conceal that thing.'

Around 6 o'clock in the evening, we dressed up, combed our hair, wore flowers and went to the temple with our elders who wore silk saris. We were carrying flour-lamps and sprouted seeds, and the entire street turned up to watch us go. It is the custom for the *pottais* (sari-clad feminine men) to gather at this temple during this time every year and sing and dance the *gummi*. So no one teased us openly, as we walked past the crowd to the temple. There were some who sniggered and some others who winked at us. Some in our group winked back and rolled their eyes. I wanted to do that too, but I told myself that I had not been operated upon and must wait until

I was a real woman. I observed the others keenly, noted their every gesture, the way they walked, and so on.

That night, after we returned home and had our dinner, the jamaat gathered. In front of all the elders, it was decided that such and such would be the chela-daughter of such-and-such elder (who was referred to as so and so's daughter). All of us sat around a plate, on which was spread a white cloth. Betel leaves and 1.25 rupees were placed on it. My guru announced that she would like to adopt me as her chela and for this, she was willing to give 5 rupees and also 1.25 rupees to the jamaat. This latter was referred to as *thandu* (fee) money. The others received the thandu money in my guru's name and placed it on the plate. They took the 5-rupee note and noted that this was 'for Revathi' and muttered, 'Five rupees for Revathi *deen deen*.' At this, the others showed their appreciation by shouting and clapping. I was to address my guru as I would my mother—I would have to call her Amma. My guru in turn announced that I was her daughter, and my name was Revathi and asked me to do paampaduthi to all the elders. I did so and after that my guru hugged and kissed me, and ran her fingers through my hair.

It was two days since I left home, my family and village. That night my guru and a few others were to leave for Delhi. I did not have the heart to return to my village. I was also afraid that my brothers would want to know where I had been and beat me up.

'I am scared. Take me with you to Delhi,' I begged my guru.

'This is my first trip to Delhi. And I am going with the others. I don't know where I'll be staying and what I'll be doing. My child, you don't have to do the sort of work pottais do. You have a family, go back home to your father and mother, study well and find a nice job. The next time I come to Tamil Nadu, we'll meet somewhere. You're my child, there's no doubting that. But you don't have to suffer like me, child.'

I must have looked disappointed, and, sensing my fear and longing, my guru consoled me, 'Look! I'll back from Delhi in six months' time. Till then you stay with your parents. If you feel sad at heart, or if a problem arises at home, you can go and stay with your *nani* in Erode (she meant her own guru, who therefore was my grandmother). My *gurubais* (sisters) and your *kaalaguru* (nani's sister) live there. They sing and dance for a living. I'll introduce you to these other ammas before I leave.'

I began to cry. I had known her only for a day, but I felt towards her as I did towards my birth mother; in fact, I felt even more torn about her, so natural did all of it seem to me. I could not bear being parted from her, she who had understood my feelings, respected me, sought to guide me. I had to leave her now and return to my family and who knows what lay in store for me there. I felt anxiety, dread and a great sadness, and kept crying.

'Look daughter, don't cry, I'll return soon and take you with me. Till then, make sure you keep your hair long.' With these comforting words, my guru left for Delhi.

four

The next morning when the group from Erode left, I decided to accompany them instead of going home. I stayed with them for quite a while, afraid of facing up to the beatings that surely waited for me at home, and afraid too that my family would not let me leave once I got home, and worse, not let me keep my hair long.

My Erode nani managed a dance troupe that performed at temple festivals in the nearby villages. A large troupe comprising nani's chelas and the chelas of chelas, they were of different ages. Troupe members danced the *karagam*, the peacock dance, the *subban-subbi* dance, the *arohara* doctor dance and also performed cycling feats. When there was no dancing to be done, they went away to Mumbai and Delhi to earn a living. They lived together in a housing-board building and all of them were sari-clad, some of them had even undergone the sex-change operation. They told me that I should remain in my lungi and shirt, ought not wear a sari and should wait for my hair to grow. I did not quite understand what they meant, but found out eventually why they had cautioned me thus. If I wore a sari without having grown my hair, I would be seen as a man wearing a sari, and that meant dishonour for the entire household. I learnt too that while we felt like women, it was equally important to look like them, and that long hair was an important marker of being feminine.

My work during this period was washing the clothes of the elders at home, fetching water, and helping with the shopping and cooking. It was hard work, but since I was the youngest I ended doing most of the chores. I was told that all those who are born pottais go through such a phase, and only if they survived this hardship could they hope to be operated upon. Even those who were elders now had started out doing the things that I did. Therefore I did not mind doing the work that I had to do.

When I took clothes to the river for washing, the elders accompanied me. They wore saris, whereas I was in my lungi and shirt. When they got ready to bathe, they would remove their saris only to re-tie them above their breasts in a manner that left their shoulders and legs exposed. They would, like women in my village did, balance their legs on a nearby rock, while applying soap or turmeric powder. Seeing them do this, I too would wear my lungi over my chest and rub soap and turmeric in the same fashion. Some amongst the elders would tease me, 'Look at this boy-girl! Such desire to be female!' Others would reprimand me saying that I ought not do such things until I had been operated upon.

After the bath, we would walk home and, always, I was teased and bullied on the streets.

'What nonsense! Look at this lad! He's rubbed turmeric all over himself, just like these women.'

They would say to the elders, 'Getting your heir ready, are you?'

Not to be outdone, some of them would retort, 'Yes, it's a new girl, want to marry her?'

We would walk home not minding the distance, happy with all the joking and teasing.

My nani, kaalaguru and my guru's sisters were all adept at dancing. They taught me all they knew. We would go up to the terrace of our house and dance. I accompanied them to a temple festival once, all dressed up and ready to dance. I wore a half-skirt and blouse, a waistcoat, a second skirt wrapped around my first, and anklets. I had long, false hair clipped to my real hair. It was then done up as two braids and decorated with paper flowers. They rubbed cream on my face, dusted powder on top of it, touched my eyes and eyebrows with kohl and sprinkled glitter. 'Since this is the first time for you, we're doing all this. But you must soon learn to do your own make-up,' I was told, as I got into an auto-rickshaw along with rest.

We danced in pairs of two, and while a pair did their routine, the rest of us sat alongside the crowd which was gathered in a circle. We got stared at a lot, and I heard people ask rather loudly whether we were men or women or Number 9s or devadasis. Some men made bold to touch us, on our waists or our shoulders. Some others pointed to our breasts and asked, 'Original or duplicate?'

At such moments, I felt despair, and wondered that people could be this way. How we could ever hope to make a living? God has made us this way, I thought, and we have no work of our own, our parents do not understand us and this world looks upon us with distaste. Yet we too go hungry. Above all, we wanted to live as human beings do, with dignity. I tried hard to ignore all that was happening around me.

It was almost a month before I thought of returning home. My sister's marriage was going to take place and I wanted to see my mother and father. I had not heard from my guru and thought that I should perhaps go home. I was hesitant though, because my family would surely ask me where I had gone, and no doubt beat me. On the other hand, I did want to attend my sister's wedding. So, bidding goodbye to my nani, I boarded a bus to Namakkal.

On seeing me, my mother wept and demanded to know where I had been for the past month. My elder brother brought a cricket bat down on my shoulders and asked, 'What happened to you? Did you go mad? We've been searching for you all over. Had you no thought for us?' He hit me again and tried to get an answer out of me. 'You wanted to go to tuition class and we sent you. Then you started coming home late and suddenly one day you went missing. What's going on in your head?'

I did not tell them that I had been at nani's place in Erode. Instead, I said that I had gone with a tuition-class friend to Madurai to see a temple festival. 'I wanted to tell you, but I thought you won't send me, so I went on my own. I thought I would return right away, but was scared you'd beat me. So I stayed back.'

'So why did you come back now? What made you think you won't be beaten a month later?'

'I wanted to be here for akka's marriage. Forgive me this once. I won't go anywhere again. What I did was wrong.' I somehow excused myself and got away with it. Since there was a wedding in the family, everyone thought it was best not stir up trouble. However, my brothers decided that since I spoke like a girl and got teased for being a girl-boy, I was unlikely to study further. After my sister's wedding I was to join them as a cleaner for the family lorry. 'No more tuition for you. You'll be a cleaner from now on. That'll teach you about life, you'll get to see how hard it is. And, by the way, why do you have long hair?'

I replied that I had vowed to go to Tirupati and so had let my hair grow. I said this, thinking that if I mentioned a temple nearby, I would be asked to fulfil my vow immediately, but since Tirupati was in another state, the family would not want to spend a lot of money right away, getting me there. My brothers said, 'All right, we'll go to Tirupati next month.'

My day as a cleaner began at 5 o'clock in the morning. I would get up, clean the lorry's windscreen, fill the radiator with water, dust the driver's seat and light an *agarbathi*. At that time it was my brother who drove the lorry. We went from village to village, picking up cans of milk to deliver to the milk factory. The cans were made of aluminum and each could hold forty litres of milk. I had to roll the cans into the back of the lorry and arrange them village-wise, and in a certain order. The lorry had to reach the cans to the factory on time, otherwise the milk might go bad. Once emptied, the cans had to be re-stacked, again in a village-wise order. By the time we were done with delivering the cans back to the villages, it would be 11 in the morning. It was hard work. If the lorry braked suddenly, the cans would roll off and I had to be behind them. While rolling a can, I would sometimes hurt one of my toes and the nail would come off. I was not offered any bandage or balm. I got used to applying brake oil to the afflicted part and covering it with a rag. My brothers did this too, if they were hurt. Once home, we ate and soon after the meal, I had to grease the lorry and wipe it clean. I usually slept for a bit afterwards, but had to be up at 4 o'clock in the afternoon to take delivery of the evening's milk. We would return home only at 10 in the night.

I continued to grow my hair for some days. I could neither talk about my condition, nor entirely hide it. Every day, my feelings died only to be reborn and to die again. I felt as though I was being whipped about in a whirlpool of emotions. I was like a worm, out in the sun, squirming and ready to die. I wanted to run away, but feared that if my brothers caught me, they would surely kill me. I was also worried that if my friends got into trouble because of me, they might reject me. I doubt if words quite capture the anguish I experienced at having to be a man, wear my lungi folded above my knees, with grease streaks on my face, hands, feet and body. Grease and oil would get into my eyes too.

In the cold months, I felt my toes throb until the pain was unbearable. As they say, it is the hurt foot that gets hurt once more, just as it is the family that does wrong that descends into more wrongdoing. When I had to get underneath the lorry and grease its innards, I would crawl out unthinking and thus hurt my head and back. If there was a piece of iron sticking out, I would emerge bruised and bleeding.

My father was not happy with my cleaning and one day, pointing to the men who worked for him, sneered at me: 'You'll learn only by drinking their piss!' I could not bear it anymore, this pain and hurt that wracked my body and mind—which I could not even mention to anybody. I decided that it would not do for me to continue to live in my parents' home.

But how I was to find out where my guru was? She had not left behind an address. When I was in Erode I heard that she was headed for J. J. Colony, Wazirpur, in Delhi. Should I go there, I wondered. But how was I to go and where would I find the money to travel? For two days, I could not eat or sleep. My hands and legs kept trembling and my heart kept pounding. I was racked by anxiety.

On the third day, around 3 in the afternoon, I found the moment I was looking for. My mother was bathing, my father and brothers were sleeping and the lorry assistants lolling about in the vehicle. This was a good time to slip away. I opened the spice box in my mother's kitchen to see if she had, as she usually does, put away some money there. There was no money but the box held a pair of earrings. My poor mother, she usually stored small change in that box for buying vegetables and provisions. Today, though, she had unscrewed her earrings and left them in the box. What was I to do with these? I did not even know how much a ticket to Delhi cost!

I made up my mind that I'd take the earrings, come what may. However, I was loath to take the pair. I left one behind, and put the other in my pocket. I went into the room in which my father was sleeping and opened the bureau and took out two of my mother's saris. I put them into a yellow cloth bag, afraid all the while that my mother would come out of the bathroom. Scared that I would be caught and brought back home if I took the road, I walked through fields, jumping over canals and bunds. Cornstalks grazed against my skin, causing it to burn. Often I almost tumbled down the path, not knowing where it rose and fell. I had to cross the dry bed of a large pond, overgrown with *elanthai* shrubs. When the elanthai's thorns caught my skin through my clothes, it felt as if a hook had gone through. Not knowing how I was going to get to Delhi, I reached the Namakkal hill-fort around 4 o'clock in the evening. If my friends do turn up, they would arrive only around dusk. Even if only one of them were to come, I could ask his advice about going to Delhi and finding my way there. I sat down on the sun-warmed rocks and waited. Soon I saw someone climbing up the hill. It was as if the god I'd come to worship had actually crossed my path! I knew him, he was one of my friends. He owned a small grocery store which his mother managed. He had dropped out of school after Class 9 and helped around the shop. I ran towards him sobbing, and sobbed even harder as I started to tell him my story.

'*Di*! Why're you crying? Where've you been all this while? The last time I saw you was when we went to Dindigul. Later someone told me you'd gone to Erode. Some problem at home? What happened? Tell me first and then cry.'

On hearing him, I sobbed more, but finally managed to compose myself and narrate all that had happened. 'Here, take this earring and get me some money. Then put me on the train to Delhi; you have to!'

He looked confused and did not seem to know what to do. Finally he said, 'All right. Stay here. I'll somehow get you the money you need,' and began to climb down the hill.

Where would he get money for the earring? Suppose someone caught him selling it and wanted to know where he got it from, and why he was peddling it, would he point to me? If he did, then matters could get bad. My family would surely get to hear of it and then who knows what would happen? Full of fear, I waited for him to return. And what if he did not come back? An hour passed and I was already praying to God, asking why He was determined to test me. I must somehow get to Delhi, I prayed, or else let me fall down from this hill and die. Blinking back the tears pouring down my cheeks, I steeled myself to face the worst.

My friend returned soon after and I heaved a sigh of relief, feeling my heart grow quiet. 'I told my mother that a friend of mine needs money to pay his exam fees, and that his mother had asked me to help sell this earring. I asked her if she could keep the jewel and give some money. She asked me to wait awhile and went out. She returned with 350 rupees.'

I was relieved, and glad that my luck had held so far. I pleaded with him to somehow put me on the train to Delhi. We both walked to the Namakkal bus stand and sat in a bus bound for Salem. Until the bus started moving, my heart was pounding so hard that seemed as if it would cleave from me.

We reached Salem and took another bus from there to the railway station. Neither he nor I had seen a railway station, let alone a train, until then. In fact, it was our first visit to Salem. Naturally we did not know where to go, neither did we know how to buy a ticket. Only after we entered the station did we see a long queue standing in front of a counter. A notice above the counter indicated that this was where one got tickets. We joined the queue.

When it was our turn, and we were at the counter asking the price of a ticket to Delhi, the man issuing tickets said that the Delhi train was expected only at 10.30 that night and they would not issue tickets before 8 o'clock. Since we had an hour to kill, my friend suggested that we should sit somewhere, maybe behind a pillar where we wouldn't be easily seen. We found such a place and sat down.

By this time my family would know I had gone missing. My mother was probably fretting and crying, and missing her earrings, saris and her son. They would of course start looking for me. 'What if they came here?' I asked my friend.

'Don't worry. Why would they come here?' He wanted to allay my fears.

My friend did not want to go to Delhi with me. He was an only son and so had decided to live at home, hiding his feminine feelings, expressing them only on the hill-fort. I was astounded that he could thus hold back his desires and emotions. He was five years older than me and had grown up in Namakkal town, so knew a little more of the world than I did. When we all went to Dindigul, he had worn a sari, but did not shave off his moustache. He tied a kerchief around the lower half of his face to hide it. He was afraid of being found out at home, yet his speech and gestures were far more feminine than mine. Anyway, I did not insist he go with me, nor did he say he wished to come along. That day, he appeared like a god just in time to save me. I thought I would never forget him or what he had done for me.

The ticket to Delhi cost 250 rupees.The tickets to Salem had cost 10 rupees and I had to give my friend another ten to get back home. I had only 80 rupees left. He left after we got my ticket. I did not know how to get to the platform where the Delhi train would arrive and had to ask my way around. Once I climbed the iron staircase and reached the platform, I sat down in a corner. My mind would not stay still, nor my eyes. I found myself staring at this and that. I was waiting for it to be 10. 30, and for the train to arrive.

five

Oh, my mother, the train was so long! Where was I to get in? I had a ticket and so I thought I could get in through any door. After the train came to a halt, I got inside one of the coaches in the middle. I saw at once that the seats in the train were not like those in a bus. They were long and appeared stacked over each other, as if they were so many shelves in an almirah. In each of the shelves lay a person, legs stretched out. I did not really understand this: Should I sleep on one of the shelves? I walked through the coach looking for a place to sleep, and finally found an empty plank and sat down on it. I kept my head lowered and finally the train started. My heart stopped beating wildly. I'd done it! I had escaped!

Then a man came up to me and indicated that I should get up from my seat in a language I did not understand. I showed him my ticket, but he did not pay any heed to it.

Instead he lay down on the plank where I had been sitting. I did not know what to do. Perhaps this is his seat, I thought and walked away. I came to the coach entrance and stood near the toilets. A tall man in a black coat appeared with a sheaf of papers in his hand. In Tamil he asked me why I was standing there, whether I had a ticket and where I was going. I showed him my ticket. Looking at it, he said that there was no room for me in that coach.

'But how'll I get to Delhi?' I asked, worried.

'With your ticket, you can't travel in this compartment. This is reserved, and only those who have reserved tickets can be in this compartment.You have to go to the unreserved compartment.'

'What is a compartment? Where is it?'

'A compartment is like a box. There are many compartments in a train. With your ticket, you can only go into the box that is next to the engine. Look, you don't seem to know anything! Are you travelling alone? You say you're going to Delhi—did someone put you on this train?'

His questions came fast and thick and I got scared. I did not reply at once.

'Why are you silent? I asked you a question.'

'My uncle lives in Delhi. He'll come and get me at the station. My brother saw me off at Salem.'

'All right, all right! Get off at the next station and go to the box near the engine, okay? You mustn't stay here.' He sounded firm.

I stood near the toilets for nearly an hour and a half. The next stop was Jolarpettai. I got off the train and started to run towards the engine. But those boxes appeared shut and were full of people, sitting close to each other. Many squatted on the floor, some stood.

'I have a ticket to Delhi. Won't you open the door for me?' I screamed.

Those inside stared at me, as though I was a spectacle to be watched, but would not open the door. I did not know what to do and kept banging at the door. Finally, it opened, but not fully. Piles of boxes and sacks lay near the entrance. I somehow got in through the half-open door. Once inside, I saw that there was no place to sit, not even near the toilets. I rested one foot on a sack and balancing another on the ground and stood in that position until dawn. When the train stopped, some people got off. I immediately moved further in and found a place to sit along the passage.

I kept asking those sitting next to me, when the train would reach Delhi. I did this by the hour and they would tell me, 'It'll take two days, maybe even three.' I never quite trusted that answer and so kept asking a new person each time. I ate only once during the entire journey, when I spent 15 rupees on the first day and bought myself a plate of idlis and vadai. I wanted to keep the rest of the money to help me get to Wazirpur from Delhi. I drank water whenever the train stopped and thus filled my stomach. Like this I travelled for two days and on the evening of the second day I found that we had arrived at a place called Nizamuddin. And that is how I reached Delhi.

I walked out with the rest of the crowd and found myself outside the station. I was amazed at how large it was. Not a word of Tamil anywhere. At that time I did not even know that it was Hindi that was up there on the announcement boards. I only knew it was a strange language. I watched people argue in that language, get into auto-rickshaws and cars. I decided that I too would take an auto-rickshaw.

I walked up to an auto-rickshaw driver asked if he would take me to Wazirpur. 'Wazirpur. J.J. Colony. Have to go there.'

He looked me up and down and asked, 'Madarasi?'

I understood this and replied, 'Yes, Madarasi!'

He showed me five fingers and said, '*Pachaas rupiya.*'

I asked in English, 'Fifty rupees?' and he nodded. I climbed into the auto-rickshaw and we left the station.

From inside the auto-rickshaw I got a glimpse of the wide roads with countless cars, buses and bikes on them, and the tall buildings and shops lined up on the sides, and was full of wonder. What a large city this was. With resolve and pride I had left home to find my guru. But would this auto-rickshaw driver take me to where I wished to go, and even if he did, could I be sure that my guru lived in that address? I kept repeating these questions in my head, when the auto-rickshaw stopped. The driver said that we had reached J.J. Colony and demanded his fare. I got out and handed 50 rupees to him, and he left immediately.

I did not know if this was indeed J.J. Colony, since there were no signboards in Tamil. I walked ahead for at least half a kilometre from where I had been dropped. I kept looking this way and that. I spotted a dark-skinned woman wearing nose-rings and with heavy anklets on her feet. She must have been around forty. She looked like she could be from my part of the world.

'Are you Tamil?' I asked.

When she replied, 'Yes, son. Are you Tamil too?' I felt great relief.

'Amma, I've come in search of my mother. She lives in J.J. Colony. You know these pottais—they go about clapping their hands like this,' I showed her how, and continued, 'She's like that. Would you know where she lives?'

The woman pointed the way. It was a small lane, and congested—people were washing clothes, bathing, some were filling water, others washing vessels. I had to walk through a number of small streets before I came to where the pottais lived, which was clearly a Tamil place. They were selling idlis and dosas on the wayside. I felt at home, seeing so many of my kind around. I stopped an older pottai and asked her if she knew where my guru lived.

'Where're you from, son? And what do you want with her?'

I did not want to tell her I was my guru's child, and instead said, 'I am related to her.' On hearing that, she held me by the hand and took me to my guru's house.

My guru was shocked and also thrilled on seeing me. My heart beat wildly; I felt tears sting my eyes as I flung myself at her and started to weep loudly.

'At this young age, you dared to leave Tamil Nadu and come this far! What if something had happened to you on the way? How would I have been able to face your parents? Or answer their questions? You could have lost your way, what would I have done then? It is God that has brought my daughter to me! I owe Him a hundred prayers.' Saying this, my guru held me tight, all the while running her fingers through my hair.

'From now on, I'm going to live here,' I announced.

Ideally, I ought to have been clad in a sari. My guru was somewhat anxious. 'You've come like a boy. Did anyone see you or talk to you?'

I explained how I had found my way to her. My guru did not want people to think that she had caught hold of a boy and forcibly made him effeminate. She wanted me to take women's clothes and go to my nani's house in Rafiq Nagar and stay there for ten days, after which she said she would bring me to her own home. She requested an elder to take me to Rafiq Nagar. I, of course, did not know anyone apart from my guru. But I had always felt close to pottais, even if I didn't know them. So I agreed to go to my nani's, and together we left in an auto-rickshaw.

I AM NOT a man now. I am a woman and I have a family with a mother, a grandmother, sisters-in-law. My grandmother lived in a housing colony which Indira Gandhi had built for the poor. There were many pottais there, and other men and women too. The house we lived in had one large room and a small kitchen. We had to use public toilets because there was no toilet inside the house. Since I had not undergone an operation, I was told I had to be very careful. I could not tell anyone that I had not had an operation, and had to make sure no one saw me naked. I was warned to use only those toilets that had locks.

We had to carry our own bucket of water to the toilet. For water to drink and to wash clothes, we went to a borewell, some distance away. Bathing took place in our kitchen. There was a small area marked out for that purpose. I learnt all this in the first two days I was at my nani's place.

Every morning, the pottais would leave to ask for money from shopkeepers. They went in a group to different areas called bazaars. After they were done with collecting money from a bazaar, they divided the collection amongst themselves. Initially, I did not go along with the rest to collect money. I stayed at home with nani. One day, I asked her, 'Why do they go like this to collect money? Can't they do other work?'

'In this Hindi country, we *hijra*s are meant to do this and not other things. We ask money from shops, collect *badaai*... In the old days, hijras waited upon queens and princesses. But today there are no queens; the rule of kings and queens has given way to the rule of ministers. But this government has not given us other work to do. In Indira Gandhi's time—God bless her memory—they built houses for hijras and other poor people.'

'Why do they call us hijras?'

'That is what we call ourselves. That's how it's been from the time of our ancestors. In this Delhi, for centuries, they've treated us like gods. They fall at our feet and seek our blessings. Our word is considered all-powerful and whatever we say comes true. When we go to shops, we clap hands and say "Ramramji! Namaste babu!" and they give us money, a rupee or 5 rupees, or whatever they want to give. We accept this money, place our palms on the shopkeeper's head and say "Be well! We hope your business goes well."'

'How come they think we are gods? How did this happen? Is there a story about it?'

'If you want stories about hijras, there are hundreds of tales I can tell you. But for now, I'll tell you just this one. You must have heard of Ramayanam, Mahabharatham and all that.

Well, when Ramar went off on exile for fourteen years, his subjects, both men and women, came to see him off to the forest. They walked with him to the forest's edge and would have accompanied him further inside, when he told them, "All of you, men, women and children, go back to your houses. I'll complete my fourteen years of exile and return to rule over you." So, everyone left, men, women and children, but a group of people stayed back and there they remained at the forest rim for fourteen years until Ramar came back. Astonished, he asked them, "Who are you? Why haven't you gone back to your homes in the city?" They replied, "Swamy! We belong neither to mankind, nor to womankind. You said then that men, women and children ought to return to the city. But you did not ask us to go. Bound by your wishes, we remained here." Rama was so astounded and moved by their sincerity that he granted them a boon. "Whatever you speak will be true. Your words will come true."

'So, from that day onwards, people here have believed that a hijra's word will come true and think of us as godly beings. They hold that it is good to start the day by seeing a hijra. Those who run businesses think that the day will go well for them if they give us money and earn our blessings.

'Since this Hindi country respects us so much, we must behave in a manner that is worthy of that respect. We must not desire men, and seek to misbehave with them. Those who think we are divine and give us money to earn our blessings should not ever think we have gone bad. When you go to ask for money, the seths are bound to be nice to you. Some will tease you, but you must not to flirt with them. Understood?'

'So that's why we go and ask for money from shops. What

is badaai, then?'

'I'll tell you, but before that you run to that beeda shop and get me an ek-so-bees paan. Here, take this.' She handed me a rupee and I went to the shop and asked for the paan that she wanted. Only then did I find out that paan was made of betel leaves. Back home, they smeared chalk-paste on the betel leaf, rolled it up with an areca nut and ate it. Here, they smeared the back of the betel leaf with chalk-paste and also something thick and red. Then they place a chunk of tobacco, add a piece of areca nut and then make a roll. A clove is used as a pin to prevent the tobacco and areca from falling off.

'Naam kya?' the shopkeeper asked me.

I did not understand his question, and said, 'For my nani,' and walked away. Nani took the paan but told me that every time I presented a paan to an elder I ought to say paampaduthi.

'Now get that *tooktani*. Make sure that you wash it clean and bright,' she added.

At my puzzled look, she explained that it was a spittoon, something that you spat betel-juice into. I found the tooktani, but hesitated to put my hands into it and wash its insides stained with red spit. Nani pointed out that I should not demur from doing such things nor consider them dirty. 'This is a service that you young things do for your elders. We used to do the same at your age, clean the spitoons of our gurus and nanis.' This made me feel somewhat better, and though I did not like it, I managed to wash the spitoon without being disgusted.

Nani chewed hard on her paan and then drawing the spittoon to her, spat into it and turned to me, 'You wanted to know about badaai. Look at that drum strung on that piece of cloth. That is a *dholak*. Hijras play the dholak, sing and dance, and this is called *doli-badaai*. They do this at weddings and during childbirth. People give them what they can afford—rice, wheat, a sari. Hijras find out where there's been a birth and send word to the family, saying that they would arrive on such-and-such a day to bless the newborn and they must be given badaai. And so they go to these homes and sing songs teasing the child's parents, thus making them happy. Towards the end they take the child into their hands, bless it and come away with whatever gifts are given. Suppose the family is rich, but gives little, the hijras insist that they've come as a large group and must be given more. And if the newborn child is a male, they ask for more money. This is doli-badaai. Similarly, hijras go to marriage halls and sing and dance, teasing the groom and bride, which pleases them, and they too give money. Usually, we split all the money we earn amongst ourselves. You'll find out more, by and by. Now take these clothes like the good girl you are, and go and wash them by the borewell.' Thus ending her story, she shooed me off.

If born a pottai, and when living amongst pottais, it is important that a person pierces her ears and nose, and grows her hair. If you merely wear press-button earrings and a wig, no one really respects you. Likewise, if you happen to see a man crossing your path, you're expected to make way for him, bend your head bashfully and make sure that your chest is covered. It is also important to learn the ways of the hijras, follow rules, respect elders, make sure that a youngster's dress does not so much as brush an elder's arm or leg, and do all that an elder asks. This is what is expected of those who want to be part of the hijra community.

After ten days, I returned to J.J. Colony with my nani. In my guru's family they don't go for badaai. I was told that only hijras living in Delhi do these things. If I or anyone wanted to go for badaai, then we would have to become chelas to these Hindi-speaking hijras and go and live with them. Our practice was to go to shops and ask for money. Nani stayed back, and only my guru and the rest of us went to the shops. When at a shop, I'd feel like buying some of the things I saw, especially clothes. I'd also feel like eating the sweets displayed in the shops. If the seth at the shop looked fair and handsome, I found myself drawn to him. But I knew I could not ever display desire. I consoled myself with the thought that we are like beggars, asking money from the shops. We can't possibly get what we want, nor do we have the right to desire them.

When I was in the house, I'd remember my family and the house in the village. I wondered often about my parents and brothers. Did they think of me? What did they imagine had happened to me? Maybe my mother was not well, and has gone searching for me. But I knew it was no use missing home. I couldn't go back, could I? I had pierced my ears and nose and could not expect to go home like that. And even if I did, surely they would not accept me as a woman. I could write to them, of course, but what if they found out where I was and came for me? They'd make me cut my hair and force me to be a man. They'd no doubt beat me too, even to death. When these thoughts struck me, I'd resign myself to the life I led in Delhi. After all, this was my world, this is what I do. I had these thoughts only when I was alone, in the bathroom or on the terrace. If the others came to know what was in my heart, they were bound to ask me questions, to try and find out what was ailing me.

Sometimes, my guru would go with some other group to the shops. At such times, she'd send me with another hijra. By then I had managed to pick up a bit of Hindi. After we were done with our work, this hijra would sit down at the end of the road, in the same bazaar where we had asked for money a while ago, and after giving me my share, spend a portion of her money on beer. The first time, I was shocked and asked her how she dared to drink openly and if it wasn't wrong to do so. She shrugged her shoulders, 'So what? Leave it. But don't you sneak on me, okay? If you do, I won't take you with me.'

While she drank her beer, I'd wander up and down the road. Sometimes, I'd stop at a cigarette shop run by a man from Kerala and talk to him in Tamil. We used to come to this area once a week and so I thought that I could perhaps write to my family and give this man's address for them to write back. Howsoever my family treated me, even if they beat me and scolded me, I could not quite forget them. I also felt guilty that I had stolen my mother's earring and at times hated myself for it.

At first, I thought I ought to take my guru's consent before I wrote the letter. But I was not sure what she would think. And if I wrote from my guru's address, my brothers would surely come and get me. As if that was not bad enough, they would think ill of my guru— that she had abducted me. She might then think that I had not come to live with her, but only to use her and find work for myself. Finally, without my guru's knowledge, I wrote to my parents, and gave the Kerala man's shop address as my own.

Dear Amma, Appa and brothers,

This is Doraisamy, writing to you from Delhi. First of all, you must forgive me for running away without telling you. I did not like it that you scolded me and beat me. So I came here, and with a friend's help got a job in a shop that sells utensils. I'll come home once I've made enough money.

Amma, I sold your earring to come here. But please don't worry, I will make enough money to buy you a new pair.

Please don't search for me, for I'm well. I've been thinking of all of you. Write to me at this address and tell me how you are.

Yours,

Doraisamy

In the early days, when I'd been in the city for only about twenty days, I'd accompanied a group to the apple bazaar. I went to observe how the others asked for money so that I could learn to do it as well as them. Sometimes, shopowners would request us not to clap our hands and gather in a group, and ask for one of us to come in and get the money. Later, I returned to this bazaar with the beer-drinking hijra. She would go down one line of shops, and instruct me to collect along another line. In some of the places, I even found Tamil speakers. For at times, lorry-drivers would sit in the offices. They would tease me, talk nicely and I'd tease them back, saying, 'Uncle, where're you from? Why can't you give me money?' and add to my collection.

It was during one such collection round that I saw a lorry-driver from Namakkal. He too saw me. He was known to my family and had worked as a driver for us. As soon as he saw me, he called out, 'Hey, Doraisamy! Doraisamy!'

I was so frightened that I turned and ran as fast as I could, out of the bazaar and into an autorickshaw and went straight home to J.J. Colony. I did not wait for my beer-drinking friend. Nani saw how afraid I was and asked me what was wrong. I told her what had happened.

'Don't worry, child. Even if that lorry-driver told your family, and they came looking for you, I'll take care of you.

Towards evening, the hijra with whom I had gone to the shops came home, looking exhausted. As soon as she saw me, she started yelling, '*Dey*! Are you a pottai or what? Why the hell do you want to dress as one? Whose cock were you sucking all this while? Where the hell did you go? I had to look for you and search all over the place! What the fuck am I supposed to think, when you suddenly disappear? Who is to answer your nani? I won't take you with me ever again!'

She grew quiet only after her anger was appeased. Nani then explained to her what had happened, at which she looked sorry and apologized for her earlier outburst.

The Namakkal lorry-driver probably went home and told my parents that he had seen me in a sari, begging at shop windows. God knows what they made of it, but they caught hold of a couple of pottais who were out on the streets in Namakkal and marched them off to the local police station, accusing them of dressing me up like themselves and selling me to beggars in Delhi. At which, the pottais had apparently replied, 'Look, we haven't done anything to your son. We don't even know if he is white or black. If you are in touch with him, write and ask him to come. Let him stand before us and say that we induced him to wear a sari and beg, and then we'll see.' The police detained them for the day but had to eventually let them off.

I did not know of this then, of course. I certainly did not know the pottais who had been rustled up. Before I left for Delhi I would never have spoken to anyone in Namakkal who was openly identifiable as a pottai. I did not want to be mistaken as one of them, afraid that I'd get beaten for wanting to be part of the group of pottais.

After the lorry-driver episode, I would occasionally visit the Kerala man and ask if there was a letter for me. One day, he handed me a telegram which said my mother was seriously ill and that I should return home immediately. As soon as I saw it, I wanted to go home. I realized that I must confess to my guru and nani about the letter I'd written home. I was very afraid of what they'd say, but my love for my mother made me tell them. They did not make much of my furtiveness and arranged to send me home. But I think they must have experienced a loss of trust in me.

six

My guru bought me a ticket to go home, and also gave me 1500 rupees. She thrust a bag containing two saris into my hand and put me on a train. This time, I wore a sari and travelled in the ladies coach. I ate the tamarind rice that she had thoughtfully packed for me and wondered about my mother, of what had happened to her.

I somehow made it to Salem and got into a local bus to go to the bus station—and then stopped to think. I couldn't possibly return home in a sari. My family knew me as a boy, they thought I was a male. If my mother were to see me in a sari, God knows if she'd be able to take it. What if her condition got worse? I should change into men's clothes, I decided.

I tried to find a room in some lodge near the bus stand, but no one appeared to want to let me in. I returned to the bus stand and decided to go to the women's toilet there. But the man who stood there to receive money for the pay-and-use toilets dismissed me as a pottai and would not let me in. When I tried to get into the men's toilet section, I was shooed away from there as well. What a mess, I thought. In Delhi, they let me use the women's toilet, but here things were clearly different. Then there was the issue of entering the toilet dressed as a woman and coming out as a man—this was sure to cause trouble. I was confused and not sure what I could do. I had to somehow get into male clothes; the question was how.

Finally, I told the man who stood in front of the men's toilets, collecting the fare to enter them, that I was a man, and had dressed up as a woman for a show. Now that the show was over, I wanted to change back into my regular clothes. He took 5 rupees from me and let me in. Startled, the men who were peeing in there started yelling. I muttered, 'I'm a man too,' and ran into one of the bathrooms, and shut the door behind me. I ought to have changed on the train, but the necessity of changing into male clothes hadn't occurred to me then. Besides, I had travelled by ladies coach—imagine what would have happened if I'd emerged as a man from the toilet!

I changed into the clothes I wore when I'd left for Delhi. I took off my earrings and nose-ring, but it was not that easy to get the copper bangle off my wrist. Finally, I had to use my teeth. I bit into the copper, thereby making a dent in it. I let my tongue hold it back, and then bit a little deeper until the bangle broke. I put all these things away in my bag safely and emerged from the bathroom as a man. My hair, though, was long, almost shoulder-length and to hide it I decided to wear a cap. I bought one at a shop in the bus stand and was soon on the bus to Namakkal.

I felt fear in my heart as I walked home from the bus stop. God knows what would happen at home, once I got there. Surely I'd be beaten up? Would my brothers cut off my hair? What was I going to tell them? My mind was crowded with these thoughts as I approached home.

I found my mother in good health. It was 9 in the morning and my father and two of my brothers were at work, plying milk. My middle brother was at home though. As soon as I stepped in, he shut the door, grabbed a cricket bat, and began hitting me, all the while screaming, 'That'll teach you to go with those Number 9s. Let's see you wear a sari again, or dance, you mother-fucking pottai!' He beat me hard mindlessly, yelling that he wanted to kill me, I who had dared to run away. I tried to protect my face and head with my hands to keep the blows from falling. But nevertheless they came down hard, and I felt my hands swell. I was beaten on my legs, on my back, and finally my brother brought the bat down heavily on my head. My skull cracked and there was blood all over, flowing, warm.

'That's right. Beat him and break his bones. Only then will he stay at home and not run away,' I heard my mother say.

I pushed my brother away at last, ran into a room and locked the door. It seemed to me then that it was better to take my own life than let my brother beat me to death. I looked around to see if there was something I could use, when my brother broke open the door and came after me again. He hit me again, till he was tired and his arms ached. Only then did he stop.

'Why don't you try and understand my feelings? Why do you hit me even before you ask me anything? I am here only because of the love I bear for all of you! What have I done wrong that you should beat me so?' I cried out loud, my voice ragged and tear-filled. My brother told me then that I had been spotted in women's clothes, begging in the apple market. This is when they caught hold of a few local pottais and marched them off to the police station. 'What've we not done for you? What comforts were you denied? You tell us that! We bought you clothes, we fed you. Why, we have men working for us and you had to go and wear a sari, join a gang of pottais and beg! How can someone from a good family do that? Do you know who we are and what caste we belong to? How could you forget all that and do what you did? How did you have the heart to do all this?' Bemoaning my fate, my mother rubbed salve on to my wounds.

I wanted at that time to get away from it all, and to save myself another beating, so I said that I had been lured away by those people and made to believe I wanted to be like them. And I had followed them, as one with a diseased mind would. 'I swear I won't do this again! I'm willing to plead at your feet! But please keep my father and brothers away from me. I don't want to get beaten again. I can't bear the pain.'

My brother responded with, 'First thing, let's get his head shaved clean. I'll go and fetch the barber.'

But my mother brushed my brother's suggestion away. 'Tomorrow, we'll go to the Samayapuram temple and there he can offer his hair to the goddess. She will help cure him, and soon he'll be free from that that seducing female demon who even now has a hold on him.'

Not wanting to meet my father or my brothers, I remained in that room the whole day. No one in the village knew what had become of me. They thought that poor boy had been gripped by a fit of madness, and so had run away, but thankfully was back now. But the girl next door, the one in whose house I had often dressed up as a woman, knew all about me and also that I had gone to live with pottais. But she did not come to see me because she was scared of what people would say. Nor did my father speak a word to me. I heard my brothers discussing me with my mother. My eldest brother said, 'Well, he's going through a bad time. Let's not beat him, poor fellow, he won't be able to take it. I won't go to work tomorrow. Let's all go to the temple and we'll get him to shave his head there.'

The next morning we got on the bus to Trichy. My brothers sat on either side of me, while my mother sat in front and I was taken to the Samayapuram temple. At the temple, when my hair was shorn off I felt more pain than I did when my brother thrashed me. I prayed fervently: 'Amma! Why must I suffer like this? Why must you put me through this ordeal? People say that you grant all that the faithful want, but in my case, I have known only pain. What have I done wrong? It was you who made me male in form, but with female feelings. And now, for your crime, I am being punished and in your own shrine! Aren't you a woman too? Can't you understand another woman's feelings? Don't you have any pity? By this day next year, you must make a woman of me, just like you. If you can't, at least make me into a man completely.'

BALD AS I was, I felt shame and hurt and did not dare leave

the house. To make things worse, whoever came home had something or the other to say: 'What is wrong with this fellow? Who denied him anything? All this comes of having it easy, of being stuffed to his gills with three full meals a day, of growing fatly arrogant.' 'Poor fellow, it's not his fault. He needs to be helped. Why don't you take him to a temple and smear holy ash all over him? That'll counter whatever bad thing has got into him.'

There is a saying that only he who has suffered hurt will know the pain and so it was for me. How could I expect these people to understand how my mind and body were bruised?

A few days later, my brothers took me to work with them. I was soon loading and unloading milk cans as before. As if it were not enough that the entire village talked about me, I found the workers at the milk cooperative, from the supervisor to the boy who washed the cans, asking me curiously, 'They say you ran off to Delhi and hung around with pottais. What did you do there?' Sometimes, when no one was looking, they would pinch my chest, run their hands over my bum and much else. I was afraid to complain to my brothers. Every day proved an ordeal and I thought to myself that all this will stop only if I leave home again, return to the pottais I knew, have the operation and become a woman.

I had to wait for my hair to grow though before I took off to Delhi again, for one with a shaven head has no standing amongst pottais. I must wait it out, I realized, and suffer my fate till I could leave again. It was three months before I left for Delhi. This time as soon as I got on to the train at Salem station, I changed into women's clothes. Since I was travelling the third time by train, I knew what to expect.

Back in Delhi, my nani and guru listened to me kindly but decided that I must leave immediately leave for Mumbai. My hair was short and I had not got an operation done. To live like that was not easy in Delhi, and if I did, I would bring dishonour to all hijras. Besides, my family would know I had returned to Delhi. For all these reasons, I was put on a train to Mumbai and sent to another house of hijras there. My guru told me that I ought to stay there till my hair grew out and I had my operation, after which she would take me back into her household. With another hijra accompanying me, and a Mumbai address in hand, I was seen off at the Delhi railway station.

The Mumbai hijra I was sent off to was my guru's mother. Amongst hijras, a guru is everything to a chela—she guides her at work, offers her a place to stay, she is with her in times of good and bad. A mother is different, for a hijra who is a daughter, the mother's home is like the natal home. The guru's home is like the marital home. In this sense, the house to which I was sent was my nani's place, that it, my guru's natal home.

seven

Mumbai was different. The people, the culture, the sea, the electric train—everything was different and not like what I had known in Delhi. My guru's mother's house was in a place called Ghatkopar. Nani presided over a large parivar or family, there were over five hundred people attached to her clan, comprising chelas, *naathis* and *sadak-naathis* (daughters, granddaughters, great-granddaughters). Some amongst them lived in Tamil Nadu, others in Delhi, Mumbai, and some in far-flung places like Singapore.

Unlike my guru's house, my nani's house was not in a poor neighbourhood, nor was it rented. She owned a comfortable house. Nani also owned a house for sex work elsewhere in the city, managed by her chela. Some of her chelas and naathi-chelas lived with her, did work around the house and went out to ask money from shopkeepers. I did not have to leave the house to wash clothes, bathe or use the toilet. I could do all these things at home, since we had all the facilities.

Throughout the week, I went to the shops. Initially, I went along with other hijras but after a month, I learnt to do this on my own. I had my own calendar. Monday: Victoria Terminus and Churchgate; Tuesday: Bandra; Wednesday: Mankur; Thursday: Sandoz Road; Friday: Masjid Bandar; Saturday: Sion Koliwada; and Sunday: Chembur. Meanwhile I waited to hear from my guru, and for her to come and fetch me.

Everyone feared, respected, and were worshipful of my old nani. When she was not at home, the atmosphere lightened and everyone relaxed, became affectionate, danced, watched television. But when they heard nani coming in, they immediately became quiet. Not that nani was cruel or anything. She too watched television, asked us to sing and dance. It was really like living with older people in one's family—we respect them, don't we? Among the hijras too, it was like that.

In Mumbai, hijras live in several places—Kamatipura, Bhandup, Sonapur, Mulund, Koliwada, Matunga, Mahim, Byculla. If you consider their occupations, many of them go to shops to ask for money, and they go for *badaai*. Unlike in Delhi, many are also engaged in sex work and there are houses devoted specifically to that purpose. Generally speaking, those who went for badaai did not get involved in sex work. If you were to look at kin relations here, you would find that there are mothers, daughters, granddaughters, great-granddaughters, milk-daughters and so on. If a hijra desired to take on another as a chela, she had to place her request before the jamaat, which then took note of her wish and granted it. There is no rule or law of the land that tells us to do this, but hijras have their own rules, culture and rituals. The jamaat is their forum for mediating and pronouncing what is good and bad. Marginalized by mainstream society, denied a legal existence and dispossessed of their rights, hijras turn to their community and its culture for comfort and for nurture. In the hijra community there is no high or low—hijras do not observe caste or religious differences and there are hijras from both poor and rich homes.

While there are no castes amongst hijras, there are houses or clans. There are seven clans or houses, and each has its own name. Hijras can choose their guru from any house and sometimes shift their allegiance to another house. This is allowed. Each of the seven houses has its own elected or chosen head, known as a *naik*. A naik's *parivar* comprises sister, younger sister, daughter, granddaughter and so on. But they don't necessarily live together, and meet only occasionally, at festivals or when the jamaats hold their meetings. I learnt all this and much more during my Mumbai days. I also came to understand that hijras had evolved a culture of their own to enable them to exercise order and restraint and also to exercise their rights.

After I had spent two months in Mumbai, my Mumbai nani's chela asked me if I would consent to be her chela and further assured me that she would arrange for me to have the operation. I felt deep regard and respect for my Delhi guru, but I hadn't heard from her and was not sure if this is how I ought to do things. Nani comforted me saying that even if I became her chela's chela, I'd continue to be my Delhi guru's chela. Besides, I was her chela in another city, where there was a different tradition. Here, I could be a chela the Mumbai way. 'So you can be my chela's chela here. Hijras can have a guru in Tamil Nadu and also here,' she added. I finally agreed and said yes.

The guru–chela system in Tamil Nadu works only there. Similarly the system in Mumbai is not valid in Tamil Nadu. In every state of north India there are separate hijra houses, each with their own parivars. Hijras from all the seven houses live in Karnataka. Tamil Nadu alone is different in this respect. A person has a guru in the state and also another one, outside of it.

To make me a chela of the Mumbai guru who lived in Kamatipura, they took me to Byculla, where the naiks of the seven houses reside. I was taken to the house where I was to become a chela. All the seven naiks were there, seated on a mat. They had asked me if I had been a chela before, and for what house of hijras, or if this was the first time I was being accepted as a chela. I said that I had been taken as a chela at a jamaat in Tamil Nadu. At which they said, 'Beta, that doesn't work here—we're asking about Mumbai, Delhi. Were you ever taken as a chela in these places?' When I said no, they declared that I was a *ghori moorathan*, that is, a person who is becoming a chela for the first time.

The naiks called the jamaat to order and announced loudly for everyone to hear that Revathi was being made a chela of such-and-such chela of such-and-such parivar. At this, all present clapped their hands. I was asked to do paampaduthi to all the elders. They call it *reeth*, this system of consecrating chelas. After the ceremony was over, I was handed a set of clothes and a box to keep these, as well as my own bed-roll. I was told where to store it. My guru then explained hijra kin terms to me:

Badudaadi – great-grandmother's guru
Daadaguru – grandmother's guru (great-grandmother)
Nanaguru – guru's guru (grandmother)
Guru – mother
Kaalaguru – guru's sister
Gurubai – (my) sister
Badagurubai – elder sister
Chotagurubai – younger sister
Chela – daughter
Naathi-chela – granddaughter
Chandichela – great-granddaughter
Sadak-naathi – great-granddaughter's daughter

I was also told that I must do whatever elders want me to do; that I should respect them, say 'paampaduthi' should I encounter them; make sure that my clothes do not touch theirs; bring them water in a jug, should they ask for it; and never be seen without bangles, earrings, nose-ring and anklets. Further, I could not cut my hair, and I could not, on any account, shave off facial hair. Instead I was to have it plucked, using a *jimitta* or plucker. I was also to share my earnings from the shops with my guru and nani. I could give them whatever I thought fit. It was all right too, to turn in all of one's earnings to them, I was told, for they would do their best by me and provide me with all that I needed.

I DID NOT live with my guru, but with my nani, and therefore turned over my earnings to her. At night, I would massage nani's feet before she went to sleep. While she slept on a bed, I would unroll a mat on the floor and sleep there. Once, while I was thus massaging her feet, nani asked me, 'Beta, do you have a *panthi* (husband or partner) in Tamil Nadu?'

I said, 'No, I do not have any such relationship.'

'Beta, I don't want you ganging up with some pottais and take to drinking and seeking a husband. If you do that, you can be sure I'll break your head! You be a good girl and listen to me, and I'll arrange for you to have nirvaanam, that is, have an operation.' She added, 'Once you have nirvaanam done, you can either stay with me or go to your guru. If you want to go home, you need to ask your guru's permission. Will you family accept you, if you return as a hijra?'

When I explained my family situation to her, she remarked, 'No thought of home must cross your mind. If you go there, they're sure to chop your hair off. For a pottai, nothing is as shameful as having one's hair cut. So don't go home yet. If anyone comes in search of you, I'll deal with them.'

I lived in this situation for six months, attending to my nani, helping around the house, listening to her advice. There were two others at home, my gurubais, who went to the shops to collect money like I did, and helped with the housework. They had been at nani's house for longer than I had. Arrangements were being made to send them for their operation.

A puja was performed in front of a picture of Pothiraja Mata, the goddess seated on a cockerel. On the morning of that day, around 8'o clock, nani called me to her, 'Beta, today you don't have to go to the shops. Put aside two saris and inner skirts.' I could not ask her if she meant to send me to some place and I did as I was told. Maybe she wanted me to accompany the pottais going for their operation and attend on them. After a while, she called me to her again and asked, 'Do you want to have an operation performed by a doctor, or by a *thayamma*?' A thayamma operation is performed by one hijra on another; an operation performed by a doctor takes place in a hospital.

I did not quite understand the import of nani's question, but felt thrilled nevertheless. I wanted to jump up and down in excitement, but instead replied, without really waiting to think about it—I was afraid that if I hesitated she might not send me—that it was all up to her and I would go wherever she sent me. In my heart of hearts I was afraid to opt for a thayamma operation. On the other hand, I knew that those who had nirvaanam done by that method enjoyed a special status and were respected. But more than anything, I was eager to become a woman and that was all that mattered to me. Back then I thought that in order to turn feminine, all I needed to do was get rid of this male object and I would become free to be a woman, like other women.

'You might not be able to bear a thayamma operation, so it is best you get it done by a doctor,' said nani.

eight

When I was wearing men's clothes, I wanted to wear what women did. But after wearing women's clothes, and trying to live like a woman, I still felt that I was a man. So, when nani sent me off for my operation, I felt that finally the female in me would be freed from her male body. I did not expect this to happen so soon and I was ecstatic. Arrangements were made to send me and my gurubai chela. Though we did not know where we were going, we were to go on our own. We were each given our tickets and 7000 rupees for the operation and put on a train to the town of Dindigul in Tamil Nadu.

Before we left Mumbai, when we had prayed to our goddess, Pothiraja Mata, we were asked by our elders to break a coconut in front of her picture, burn camphor as an offering and light incense sticks. Tiny yellow cloth bundles containing a rupee and 25 paise were then tied to our wrists. We were also given a coconut and lemon each and asked to keep these with us. These would help ward off whatever evil awaited those who undertook nirvaanam.

We reached the hospital in the morning at around 8 o'clock. It was actually a small house. There were many women and men occupying the beds, accompanied by their families. We realized that this was a regular hospital where people came to get treated for different ailments. Within the hospital compound, there was a smaller building with a red-tiled roof. We found out that this was the place for our sort of operations.

The doctor came at around 11 o'clock in the morning and asked which of us was to have the operation. We told him we had both come for that purpose.

'Has no one else come with you? For help?' he asked.

We said, 'No.'

'Each operation will cost 2500 rupees. You'll have pay extra for the injections and the medicines.' (This was 1986.) He added: 'There is an older woman here, an ayah who'll help you. She can fetch food and medicines for you for a fee, and look after you. Pay up 5000 rupees now and sign on this paper.'

We had to decide which one of us would get operated upon first. My gurubai chela pleaded, 'Amma, you are an elder to me. If I get this done first, you'll be able to look after me. If you have it first, then there'll be no one to attend to me. Could I go first?' My Mumbai nani had actually told me, 'You're the elder one, so you should be the first to have an operation.' And here she was, my gurubai, saying the opposite. But then she was younger, poor thing, not in age, since we were about the same age, but in hijra kin terms, she could be my chela. Because she asked to go first, I agreed.

The doctor finished his examination of our organs. At 7 o'clock that evening, my gurubai chela's pubic area was shaved. The barber had to be paid 50 rupees. After this, they gave her an enema and she could not eat anything after the procedure. She had to use the bathroom several times after this.

Neither of us could sleep that night at the hospital. We had brought with us a small picture of Pothiraja Mata which we put up on the wall. We kept gazing at it all night and praying for protection through this ordeal. My gurubai chela entreated me to stay with her during the operation. 'Amma, if anything happens to me while they are doing the operation, please make sure that you take me back to where I ought to rest finally.'

I assured her that I would stay with her, 'Don't worry beta, nothing will go wrong. She whom we worship will look after us. Wait and see, how well your operation goes. Don't forget, when it's my turn there's going to be nobody to look after me!'

I wondered then why nani had not sent anyone to be with us. Since both of us were undergoing the operation, it would have been comforting to have another person around. My thoughts turned to my parents and I felt tears fill my eyes. This was a major operation: the very core of my life was to be removed and who knows if I would survive it. It hurts to death, even if one were to hold the organ tight. Imagine how much more it would hurt if were to be operated. I felt great fear. If only God had created me a woman, I wouldn't have to suffer through all this. What if I died? Perhaps I ought to have visited my father and mother before I opted for this. But of course, that was not possible. I had no choice but to trust God—whatever happens, whether I live or die, I would do so as a woman.

I barely got any sleep. The morning after, at about 8 o'clock, a fifty-year-old woman came up to us. 'Which one of you is not well? Who should I look after?' When we said that both of us needed care, she wanted to know what ailed us.

'I am going to be operated upon tomorrow, and she goes today. We need someone to fetch food for us, buy medicines. That's why they must have sent you,' I said.

'Oh! Now I know what operation you mean. Why, just last week two others were here, undergoing the same operation. I cooked for them and brought food over. I can do that for you too. I'll bring lunch and dinner. I'll come by in the mornings too and get you whatever you need. You'll be here for seven days, so you need to pay me 500 rupees in total.'

We gave her the money she asked for right away.

AROUND 11 O'CLOCK, they took my gurubai chela to the operation theatre. She was pale-faced when they took her in, and entreated me to look after her. I was scared too. I hope all goes well for that pottai, I said to myself. Only then would I consent to go in for my operation.

I was not allowed to go into the operation theatre and I waited outside, my heart beating fast as I wondered what was going on inside, and how they were going about it. After two and a half hours, they took me in to see her. There she lay, her legs wide apart, a tube fixed to where her organ once was, stuffed with blood-speckled cotton. There was the scalpel, and the knife too, and in the room were the doctor and the nurse. I felt my head whirring, my eyes closed of their own accord, and darkness swept over me. I fainted.

A while later I felt the doctor shaking me awake. 'Nothing to worry. Come, look at your friend, her operation is over. Tomorrow we'll be doing this to you. You won't know what's happening, that's why I wanted you to see this.'

My gurubai chela spoke too, 'Amma, look at me. All is well. It's all over and I'm fine.' She looked at me, her eyes wide open. 'Here I am, able to smile, and you are afraid! There is no pain at all.' I was surprised to hear her say this. After all, they had removed the penis entirely and here she was smiling away and claiming she was not in pain. The doctor shooed me out, saying that I should wait outside till she was returned to her bed, and then I could talk to her. The door shut behind me.

She was given an iron bed, on which they had spread a sheet of plastic. For the first half hour, she seemed fine. Soon, however, she started screaming in pain, and yelled that she felt a burning down there. I was thoroughly frightened now. All this time, she had seemed fine. I tried to comfort her, saying that it should be all right soon, at which she cried out, 'Amma, it's burning, I fear I'll die from it. Can't you ask the doctor to give me an injection to make the pain go away?' I went looking for the doctor, but was told he had left. When I asked the nurse about an injection, she said that the pain would recede after sometime.

My gurubai chela lay crying and thrashing about. I felt her

pain and burning, as if they were my own. The ayah brought a cup of black tea and I made her drink it. After a couple of hours of crying and screaming, she slipped into an exhausted sleep, and slept through the day

By late afternoon, they took me away to be shaved and gave me an enema. From then until evening, I kept going to the bathroom. Once the enema had been given I could not eat anything. I watched my gurubai and wondered if I would also have to suffer the same. She was asleep, but I felt fear. Was it mere sleep? Was she alive? The night passed without me sleeping a wink.

The next morning at 9 o'clock, they took me to the operation theatre. I wanted to say goodbye to someone before I left—my gurubai chela, though, was still asleep. There was thus no one to see me off, no one to tell me it would be all right. Inside the theatre were the doctor, a nurse and a compounder. First, they asked me to take all my clothes off. I was to only keep my inner skirt on, which they told me to raise and tie around my chest. Then I was seated on a table, and asked to raise my knees to my chin, so that my back was bent in an arc. The doctor said, 'We're going to give you an injection in your back, so you don't feel the pain while we carry out the operation.'

This took a long time and I figured that the doctor was not quite able to put his needle through, that he was perhaps searching for the right spot, for a nerve end or whatever. I got scared. What if the injection did not find its way to the right spot and it hurt while they were operating? I felt suspicious too. But it was soon done, and I was asked to lie on my back. The doctor pushed my legs apart and then asked me to count up to ten, which I did. He then took hold of a small hammer and hit me on the leg with it. 'Does it hurt?' he asked. I said, no. He said that I was ready to be operated upon. 'Think of your Mata and all will be well.'

'Doctor, will it hurt?' I was petrified that it would, when he put his knife to it.

'No, it won't. That's why I've given you an injection.'

'But why am I not unconscious then? I feel normal, I can see everyone, I hear everything.'

'This is not that kind of an injection. It makes you go numb, especially below the hip. But you don't end up unconscious.'

'Careful, doctor. I'm scared. What if it pains?'

'Is it paining now? We are in the middle of the operation already…'

'No!'

The nurse covered my eyes with a strip of cloth and asked me to say, 'Mata, Mata', and I did. I kept repeating the goddess's name. The doctor continued to talk to me, even as he did the operation. I could not see anything, but I heard the sound of the knife scraping.

'So, your name is Revathi? Are you a brahmin?' asked the doctor.

'No, I'm from the gounder caste,' I said.

'Do you want me to arrange things so that you pee like women do, from below? Or as men do, from above?'

'I want to live as a woman, which is why I wanted this operation. Please make it like it is for a woman.' I did not know how women peed, but I wanted to be a woman.

After two hours I was told it was all over. They made me

sit up a bit and placed a pillow against my back, so that I lay with my head raised. The doctor brought me a cup with pieces of flesh in it. 'Here, look at your organ. We've cut it off and made a woman out of you.'

The compounder carried me as if I were a baby and put me on a bed next to my gurubai chela. She was still asleep. A tube was attached to where my organ once was and a bag hung at its other end. This was for my urine. The compounder tucked the bag away underneath the bed. (At that time these two beds were in a hall, against a wooden screen which partitioned them from the rest of the room. The cots we lay on had no mattresses. Neither did they use stretchers to carry us. I wonder how it is now in that place.)

I WAS ECSTATIC—I was at last a woman. But I felt apprehension too. When would it start to hurt? My heart thudded away. It lasted for an hour, the effect of that injection, after which I felt a great burning down there and also pain. Initially, I held back, gritting my teeth. But soon, in spite of myself, I began to scream.

'I can't bear this! It's burning! Can't you give me an injection? Please, someone come to help! I don't think I'll live through this!'

Hearing me yowl, the nurse came over and calmly said, 'Why are you screaming like this? Do you want those around you to know what sort of operation you've had? Just shut up and put up with the pain.'

An old woman who was attending to someone who lay on the other side of the wooden partition had come over too, attracted by my screams.

'What's wrong with this girl? Why is she shouting so much?'

'Stomach pain. We've operated on her stomach and it hurts more in such cases,' explained the nurse. I understood then that this sort of operation was done stealthily.

The ayah came and gave me a cup of black tea. 'Drink this. There's more, if you want. I'll leave it next to your bed.'

Hijras who undergo this operation do not eat fruit or drink milk for forty days. On the fortieth day, they offer puja to Pothiraja Mata. They carry a pot of milk to appease the goddess and only after they have ritually mixed it with the water of a river or a pond, do they eat fruit and drink milk. Older hijras had told us about this. They'd also advised us to drink a lot of black tea, which would help us pee easily. In any case, I was told that because the tube that was attached could only be removed after three days, I was not to eat anything, or even drink anything except for black tea.

The woman who had come rushing in on hearing me scream took pity on me. She was looking after an elderly man, but she began to take care of me as well. From time to time, she came over and consoled me, and poured me a cup of tea. Her loving care made her seem like a goddess to me. I thought of her as our own Pothiraja Mata.

I lay writhing in pain for nearly two hours and then felt this huge pressure on my chest. Bile rushed up to my throat and I threw up the black tea. At that time it seemed as if I would surely die. But actually, I felt better, the burning was less acute, the pain too was bearable, and my heart had stopped beating wildly. I felt like I had been born again. I slipped into a dreamy sleep and did not know who cleared up my vomit and cleaned me.

I woke up the next morning after at 7 o'clock. I saw my gurubai chela sitting up on her bed. She was talking to the ayah and eating a bowl of rasam and rice. 'So, how're you feeling?' she asked me, smiling.

When the ayah gave me a cup of black tea, I asked her how she knew that we had to be given only black tea.

'What, sami! How many people have I taken care of here, cooked for them with my own hands? Won't I know even this, sami?'

On the third day after the operation, they remove the tube and we are expected to pee normally. We did not even have a nightgown those days and had to go the bathroom in our saris. Holding our saris high and away from the operated area and walking with our legs far apart, we had a time of it. If the pee did not flow freely, we had to be careful and not force it out, for the pain would be unbearable and there would be bleeding. When I think of that time, I shudder even today. As for shitting, that was an ordeal and if I had to take a deep breath to force things out, my nerves felt as if they would snap. I was also scared that the stitches would come off.

On the seventh day, they removed my chela's stitches. It was my sixth day but I insisted on having them removed. We were down to 500 rupees and had decided that we would leave for Mumbai as soon as possible.

I asked the doctor if removing the stitches hurt. 'Only slightly,' he replied. He said he would remove a portion of the stitches and the rest would fall off on their own. It felt like a sharp and painful pinprick when he unpicked them. I closed my eyes and gritted my teeth as before. I had to put up with all these painful procedures, if I wanted to become a woman.

From the meagre amount left we had to part with a certain sum to the nurse, the compounder—both of whom hung around us, scratching their heads, now that we were leaving. Unsurprisingly, they were never there at other times, not when we yelled and screamed and asked for help. When we came for the operation, they welcomed us and attended to us with care before it was done, but once the operation was over, they did not really care. Now that they knew we were leaving for Mumbai, they turned up, expecting to be paid. Not knowing what to do, but having to pay, we gave 50 rupees each to the nurse and compounder and left, clutching our precious 400 rupees.

nine

We took an auto to the Dindigul railway station. At the station, as soon as we got off, we noticed that the auto-rickshaw drivers were pointing at us and sniggering. Some other people too were laughing. We did not have the energy to argue or fight back. We were in great discomfort, could not walk properly and, besides, were weak from not having eaten proper, nutritious food. But we understood that they knew we had come to have the operation and were laughing about that.

The train we were meant to take that evening arrived late. It was very crowded and left before we could manage to get in. We therefore decided to take a bus to Chennai and take the train to Mumbai from there. We did not get seats in the front on the Chennai bus and had to sit in the last row. We had taken care to place cotton wads on our wounds and pad them up with a loincloth of sorts. Two inner skirts offered double-layered protection, but we had an uncomfortable journey as we were at the back of the bus. We felt every jerk and turn in our wounded flesh. We sat with our feet planted firmly on the floor of the bus and held onto the iron rod of the seat in front of us to protect ourselves from being thrown up with every bump on the road. But if we let go and relaxed even for a moment, because it was a strain to hold the position, the wound would begin to throb again. We kept praying to our Mata, muttering her name in our hearts all the way to Chennai.

It was 9.30 in the morning when we reached the Chennai Central station and found out that the next train to Mumbai was only at 4 o'clock in the evening. We wondered what to do until then. We could not use the railway waiting room, because we learnt that it was reserved for passengers with confirmed tickets. There were people in the main hall of the station though and we decided to sit in a corner. But we could not sit for long; neither could we lie down and sleep, though we desperately wanted to. We would have liked to sit, leaning against a wall, and stretch our feet. But wall space was taken up by shops and offices. We sat in the main hall, and found that people who walked by as well as those who sat around, looked at us as if we were oddities. There was, of course, no one to fetch us tea or buy us some food. We were so tired from our bus journey that we could not imagine getting up and walking. Watching people stare was also exhausting—we ended up wondering why we had wanted this operation done at all! We prayed, pleading to God to somehow help us get away and reach Mumbai.

My gurubai chela was hungry and decided to brave it to the food stall and buy some idlis. We ate these, but soon I had to use the toilet. I got up slowly to go, but was worried that if people saw me walking with my legs apart, they might get wind of the fact of my operation and prevent me from boarding the train. I decided to hold my breath, walk normally and somehow bear the pain.

I reached the ladies' bathroom. The woman police officer stationed outside looked at me scornfully and said, 'I can see that you've had an operation. Why can't you be like other men? Why can't you be normal? Find a woman, get married, and be a good householder, who works for a living?' I didn't think she would understand me or my troubles. She made it seem easy, this business of being a normal man. I did not have the energy then to explain matters to her and so, without replying, staggered into the nearest bathroom and shut the door.

I lifted my sari up, and bent down to remove the cotton wad. I was shocked to see it soaked with blood. My wound was still raw and fleshy red where the stitches had been removed. Blood continued to ooze from it. What was I to do? If I could find some hot water, then I could clean the wound and use a fresh wad of cotton. I threw aside the bloodied cotton, and peed and cleaned myself, all the while making sure that the wound remained dry. I took another wad of cotton, cleaned the wound on the surface and applied boric powder. I put fresh cotton on it, and packed the wound in a loincloth. By the time I finished, my head was spinning.

My gurubai chela said that her wound was not oozing blood, nor was her flesh raw and red where the stitches had been. She felt tired though, and very weak. Unable to sit or sleep in that hall, we walked to the platform from where the Mumbai train would eventually leave. We asked where the ladies' coach was likely to be, went there and sat down in a corner. We tucked our bags beneath our heads and tried to get some sleep. We did not have enough money for our tickets. We had spent nearly all our money and this made me wonder why nani had not given us more. Without a ticket we would not be allowed to board a train, and the ticket collector could well ask us to leave, and even have us thrown out. I lay there, plagued by these fears.

Eventually the platform began to get quite crowded. We were ready this time and determined to board the train. We had to find seats somehow. Just then we spotted four hijras, all set to go to Mumbai. Obviously they had not had operations, or perhaps they'd had them earlier. As soon as they saw us, they exclaimed, 'Oh, these are pottais!' and came over. They wanted to know our names, where we were from, whose chelas we were... We said that we had just had nirvaanam done, and were returning to Mumbai. We gave them nani's name and identified ourselves as her naathis. We also told them that we did not have money to buy tickets. We felt better, just talking to them and sharing our troubles.

The train arrived, and along with the four, we managed to get in and find seats for ourselves. They were from in and around Chennai, we found out, and they lived in Mumbai, and collected money from shops in their area. They were returning after a visit home. They shared their food with us and even let us rest our heads on their laps.

After a while, the ticket collector came. The four of them

had tickets, but we did not. They told him, 'Aiya, we are pottais, as you can see. We're going to Mumbai to beg, to earn our livelihood. We have no money on us, which is why we have not been able to get tickets for these two. They have had stomach operations and must rest. We hope you will be generous and help us.'

'I can let you travel, but when they ask you in Andhra, what'll you do?' he said, and walked away.

'Good man. May he live long and well!' one of the hijras thanked him. She added, 'For pottais, an operation is a veritable rebirth. Those who get nirvaanam done win special praise in the community. If we want to live as complete women, that is possible only after we undergo this operation. See, it's not easy to become a woman. You have to suffer to be one. What would you two have done, if you'd had to undergo a thayamma operation? You think this operation by a doctor is bad, but if you'd had the other? What can I say except that our Pothiraja Mata is there for us and it'll all end well. Don't be scared. Once your wounds heal, you'll feel better. And since you've joined us on this journey, you are our responsibility. We'll take you to your nani's.'

Mercifully, we were not asked to leave the train. Though we were in pain, being with other pottais helped us bear with it. For us pottais—whether or not we own things or know people—it is knowing a pottai that counts. Only a pottai knows another's feelings, pain, loss and anguish. Even when they didn't know us, didn't these pottais come to our assistance? Pottais stand by each other and, believe me, a pottai looking for consolation is sure to find it, and often only in another pottai. We are, in a sense, like a flock of crows. We stick together.

ten

Mumbai Dadar, Chennai Central—the things I saw at these places filled me with sorrow. Men and even women stared at us and laughed, and heckled us. I realized what a burden a hijra's daily life is. Do people harass those who are men and women when they go out with their families? Why, a crippled person, a blind person—even they attract pity and people help them. If someone has experienced physical hurt, they are cared for both by the family and by outsiders who come to know of it. But we—we are not considered human.

After we got off at Dadar, in order to get out of the station, we had to climb a flight of stairs and walk across the bridge that connects the many platforms. The looks I got then and the things I heard hurt me more than my wound. I wondered too, if I had not actually asked for this. Maybe I would have been better off as a blind man or woman, an invalid of either sex, than what I was now. I found myself asking the same questions again and again: Why did God give me these feelings? Why must we be tortured by people's looks? If we, my gurubai chela and I, had not met the four hijras at Chennai Central, we would not have reached Mumbai alive. In fact, I am convinced we would not have made it.

We reached my nani's house in Ghatkopar and were welcomed with burning camphor stuck on a coconut and an *arthi*. Nani said, 'Enter, you women!' The four hijras who had seen us home safely were likewise welcomed, and with great respect. My kaalaguru prepared warm water for us to bathe, and everyone crowded around us, enquiring about our health and well-being.

When we narrated all that we had undergone at the hospital and afterwards, to our nani and kaalaguru, nani responded, 'Well, its not easy, becoming a woman.' She added, 'You say you were in great pain, but what if you'd had to undergo a thayamma operation?'

Our kaalaguru then helped each of us bathe in turn. She cleaned the wound and dusted boric powder on it, and expressed her opinion that the operation had been done with great skill. Later, the hijras who had accompanied us were seen off ceremoniously.

WHETHER A HIJRA undergoes a surgery or a thayamma nirvaanam, she has to abide by certain rules for forty days thereafter. We have to abstain from having milk and fruit. We were told it was good for us to eat chappatis and bitter gourd. Mutton soup and the head of lamb were good as well, we found out. We could not bring ourselves to eat bitter gourd, but nani stood watch over us, stick in hand, until we had eaten it all up.

We had to sleep with our legs apart. If not, the hole through which we had to urinate could close up. We continued to drink copious amounts of black tea in order to be able to pee with some ease. We were told not to look into a mirror, to see men or to comb our hair. We had to refrain from doing paampaduthi to elders.

We bathed in warm water, after which we applied medication on the wound. This usually caused the wound to ooze. We would then use cotton to wipe ourselves clean. Once again, we would wash with soap and keep the area dry with a clean cotton cloth. At the end of all this, we dusted boric powder. Every day, for fifteen days, we saw a local doctor who gave us penicillin injections. Our kaalaguru helped us through this period of healing. May she live a hundred years, wherever she is! She did not mind that I was much younger to her, and she even washed my blood-stained clothes.

On the twelfth and twentieth days, hijras in the neighbourhood are invited to come and pour water over our heads. On those days, the elders at home, as well as our peers, rubbed turmeric all over our bodies, performed arthi for us and filled our mouths with sugar. Hijras who came to see us brought gifts of wheat, sugar, ghee and sometimes even tea. Apparently, it is good for us to drink black tea with a dollop of ghee. By the twentieth day, the day of the second ritual bath, the wound is mostly healed. A scar remains though. And once our wounds had healed, we were asked to help around the house, as before.

As the fortieth day approached, we noticed that we seemed

feminine, especially in certain parts—the face, the legs and the arms. We longed for the fortieth day to dawn, feeling trapped at home, unable to move about freely. It was only after the *haldi-mehndi* ritual, followed by a puja to Mata and another ritual similar to the puberty rites done after the first menses to declare the girl free from pollution, that we could leave the house.

The fortieth-day ceremony was held at nani's house in Bhandup, which was devoted to sex work, not at her Ghatkopar house. And nani did not participate in the ritual. I came to know about this only on the day of the ceremony.

Hijras in rich, colourful saris, older and younger hijras, and a few sex workers came to take part in the ceremony. We were seated in a separate room and did not know what was happening outside. But we heard a number of people come and go, and heard happy, jolly music and the sound of dancing feet. There also seemed to be a lot of cooking happening that day.

Some of the visitors came into the room to see us. They ribbed us in a comradely manner, 'So, where is the ceremony and where are these women?' All of them stayed to eat—we too were served food in our room. At around 2 o' clock in the morning, they made us both wear skirts, which we tied high on the chest. They sat us down, and we were anointed with mehndi and turmeric. Meanwhile others were preparing for puja, cleaning and decorating Mata's image.

The custom was that the guru gifts her chelas who had undergone nirvaanam with a *jok*. The jok comprises a green sari, a blouse and an inner skirt, and a nose-ring, anklets and toe-rings. Our hijra friends bathed us, braided our hair, decorated the braids with flowers and then made us wear the jok. They pulled the ends of our saris over our heads to cover our faces. Clad thus, we were led up to the image of Mata. The smell of incense and camphor merged with the sounds of voices singing Mata's praise. A coconut was broken and a puja performed. *Jani Jai Santhoshi Mata* sang the hijras, full of emotion, as they placed garlands on us and tied small bundles of betel-leaves and areca nuts into the folds of the green sari. We remained there, waiting for Mata to descend on us, while the others whirled around, praying and dancing. We too were asked to chant her name, which we did.

It must have been around 4 o'clock in the morning. The hour, the fragrance of burning camphor, the hijras all around us clapping their hands and calling out to Mata—I was profoundly affected by the experience, I felt my body beginning to sway to the rhythm. As if they had been waiting all along for that instant, the hijras took up the Mata chorus even more loudly, and chanting, they lifted a pot of milk and placed it on my head. Two hijras stood behind me to help me balance the pot. The same was done for my gurubai chela. Attended by other hijras, the two of us were taken to the nearest well, balancing milk-pots on our head. We were asked to pour the milk into the well, but without taking the pot off. We had to bend our heads to do this. Then we were asked to fill our pots with water and pour it back into the well. This happened about two times, after which we filled our pots with water, balanced them on our heads and retraced our steps.

Back in front of Mata's image, we were asked to uncover our faces and look at her glorious image. We were asked to recite: 'Take me away and give yourself to me.' She looked gorgeous and her face glowed, as if it were made of gold. As I whispered, 'Take my form away and bless me with yours,' I felt tears sting my eyes. A moment later, I was asked to bend low and offer obeisance to the image. A mirror was then thrust into my hands—I had to look at myself, and I had not looked into a mirror for forty days. The mirror was of such a size that I could view my face and Mata's face. Beguiled by her rich beauty, I could not recognize myself. My face had changed! I felt like a flower that had just blossomed. It seemed to me that my earlier male form had disappeared and in its place was a woman. I felt exultant.

'ALL RIGHT, ALL right, you pottais now have to eat what you like best,' said a hijra, pointing to the heap of offerings in front of Mata. There were nine kinds of fruit, fried snacks, sweets, broken coconuts... On both sides of the image were mounds of rava kesari, with 'Om' inscribed on them. We stared, wondering what we should to eat, while the others waited eagerly. Several were waiting to eat the offerings, but we had to eat first. Unsure as to what I ought to eat first, I reached out for one of the kesari mounds, broke off a small bit and put it into my mouth. At once, all the hijras present started shouting, 'Seesaa! Seesaa!' My gurubai chela took an apple and bit into it and was rewarded with the same shouts of approbation. After this, everyone attacked the food heaps, searching for their favourite titbit.

Hijras believe that our future would be as the food we chose to eat. For those who chose sweets and fruit, life would be pleasant. No one tells you about this before though and so many of us don't know what to eat first. If I had witnessed this ritual before, perhaps my choice would have been informed. The first ritual I participated in was my own! After the ritual was completed we were asked to say paampaduthi to everyone present. We also fell at the feet of our elders. Each blessed us in her own way.

'Be well, beta. From now on, your guru's parivar is your own and you must make your guru's name proud. Listen to what your guru says. Remember you've had nirvaanam done to you. So, no lifting your skirts in public! You have to respect and abide by the codes that hijras live by. You're a woman now and so must learn to act like one. Cutting your hair, running away to your home—none of this is allowed. And don't spoil your life by taking on a husband.' We were subject to hundreds of such homilies. The older women in the Bhandup house called us 'pinjus', implying we were still tender and young. Some of the younger girls however called us 'amma'. We realized that in these places, the women followed the culture of hijras.

After we had received blessings from all present, my gurubai chela and I, still in our jok garb, left for nani's Ghatkopar house. We had to take her blessings. As soon as we entered nani's Ghatkopar home, she exclaimed, 'So here you are, women!' We rushed in and fell at her feet, and said 'Paampaduthi nani.' To which she replied, 'Paampaduthi daadi! Jiyo beta, be well.' She also said, 'Beta, now that you've undergone nirvaanam, you must not think you can behave badly just because you don't have a thing dangling between your legs. You must not lift your skirt and exhibit yourself, whether you are fighting with other pottais or with a shopkeeper who hasn't given you money! No arrogance to be displayed! We do all this because we want to live like women. Not because we want to flaunt it in front of the world and shame ourselves thereby. So be careful.'

Nani then gave us each another sari to wear, 'Now take off your green sari, and the blouse and skirt. You can wear the jok only today. Tomorrow you should give it off to those *akuva pottais*. I'll buy you another jok.'

Nani had in fact booked our joks out to various akuva pottais, that is, those who are yet to undergo nirvaanam. They believe that if you wear the jok of those who've had it done, Mata would descend on them as well. My jok was given away to one of my younger gurubais, who lived in a sex worker's home in Kamatipura. My gurubai chela gave hers away to her gurubai who lived Bhandup.

'A person might be able to afford nirvaanam and plan for it. Ultimately, the time has to be right—the hour has to beckon you. If the moment is not ours, then we won't be able to do it, and will encounter all sorts of obstacles. Mata has to descend on us, otherwise it never happens. Look how you've had it done, just like that. You've been here only for six months, but in that time you've become a woman. Some of us have been here for three years and yet we haven't been able to attain that nirvaanam stage. Your nani has not seen it fit to send us, but she chose you. Your gurubai chela has been here two years and she was chosen only now. It all depends on Mata's grace—when one gets to have the thing done. Because her grace favoured you, you had it done early.' So spoke my kaalaguru. Hearing her fervent words, I understood her faith and was moved by her devotion.

As far as I am concerned, I feel that while there is much to be said for faith of this kind, there is also the fact that I had been a good chela. I did all that nani asked of me. I was respectful and nani approved of my behaviour and attitude. I felt therefore that for these reasons too nani might have sent me for my nirvaanam.

Soon my gurubai chela left for her guru's house in Bhandup. But nani kept me with her and, as before, I started helping around the house and going to the shops.

eleven

Before I got nirvaanam done, I was beset by a strange fear. I felt a pinprick of disquiet, going to the bathroom, or going out of the house. I could not think of myself as a complete woman. But now, all that was gone—the fear, the sense of unease that haunted me. Deep within myself I recognized that I was now a real woman. And I felt joy about it. After the nirvaanam, when I went to the shops, shopkeepers and others who knew me observed, '*Kya, chikni ho gayi*?' (You've become beautiful?) For us hijras, the shopkeepers were *maliks*, veritable gods. They saw us as gods too. Only a few got taken in by my looks and tried to befriend me.

Since I went to the shops on my own, I would be mistaken for a customer and asked if I was looking to buy something. I would then clap my hands, as hijras do, and only then did they know that I was a hijra. I could have passed for a woman.

Amazed by my changed looks, a few shopkeepers even tried to get fresh with me. When they handed me money, they would hold my hand a little longer. If a shopkeeper was alone, he would make me sit me beside him and we would laugh and chat for a while, and then I would be sent off with five or ten rupees. I felt no fear, sitting with them, like I used to earlier.

Rain or shine, we would go to the shops. During the monsoons, it never stopped raining and sometimes there were storms. Even in that foul weather, I would go and feel good about it. In the ladies' coach, I could at last breathe easy and stand without fear near a woman. Usually hijras travel in the ladies' coaches, sitting on the floor in a huddle. But we were never asked to show our tickets and did not buy them ever. We went, as other men and women do, to work—going to the shops was my occupation.

My nani trusted me and thought well of me. I couldn't have done anything without her knowing about it. I learnt many good things from her. From my kaalaguru, I learnt to cook well. On Friday evenings I went to the market in Mulund. I would go to the stalls and ask for vegetables. Carrying a sack, I went from one shop to the next and held it open to be given a few tomatoes, vegetables and other items. I would return to Ghatkopar with a full sack of vegetables balanced on my head. I would sort out the vegetables neatly in plastic bags and store them in the fridge.

Like me, other hijras too came to the market and asked for vegetables, and like me, they too, filled their sacks. Some hijras would insist on being given certain choice vegetables. But if they were highly priced, shopkeepers would refuse to part with them. Some hijras would start a fight, try to make off with the vegetables, or clap their hands loudly to attract attention. I knew what a difficult time shopkeepers had with their produce, so I usually took what was given to me. If I wanted something specific, I would bless the shopkeeper's enterprise, wish him a good profit and then ask for the vegetable of my choice. A few shopkeepers would say in response that it cost a lot and they could only give me a small measure. Some offered me old or rotting vegetables. My kaalaguru scolded me if I returned with spoilt vegetables. I don't think she understood the trouble it took to get the vegetables in the first place, neither did she understand the travails of the shopkeepers.

When going to the market, or the shops, my heart would skip a beat on seeing a face I liked. I would then want to stop and talk to these men—to fall in love with them, be with them. But I did not dare say this aloud. I was a hijra, and I went begging from one shop to the next. People would surely wonder: can a hijra afford to fall in love?

Like my mother and sister wished, I wanted to marry and settle down. But how does it matter what I want? Who would want to marry a hijra? I kept these questions—and my answers—to myself. Some hijras boasted that they had husbands. This did not mean they were married. It only meant that two people liked each other and so had decided to live together in the same house. Even if I were to find myself such a husband, my nani and my guru would never approve of such an arrangement. There are hijras who do not mind alienating their gurus. And there are hijras who are on their own and could live as they pleased. But I was not like them—

I was part of a household; a household with not even a trace of a man. Nani did not have the heart to send me to a house where sex work was done. At that time, I too did not want to do sex work. Till I had my nirvaanam, I had not acknowledged my sexual feelings. Whatever I felt within, I kept to myself. I had learnt to suppress desire and had told myself that it was important for me to become a woman first. Everything else would come later.

When I went to the shops, I met other hijras and heard harrowing tales of how some of them had suffered at their husbands' hands. I have met and spoken to those whose faces had been scarred by a nasty blade, who had poison forced down their throats and those who had been burnt and were still raw from it. Why must hijras suffer so, I wondered. But I did hear stories of happy marriages too. In any case, I did not think then of falling in love and getting married. Even if I got married, I would not be able to have a child. And I knew of so many who had been beaten black and blue by their husbands, and had lost their money and been left to suffer.

There was my friend, Shakuntala. We met on visits to the shops at Masjid Bhandar. The practice was for us hijras to gather in a tea shop, have a glass of tea, and start our day by asking money from the owner of the tea shop. After that, we would go to the rest of the shops. Like me, Shakuntala came to the shops unaccompanied. She could have been my gurubai, but she did not belong to my parivar. She was from the Chauhan house of hijras. She had come to Mumbai four years ago. In spite of going to the shops regularly and earning for her guru, she was not sent for nirvaanam. Her guru promised that she would send her the next day, then it was the day after and so on. Finally, Shakuntala got tired of it all, quarrelled with her guru, and left to set up house on her own. She started going to the shops on her own too, saved up for her nirvaanam and finally got it done. After which, her guru conducted the mehndi ritual for her. After all, it is the guru's duty.

Shakuntala's guru insisted that even if she lived on her own, she ought to give her guru a portion of what she earned, at least once a month. In the past she had given all her earnings to her guru, but Shakuntala did not want to continue the practice. She wanted to keep some money for herself. She wanted to visit her parents, and save for her own needs. If she were to attend a hijra ritual she would need money to buy presents, to gift a bit of gold, for a bangle or a chain. She told her guru she would give what she could, and that because she was her guru's chela.

Shakuntala's guru would have none of it. Glowering, she had said, 'Why, how much I've done for you! Have you forgotten how you were, when you came here, with your cropped hair, not knowing even how to wear a sari, like a *byrupi*? Now that you've become a *masoka* woman (that is, a woman in good circumstances), you've grown vain. I am the one that got your ears pierced, made you wear nose-rings, taught you how to tell right from wrong—and all this, when you knew nothing and came here as an ignorant pottai. But now you've become bold enough to talk back to me, you dare question me?' After the scolding, Shakuntala's guru had also beaten her. Shakuntala waited for her guru's anger to exhaust itself and then left.

Nothing changed. Her guru continued to demand money from her and was believed to have said that she did not mind Shakuntala living away from her, but she must definitely bring her money. So Shakuntala continued give her guru whatever she could—perhaps not what her guru wanted from her, but what she could afford.

There was a local rowdy where Shakuntala lived who had taken to shadowing her. He whispered sweet nothings into her ear and declared that he was in love with her. At that point of time Shakuntala did not know he was a rowdy. One day, he stubbed a burning cigarette-end on his arm to prove his love for her. Shakutnala too appeared to have grown fond of him. (She did not accept his love, since they both lived in the same neighbourhood and she did not want trouble. But people came to know of it eventually.) He took advantage of this and started demanding money from her. He would take her cash, blow it all up in a gambling den, come to her house and beat her up. He got drunk often and would rush to her house and demand money.

Shakuntala did not know how to handle him and continued to hand him money when he asked. Eventually she got tired of losing her earnings. Why should I work hard and give it to him, she thought, and decided that she would not go to the shops for a week, on the pretext that she was ill. But he did not let her get away with that, and beat her up. When she said she wanted to put an end to their relationship and asked him to leave, he had retorted, 'What do you mean, let's part? You mean to get rid of me and take up with another man? You talk like this because you know you're beautiful.

But let me tell you this: wherever you go in this Mumbai city, I'll follow you. And watch it, I am going to throw acid on your face.'

Scared and vulnerable, Shakuntala now had to earn both for her guru and for this man. She bemoaned her fate, 'Why must I slog to give money to these two? Why do they use me like this?' She was afraid to leave that man. She contemplated telling her guru, but feared living with her in her house. All she could do was wail, 'Oh, why did I become a pottai?'

Shakuntala was dark-skinned, with large, expressive, oval eyes. I learnt that beauty can harm a person. Whenever Shakuntala went to the shops, she would smile with her eyes and lift her eyebrows bewitchingly. I used to feel jealous of her: what a smile she had! But behind that smile lay much sorrow. And so it must be with every hijra, I mused, each of us probably carries a lot of hurt and pain. Yet we continue with our lives.

Shakuntala wanted to leave Mumbai and go away to her parents, if they did not mind having her back. She was to tell me all about her parents some time. But that never happened. We did not meet again and I didn't know if she had left for her village. The hijras from my house did not like me talking to Shakuntala. They would complain to nani, and I would get scolded. 'You should mind your own business. Go to the shops, finish your work and return home. If you feel like chatting, talk to hijras in your own house. Why go and talk to that Chauhan-house woman? She does not know how to respect her guru. She has set up house on her own and taken in a rowdy. Why talk to someone like that? Do you wish to become a chela in that household?' The hijras of my house feared that if I talked to pottais from that household, they would poison my mind and make me a chela to another guru in their clan.

If a hijra does not like her guru, then she must move out and be on her own. But as I had seen, living alone was not easy and brought with it a host of new problems. A hijra can become a chela to anyone, but must ultimately live only with her nani or guru and abide by what they say. A hijra must necessarily follow the rules of the community: if she fails, she is bound to suffer. These rules are by and large good. Gurus and nanis, when young, had obeyed their elders, respected them and listened to them before they became gurus and nanis themselves. So it would be for me. If I listened to my guru and nani, I too would attain their status and achieve the freedom they possessed, when I was their age.

twelve

I was twenty years old and troubled by desire. It seemed as natural as hunger, this hankering of the flesh. I could not get married, my nani would object... Perhaps I could have fulfilled my wishes if I'd lived in a house for sex work. I did not dare talk to my nani about any of these anxieties. I wondered if I should become a chela in another house. But where was I to go? How was I to know who was from the Chauhan clan? What if, by mistake, I went to hijras from my own house? What would happen then? I felt confused and did not know what to do.

One morning, I woke up while the others were still asleep. I swept the frontyard, cleaned it with water, drew the kolam and threw the garbage into the bin. Then I walked away. I had nothing on me, except the sari I was wearing. I was scared that they would come after me. I did not have a place to go to, and finally ended up in Byculla where they had done the mehndi ceremony for me. Hijras live with members of their own house, they do not live with hijras of a different house. I was scared of ending up with those of my own house. I looked around for a Chauhan house, but not knowing what was what, I just slipped into a building.

Voices greeted me, 'Come child, who're you looking for?'

'I've come to become a chela,' I said.

'Where're you from? In whose house were you a chela?'

I gave them the details of my house.

'All right, child. But you must tell us whose chela you want to be.'

I said that I did not yet know whose chela I wished to be, at least not in that house.

'Well, then you have to go to Matunga or Mahim, where you'll find pottais from our house. Choose from among them a guru you like and bring her to us. We'll then do the ritual after we know the details of the parivar to which you'll be a chela. If you come like this, on your own, we can't do the reeth ritual for you.'

I left immediately and took a train to Mahim. I went straight to a hijra living in a *jopdi*. You would find these jopdis all along the railway line, from Mahim to Matunga and Dadar. The houses have no walls, instead they are held up by the railway fence on which the inhabitants had flung sacking, large sheets and screens to shade off the insides of their homes. When I expressed my wish to become a chela, the hijra said that her guru resided in Matunga, which was not far from

Mahim, and that she would take me there. I was to talk to the guru myself.

Opposite Matunga station was a line of jopdis. Behind the houses stood the railway station, and in the front, they opened onto a road. Casual workers, both men and women who laboured for a daily wage, lived in these tenements. Opposite these jopdis, on the other side of the road, were tall buildings with shops and flats. The guru we went to meet had two jopdis, one was meant for sex work, the other served as a kitchen. The hijra left me there and returned to Mahim.

The guru took a fancy to me and agreed to make me her chela. This made the others somewhat jealous. My new guru admonished them, 'Why be so blunt and rude to her? The pottai has come looking for us. Come on, talk nicely to her, be kind.' She turned to me and said, 'See you are fair-skinned, pretty like a woman. They're jealous that they won't get any customers.'

She then questioned me closely about how I had come, who had brought me to her place, where was I from, from whose house had I come and whose chela I was. I replied as best as I could, but did not tell her everything. I changed a few details. I mentioned my nani's name, the name of her house and my guru's name. I told her that I wanted to visit my parents and they denied me permission, so I had decided to leave. When the guru asked me who had done my nirvaanam for me, I truthfully said my nani had arranged for it.

'Were you into danda?'

I told her that I went to the shops and had not done sex work. I also said that I might want to go home and see my parents, should I miss them. She said that I could do so, but must inform her before I leave.

I had to live with my guru, two gurubais and my gurubai chela in the jopdis owned by my guru. The roofs were made of tarpaulin sheets, the walls of rough woven bamboo, and both houses had tin doors. My heart sank when I realized what it would mean to live there. But I could not really go back and I realized there was no other way out. There weren't any separate rooms for bathing, eating and sleeping. Everything had to happen in the one room that was there. It contained a cot which was screened off and nothing else. Sometimes one would even have to sit outside, on the road. One had to walk up to the railway track to piss or shit, when no one was looking. A water pipe ran along the railway line and water had to be brought from there to bathe inside the jopdi. As for sleeping, there was the road that ran in front of the jopdi.

I WAS NOW a chela to my new guru and neither my first guru nor nani could make any claims on me. If I had merely come to the new guru and not become her chela, then perhaps, according to the laws of the hijras I might have been returned to my first guru. Since that was not the case, I had nothing to do whatsoever with my old guru now. The hijras were bound by, and honoured, such rules. When the chela ceremony was done, they, in fact, addressed these aspects. Thus, if a person were to become a chela to another guru, she would be asked if she had with her things from her previous guru's house or if she had accumulated bad debts. If the latter was indeed the case, they would arrange for the old debts to be repaid.

All this happened under the tutelage of the seven naiks who sat together and decided on such matters.

During my ceremony, they asked me why I had left my earlier guru's place. I explained that I did not like the way things were.

'Were you given money or jewellery? Have you brought anything from that house?'

'I gave all of my earnings to the household. They arranged for my nirvaanam and presented me with a nose-ring, *lajja* and anklets.'

'You must return them. Is there anything else of theirs that you have?'

'There's nothing else that I have.'

'Do you know whose chela you're going to become? Do you want to be her chela? Or are you being forced to become one?'

I pointed to my new guru and said, 'I want to be her chela and I am doing this on my own. No one's forcing me into this.'

I handed over my jewels and things to the jamaat and these were given to the naik of my previous house. My new guru paid a sum of a hundred and fifty rupees to the house that had arranged for my nirvaanam. After this I was declared a chela of my new guru.

My heart alone knew the truth of all this: that when I was at my nani's place, they had looked after me well. I lacked for nothing. I became a chela to my new guru because of my desire for sexual happiness, in order to fulfill my sexual longings.

EVERY TIME A train thundered past, the jopdi's floor would rattle. From inside the house, I could see the railway station and the people waiting on the platform. To solicit a customer, you would have to draw the screen away from the cot and look out. Our neighbours said nothing though they knew that we did sex work.

After many days, for the first time since I came to Mumbai, I applied lipstick and touched up my cheeks with rouge. I was not allowed to do all this at my nani's house in Ghatkopar. In this place, they seek out newcomers. In fact, customers flock if they come to know that a new person has joined the trade. My gurubais would collect money from customers and hand it over to our guru who sat outside. If a customer offered to pay only thirty or forty rupees, my gurubais told him that he would have to go to them for that amount and not me. I was told that I should not agree to anything less than a hundred rupees. For the customers who came there that was a large amount.

In the beginning, as it was only a few months since I had undergone nirvaanam, they spared me from sex with men who were prone to be rough. On those days I had to make do with small tips, usually ten or even five rupees. I would use the money to buy a lipstick or a tin of talcum powder, or stitch a new blouse.

Those who came were mostly drunks and men who could not afford to spend more than fifty rupees. Sometimes my gurubais would send such men to me, if they especially wanted me. I did not care for a majority of the customers. Those I liked I never really got to see all that much. But there was nothing to be done. After agreeing to be in this business, it won't do to say that I won't go with this person, or I dislike that one.

I did not like doing sex work, but now found myself doing it. I wanted to experience sexual happiness, but I found myself having to treat sexual experiences as work. We had to make do with the dark, with often only a lamp to illumine our world, when we carried out our trade or sat down to eat. In nani's house at Ghatkopar there were separate rooms, and the bathroom was inside the house. We could even watch television, should we want to. But there was work to be done, much work to be done, in fact. It was, however, a gilded cage. I felt that I was breathing freely now that I was out of that cage.

We had to sleep in front of the jopdi—we'd spread a sack on the ground and sleep on it, drawing a blanket over ourselves. If there were rowdies troubling us, my gurubais would handle them. They never involved me in this; in fact, they made me cover up fully and feign sleep if I happened to be awake. My guru would repair to Dharavi every night and come back drunk. She would bring some booze for my gurubais as well. They offered me the stuff, but I declined, saying that I was not in the habit of drinking. They did not compel me. Though we lived poorly and in a hut, I was indulged by all, and was the darling of the household, chiefly because I was fair and pretty and spoke nicely.

OPPOSITE OUR LINE of jopdis lived a rich drunk. Every time he came our way, he would look me up and down. But he was also scared that his family would come to know of his interest in us. In spite of his fear, he would come up to us, especially when there was no power and the road was dark. We never welcomed him, but we couldn't antagonize him either. We would address him as 'brother', tell him that we looked upon him as our protector and plead with him to think of what his family would do to us, poor people living in huts, should they know he had come to visit us.

'You think I don't know what you do? Why, I can pay you too. Won't you come to me, gori?' he would proposition me.

'Sir, sir, she's just come from the village. She's not well. Please sir, don't stand here. If someone from your house spots you, they won't let us live here!' Somehow we would manage to fend him off.

Some nights, he and his friends would come around when we were sleeping and throw lighted matchsticks on us. We would be jolted awake by the heat of the flame on our bodies, get up shrieking and put the fire out. He and his friends appeared to enjoy our shock and discomfort. After this happened a few times, we decided to take turns, except for me, and keep watch all through the night. The man was mad, we knew, especially when drunk. We were poor, and besides, we were hijras. We were afraid to go up against him or report him to his family. They were all Marathi-speaking locals and we would not be able to live here, if we opposed them. We did not dare beat him up, neither could we go to the police. We knew the police would give us no support. Besides, we were in a trade that invited such affronts, and so we carried on, afraid and unsure how to handle him.

Many such things happened in a day and we lived in constant fear. To get over this feeling of vulnerability and to be able to sleep, I too took to drinking. Initially I found the taste bitter and I experienced heartburn, but once I got used to it, I found myself waiting for the hour when my guru would bring me the stuff from Dharavi.

WE WERE VISITED not just by these rich fellows, but also local rowdies from the jopdi. They would come by and threaten our guru into giving them money to drink. Once a large, dark rowdy tried to force me into having sex with him. I ran into the hut, but he followed me. My gurubais ran away and my guru could not do anything under the circumstances. She could not come in or ask for help.

I felt trapped and not knowing what to do, I had to accede to his demands. I held onto his legs and pleaded when he wanted me to do things that I did not like doing. (He wanted me to have anal sex with him.) He spat abuse at me and forced me into the act. When I screamed in pain and yelled for my guru, he shut my mouth with one of his hands, whipped out a knife with the other and threatened to take it to my throat. I was hurting all over, and yet had to give in and do as he told me. The skin down there felt abraded and I was bleeding. Unmindful, he left, but only after he had snatched my purse away from me. Men like him will understand the terror and pain they cause only if they become hijras and are hurt by rowdy men such as themselves.

After he left, my guru came in to see me. She asked me if I had ever had sex in this fashion before. When I said no, she said that if I were to do this sort of thing, I must apply oil in that area. I cried out that I did not want to have anal sex, that I did it only because that man held a knife to me and forced me. I understood then what had happened to my friend that evening up there in the hill near my village. She must have suffered as I suffer now.

My guru said, 'Beta, if we are to live here and make a living in this place, you'll have to listen to what people like him say. Do as he wants you to do and make him happy.'

What else could she say, poor thing? I reckoned my gurubais had suffered this before. I asked myself why we pottais were treated with no respect. Would a time come when we would be freed from being humiliated thus?

My guru took me to a doctor she knew in Dharavi. She took me there because he was used to examining hijras who had been hurt in this fashion. He did not ask to see my wounds. My guru said a few words to him, after which he gave me an injection. He also wrote out a prescription. Back at the jopdi, I heated water in a broad vessel and poured dettol into it. I sat athwart the vessel in such a way that my wounded parts were immersed in the water. It helped to do that, at least it lessened the burning. I had the tablets on time and tried to take care of myself through a period of hardship and hurt.

Five days later that rowdy was back again. He claimed that his gold watch and five hundred rupees had gone missing in our place and that I had taken them off him. 'If you do not return them,' he threatened, 'I will slash your face, even burn your hut.'

I was stunned at his behaviour—after he had forced me to have sex with him and taken my purse away! But what could I do? He was a thug. Now it appeared that he was determined to take more money from us. My guru looked at me. 'Amma! I took nothing!' I cried out and fell at the rowdy's feet. He said that he would return in the evening, by which time we were to have the money ready. And he left, but only after he delivered a well-aimed kick at our tin door.

My guru tried to console me. She said that he was known to harass anyone who was beautiful and that he would not come again. She added that he was trying to frighten us and that I was not to give in and get scared.

I had not chosen sex work in order to make money. It was because I could not really repress my sexual feelings that I had opted for this life. I was beginning to discover the horror and violence of this choice. I cried and confessed that I wanted to go home to my parents, that I would fall at their feet and beg to be taken back.

My guru would have none of it. 'You've been here only for two months, your gurubais have been here for two years and I haven't yet let them visit their families. How can I let you go?' she reasoned.

I assured her that she did not need to give me anything. I told her that I didn't feel right in my heart, and asked her let me go for at least ten days.

'What'll you do if your people don't accept you? What if they shave your head and beat you up?' my gurubais wanted to know.

'When I went home from Delhi, I hadn't had nirvaanam done. But now that's not the case. I'll speak to my mother and father. Plead with them to accept me. Do you think they have no love left for me?' Brave words, but I knew I was only mouthing what needed to be said. I felt I could no longer stay in that house. Not even for a minute. I wanted to leave, for this reason, for any reason.

My gurubais advised my guru to send me home. 'See, the

pottai's got scared because that rowdy threatened her. If you don't send her home, she is sure to run away and become a chela somewhere else. So send her home for a few days.' My guru relented and gave me a thousand rupees and five saris, and bought me a ticket on the Kanyakumari Express. She and my gurubais saw me off at Victoria Terminus. As the train left, my gurubai reminded me to return in ten days.

THE FIRST TIME I left my village for Delhi, I was anxious about finding where hijras lived. On my return home, after hearing my mother was ill, I was not too worried. At that time, my family did not know I was a hijra. When I got home, of course, everything changed and I had to leave again. It was now a year since I had come to Mumbai and I was returning home, yet again, but as a woman.

I was admittedly confused. How would the people in the village look at me? What was I to expect at home? What would my friends from school have to say? What would my neighbours think? I had wanted to become a woman and had become a woman. Yet my village knew me as a man. It knew nothing of my feelings, the reasons why I wanted to become a woman, the relationships I have with hijras... What if my family accepted me, but the village did not? I was filled with questions, doubts and some possible answers.

In all this I forgot hunger. I was rehearsing questions and answers. I should say this, if I'm asked that; I would answer thus, if they wanted to know of that...

thirteen

I entered Namakkal town as a woman. It was my first time in a sari. No one seemed to recognize me. I took an auto to my village and got down in front of my house. I stepped into the house and my mother knew who had arrived. She began to wail immediately. 'I thought you were dead. Would that it was true! What is this guise you've come in? We feared this would happen and we shaved your head back then. But you ran away without telling us. How dare you appear in this state before me? What hardness of heart…'

My brother, who was sleeping inside, came out on hearing her. 'You pottai motherfucker! So you're not content with casting our honour to the winds! You've come now dressed as a woman. What guts!' He rushed towards me with a stick.

'Look! I've had an operation and I'm a woman now. From now on, I'll live as I wish. You can't beat me as before, you have no right to. Don't you know that there are laws in this land that'll punish you if you hit a woman? If you dare hit me, I'll go to the police,' I warned him.

Undeterred, he raised his stick, 'Think you're a woman?'

At which I lifted my sari and showed him. 'So, tell me am I a woman or a man?'

'Think you're a woman, just because you've cut your bud off?' My brother kept the stick raised, but did not dare hit me.

Seeing me lift my sari, my mother hit her mouth with her hands and bawled out, 'He's cut it all off, the two and the third! Oh, how did he have the heart to? How is it that he's still alive? When he was a baby, I used to fondle and kiss his bud. How could he do this and come and stand in front of me like a barren tree! How dare he lift his clothes up and show it all in front of his mother and hurt her so... and he's here alive still, even after what he's done...'

Crying, she fainted. Hearing her keening, the neighbours crowded into our house. The girl next door exclaimed on seeing me, 'Doraisamy! What sort of disguise this? Have you really changed into a woman? Have you no thoughts for your father, mother, brothers and sister? What has happened to you?'

'Look! I'm not a man, don't call me "dai". My name is Revathi and that's what you should call me from now on.'

'What?! How many times would we have called you Doraisamy in the days past? How can we all of a sudden address you as Revathi? Just because you've worn a sari, we can't think of you as a woman! Come on, get rid of this costume before the entire village comes of know about it.' She had hardly finished saying this when my brother handed me a lungi and a shirt.

'Come on change! Motherfucking pottai!'

I refused.

'You want the entire village to laugh at you? Come on, change into male clothes!' he insisted.

I experienced great anger at that moment, but did not want the rush of feelings in me to burst out. I will stand my ground, come what may, I decided, and said, 'Disguise? Costume? What're you all accusing me of? What I'm wearing now is real, true. Everything that happened before, the clothes I wore, the life I led, the way I had to be—that was when I was in disguise, when I wore a costume. Whatever you say, whatever anyone thinks, I shall remain what I am now.' My voice was loud and clear.

'You've grown fat on your own vanity! Went dancing about the village in a girl's guise first and then you had this operation done! You've all but destroyed your life and yet you say this is real and true. You've buried our honour deep and clothed us in shame. How does it matter to us if you're alive or dead?'

'It's not my vanity that made me cut it off! I felt like a woman—I wanted to stay true to my feelings, so I changed into a woman. And I'm going to live as one.' I sounded quite firm.

The women attended to my mother. They splashed water on her face, gave her some water to drink and made her sit up. My mother must have been listening all the while. She lamented, 'Is it not enough that all of us born as women suffer? Many in this world long for and are willing to do penance for a son! And here you are, born a man, who has decided to become a woman halfway through his life! What'll the world say? Will anyone accept you? Do you think we can walk with our heads held high in the village any more? It might not matter to you, what the world or anyone else thinks. What about us, though? We have to live here, have our marriages and our funerals here, and in the course of all this, if people were to say, "That Doraisamy has become a woman, has he?" what can I do, but lower my head in shame!' So she went on.

I replied that that this world would talk ill not only of me, but of anyone who is not seen as normal, anyone who is disabled, anyone has been violated. Each one of us, I pointed out, would be discussed and gossiped about. Why should I be afraid of or care for the world? 'And why should you feel shamed on my account? I came here only because of the love I bear for you. If you think my presence causes you shame, if you feel that you've been lowered in the eyes of the world because of me, then I'll leave and be with my own kind. I want nothing of your property or your people. I'll sign away my interest in what you own and leave. No one needs to feel ashamed because of me. In future think you have one son less.' As I spoke these words, I felt the pain of them deep in my stomach.

'Even if a woman were to smile at a man or talk to him, this world construes a relationship between them and talks ill of them. If you were to go into the village wearing a sari, the world would talk ill of not only you, but of me, along with you. It is bound to ask, "What sort of woman is that who has raised her son this way?" Son, give up this dress. If you must, wear it when you're with your own kind, but when you are here dress like a man...'

My brother intervened, 'Amma! Why must you plead with him? Let me get out my knife and cut his hair, and land him a blow or two. He'll have no choice but to come around and dress like a man!'

Just as it seemed we were in the middle of a war, I heard my father ride up to the house on his motorbike. Hearing the sound of his bike, the neighbours quietly slipped out. My brother and mother remained silent. I felt my heart thud uneasily against my chest. What would I say to my father? How was I to greet him in this new guise? I stood with my head bent in fear.

He came in, looked at me and asked who I was, and why my mother looked the way she did. 'Can't you see? It's him—remember how much we loved and indulged him when he was young? Here he stands, having betrayed us all. He wears a sari, says he's had an operation and that he's a woman.'

My father did not speak to me. God knows what he thought, but he went in, changed his clothes and came out. 'Look, we tried our best. We beat him, cut his hair, shaved his head. He would not be deterred. He has not been with a woman or had a child—none of that has happened. It seems this is his destiny. Who can change what has been ordained? There's nothing we can do. Nothing we do will make a difference. All our other children have their wives, their families, but he'll have none. As long as we are alive, he'll have us for family, but after our time, he'll know what it is to be alone. So people will talk, that he is a man in woman's clothes, that he's had an operation... whose loss is that? If that's what he wants, let him have it. Things will happen as they must. Let him be and eat of our food.' My father's eyes were moist with tears and his voice betrayed a deep sorrow. After that, he went out of the house.

Everyone feared my father. So did I. After he made it clear that I should be left alone to lead my own life, I did not speak to him. I could not bring myself to speak with him. Deep inside my heart, I yearned to fall at his feet and cry. But a strange kind of fear held me back. Meanwhile, my mother and brother laid down a set of rules for me. I was not to roam around the village, nor was I to take part in public gatherings. Most importantly, I was not to hang around with men, talk to them or go out with them. My response was silence.

I felt fear, shame and confusion. What would people say? I wondered especially about my classmates and my relatives. It was my eldest brother who was tough on me. He didn't live with us and he was not even working with my father. He was a driver with another lorry service. After his wedding, he had set up house on his own. My other two brothers were single and still in our family business, taking milk cans around.

Everyone at home continued to call me Doraisamy. I felt bad about this, but what could I do? I thought that it was remarkable that they had accepted me wearing a sari and being a woman.

MY SISTER GAVE birth to second child around that time. She lived with her husband and child in her mother-in-law's home in their village. My brother-in-law was kind and affectionate towards me and my five-year-old nephew called me 'kudumi mama' ('the uncle with long hair').

I used to visited my sister at her village. The people there thought that I was her younger sister. Only she and her husband knew me as Doraisamy. I was happy to be in their house, playing with my nephews and helping my sister take care of them. I often thought of them as my children.

My sister did not ask me too many questions. Sometimes she would say that this must surely be fate's doing, or someone's sin that was being visited on me. Why would I have changed otherwise? At other times, she reckoned I was like an ascetic, for I lived a life that knew no pleasure. Though we fought a lot when we were children, she had become different after marriage. She was responsible, even-tempered and calm. When I was with her I thought that if I had been born a girl, I would have lived just like that—married, with children and happy.

Though I was my usual self in my sister's house, I would lower my voice when there were visitors. Sometimes, I stayed inside and did not come out to meet them. In any case, I never stayed at my sister's place for long, maybe a day or two at the most. I went in the morning and returned by evening.

When I wanted to visit my sister, I would go to Namakkal town first and take a bus from there. Usually, my father or one of my brothers brought me to town and waited until I took a bus. People in my village would wait, at such times, to catch a glimpse of me, as I left the house. But no one recognized me in Namakkal back then. I went about as any woman would. Only my voice was like a man's. I tried to hide it, and when on the bus, spoke softly to ask for a ticket. I was afraid that my voice would give me away and I would be identified as a pottai. I never spoke to the women who sat next to me, and even when they spoke, I mostly remained quiet and got by saying very little.

In my sister's village, whenever I was sent out to buy things, say biscuits for my nephew, I would go to the shop in the bus stand, where I was sure I wouldn't be found out. That shop was run by a man who was both deaf and mute.

I was petrified of being exposed and teased. What if I got angry and fought back? Then people at home would come to known of it and god knows what they'd say. I lived in the silent shadows, half hidden.

MY MOTHER'S PARENTS died when she was a child and she was raised by her grandmother. The old woman had worked as a labourer—carrying sand and soil for roadwork, whitewashing trees roots upward with lime, and other such tasks. She had also died some years ago. My mother's family now comprised only of her aunts, their husbands and children. They lived about twenty miles from our village and visited us often. Every time there was a temple festival in their village, they invited my mother. Mother's relatives were mostly poor—small peasants and labourers. On the other hand, everyone was rather well off on my father's side. His two brothers lived close by and their four sisters lived in Namakkal and Salem.

My relatives came to know about me. When my father's family came home, they did discuss me. Some even supported me. Well, if he had remained a man, they'd reason, he would have got himself a wife, had children and lived happily with his family. What to do, though? It is written in his fate that he should change mid-life into a woman and who can change what has been already put in place? They would try to console my parents by assuring them that in time everything would be just fine. That people would eventually stop talking about me. Besides, if I had been a woman and had come home from a bad marriage, would they not have supported me? So it must be now as well. 'Don't say anything to hurt him,' they'd add, 'he is close to God.'

Whenever my father's family planned a festivity or celebration, they made sure to invite my mother and father, my brothers and sister. But they never asked me to go. My mother's family though would insist that I came along for every occasion. 'You must come,' they said, 'no one will be able to tell looking at you, and we won't tell them. We'll say you're a woman.' I felt secure in their affection and concern. My father's relatives, I felt, were merely saying things, their words rolled off their tongues too easily. Maybe some of them did mean well by me, perhaps they were afraid that their status and the respect they enjoyed would be affected if they were seen welcoming me.

In the beginning, I hesitated to visit even relatives on my mother's side. My family, too, didn't want me to go. Whenever I was invited to one of their homes, I accepted politely but did not ever go. Eventually, I did begin to pay them visits. In the village where my mother's people lived, there was an annual temple festival. I sought my family's permission to go to the festival. I wanted to go dressed in a sari. I had been to those festivals earlier as a boy, but this was the first time that I would be going as an adult and as a woman. I went, wearing my sister's jewels. I visited the homes of kin whom we referred to as uncles, aunts and grandmothers. When they addressed me as 'Doraisamy', I entreated them to call me 'Revathi'.

I went with my grandmother and aunt to the temple to offer worship. When asked who I was, my aunt mentioned my mother's name and said I was her daughter. There were people who knew our family who then came up to me and said, 'Where is your husband, my girl, and your children?' I had to tell them that I was not married. Listening to them talk to my aunt, I figured they mistook me for my sister, for I heard them wondering aloud, 'But isn't her daughter married?' I immediately said I was the younger daughter. My aunt and grandmother smiled uneasily, and muttered under their breath, 'Actually this is Doraisamy, but he has become like this.'

My uncle's son whizzed into town on his motorcycle, with me riding pillion. He showed me off to his friends, 'How's she? I mean to run away with her!'

'Who's she?' His friends were curious.

My cousin laughed and said, 'Actually this is Doraisamy. He went off to Mumbai and returned like this!'

His friends were a bit puzzled, but nevertheless nice to me. They told my cousin that since he had found a nice girl, he should perhaps speak to my mother and ask for my hand, but only after ascertaining if my mother had put aside a handsome dowry and some jewels at least!

I was touched by this banter, so open and ingenuous it was. I longed for it to come true. Though I thought of myself as a woman, I felt that I was a man who had become a woman. Could I bear a child? Would I be able to marry? These questions bothered me and I felt them as so many insistent pinpricks. One can joke about marriage, but I knew deep down that none of this would come to pass in real life.

People would look at me curiously, but no one teased me, or made fun of me. Women appeared eager to talk to me, wishing to get to know me better. Since I knew they saw me as a hijra, I felt abashed whenever they spoke to me. My aunt hesitantly asked me if I had breasts like her and other women. When I said I did, she wanted to know how I got them. 'There is an injection they give you which makes them grow.' In truth, at that time I had not developed breasts. But I could not tell them that. I therefore lied.

Usually I avoided spending the night at relatives' houses. In my aunt's house you bathed in the bathroom, but to pee and shit you had to go to the fields. The women in that village went to the fields but I felt shy about going along. I also knew that though they did not say anything to me, my relatives did discuss me amongst themselves and noted that I was indeed a man in a sari. Some of my cousin's friends who drove lorries and had gone up to Mumbai had seen people like me begging, doing sex work and running houses where sex work happened. They did not speak of this to me, nor did they tease me, but I knew that they discussed these things amongst themselves.

In any case, how long and how often could one stay with relatives? It was all right to visit during the temple festival, and also because I was invited to their houses. But I couldn't possibly stay anywhere for long, even if I was asked to. I did not want to feel that I was a burden. Besides, there was the problem of the bathroom and toilet. It was different at my own house, with my parents. That was a story I knew and was familiar with. Even if I was beaten and scolded, I had a right to be there.

THE PEOPLE IN my village talked about me. They were curious. Many wanted to come and see me. And how long could I remain trapped within my house? I began to step out and gradually took to sitting a while on the veranda. The village water tap installed by the panchayat was outside our house. Women from families that lived on my street and from the adjoining streets would come to the tap to fetch water. (We did not use the tap, since we had installed a motor that pumped water from our well into a tank.) The women who came would look at me and whisper among themselves, and if anyone of them was new, they would be told, 'Look at that, a man sitting there dressed like a woman.' I felt odd when looked at and spoken about in this fashion.

Sometimes I got angry. One time, a girl in our village got married. The marriage procession was passing by my house. I stood by a half-open door to watch them go. As the procession went by I could sense that some people from my village were staring at our door. I also noticed that they made signs to members of the groom's party, asking them to look at me. Abashed, the bride lowered her head but yet whispered to her husband, who then turned to gaze at me. My heart grew heavy. I understood then that there were many people out there in the world eager to criticize and find fault with others. For such people, I was a thing to be looked and laughed at, an oddity, a comic figure. It was not only this newly married couple, but also others who went by who stared at me. A motorcycle had only to speed by and if the driver had perchance missed seeing me, his pillion rider would say something to him, and he would turn and gaze at me. Whenever that happened, I was petrified that there would be a road accident. I often saw people go down our street, then turn back to look at me, while they continued driving.

Those walking on the street also stopped to stare, including children who stopped by and asked me for water. My mother would bring them water, and often had to reply to questions about me. She would mutter her replies. Once I heard someone ask her, 'Amma, why is Doraisamy standing in a sari? We heard that he has had an operation ...' My mother said that someone had poisoned my mind, made me go mad and then had done this to me. 'I have no one to blame, but my fate,' she added, 'I don't know whose sin is being visited upon my son.'

I ASKED MY mother to take me to the Mariamman temple in Samayapuram. We walked the half a kilometre distance from my house to the bus stand to catch the town bus to Namakkal. I wore my sister's wedding sari and her jewels. People walking on the road looked at us in astonishment. Some women came up to my mother and said, 'We see you have two daughters now.'

My mother smiled and said, 'Yes.'

They looked at me next and said, 'No woman can vie with you and win! What do you call yourself?'

'Revathi.'

'So we should call you Revathi hereafter and not Doraisamy, is it?'

'Yes.'

As we waited for the bus, more passers-by, students going to college, local shopkeepers and many others stared at me. Since this was my village and my mother was with me, no one dared say anything. My eyes scanned the road restlessly, noting who was staring at me, who was whispering. I kept wondering what people were thinking as they looked at me. In turn, I felt peoples' eyes on me—clearly they were unable to tear their eyes away from what was before them.

On board the bus, all my actions—the way I held onto the railings, adjusted my sari around my waist every time I felt it slipping, my manner of mopping my face with a kerchief—earned a persistent stare. There were some Telugu-speaking dalit women in the bus who talked about me among themselves. They thought I wouldn't be able to understand what they were saying, but I could. They remarked that I did indeed carry myself like a woman. 'How did this happen? Who is he and what is his family?' At this, one woman cautioned them all to lower their voices, saying that they should talk softly. Another continued, saying that I was Revathi and liked to be called only by that name. At which one of the women asked me, 'Revathi, are you well?' I said I was.

College students on the bus too stared at me. They did not dare tease me but one asked the other, 'Ay macchan! What's the time?'

To which, the other replied, 'Nine, da!' All this in an undertone that neither I nor others in the bus could hear clearly.

'What about Bus Number 9?' quipped another. Through barely concealed taunts, and by making eyes at each other, they spoke about me. I felt rage in my heart. I gritted my teeth and thought, 'They are so thrilled to be making fun of me! What if their brothers were like me? Would they talk of them?' My palms burned to slap them hard on their cheeks.

From Namakkal we took the bus to Trichy. No one appeared to notice me on this bus. In fact, those who had not seen me before would not be able to tell I was a man dressed as a woman. But I was nervous and as always my eyes were restless, darting, trying to fathom how those on the bus looked at me. But really, the men who stared at me stared as they would at any other woman. The women on the bus, I realized, were more interested in my sari and jewels than in me. They did not look at me or whisper among themselves. I imagined they saw me as a woman.

The last time I came to the temple, I had lowered my head in shame, filled as I was with unfulfilled desire and sadness. I had been weeping inside, as I was forced to cut off my hair and offer it to the goddess. I had demanded of the goddess that if she was indeed all-powerful, she should make me anew, to be like her. Mariamman had not played me false, for she had given me a woman's form and I was standing before her as a woman. I felt the prickle of tears as I prayed, 'Amma! You are unique in your compassion. You are all-powerful, as they say. Not only have you helped me realize my wish, but you've united me with my family. I don't know how to repay your grace. I will never forget you, Amma.' I fell at her feet and returned home, clutching a photograph of the goddess in my hand.

fourteen

My mother often said to me, 'You'll be fed as long as we are alive. You are safe until then. But what'll happen to you after we die? I fear for your future. Who'll take care of you?'

My mother spoke the truth. Who was there for me? People might respect me if I had money at least. I had become a woman, but would I be able to marry? Or have children? My brothers will look after their own children, their families. If I had money, maybe, they would respect me, treat me well. But what if they allege that I am eating off them, that it's a waste feeding me?

Besides, I needed things—soap and powder, kohl, sari and blouse. Every time I needed something, I didn't really expect a helping hand to reach out and give me things. Fine, my parents fed me, but I did not want them to get these other things for me. I didn't want to trouble them. I was young, and I should be able to fend for myself. Once I had money, all other things would fall into place—respect, consideration … I could not expect to achieve this later, after sitting out my youth in laziness.

I had not even passed class 10. Who would give me a job? Who could I possibly ask? I could go back to Mumbai, but I would have to deal with rowdies as before. I had left saying I'd be back in ten days and it was three months since I came. What will my guru say, if I were to go back now? Should I return to my old nani, the one that helped me to get my nirvaanam done? I was scared that I would be yelled at and hit for leaving that house without telling anyone, and becoming a chela to another guru.

My brothers were earning. I was idle. As a matter of course, almost routinely, they found fault with me. I had to endure scoldings and beatings. I had no one supporting me. I could not assist in the lorry; looking like a woman, how could I be a cleaner? I felt grim and unhappy. I kept thinking that I should indeed return to my old nani. After all, there were others, hijras, who ran away, returned home, went away again… Why should I imagine I would be beaten? I could explain things to nani and make her take me back. She might like that, it might make her happy. It is common, as I said, for hijras to leave the house where one was a chela and become a chela at another house. It was best that I went back to my old nani. I could earn by going to the shops. Having resolved to go back, I told my mother about my decision. I would go back to my own kind, perform like them and earn my keep. Thus would I be able to stand on my own two legs.

I left for Mumbai soon after.

ON REACHING GHATKOPAR, I went straight to my nani's house. My kaalaguru greeted me warmly. 'Revathi! Welcome home! Amma, Revathi's here!'

I followed her into the house. My guru and other elders were there. I did paampaduthi to them and then fell at my nani's feet, weeping. 'Nani! You must forgive me. I ought not to have gone away without telling you.'

'You stole away when we were sleeping. You might as well have thrown stones at us! What did we do to you? What were you lacking in this house? You seemed all right. Didn't nani arrange for your nirvaanam and offer you the ritual milk? You cheated us and ran away to become a chela in another's house! You gave me grief, girl.'

I told her all. I told her how I had felt then, how I'd wanted to get married and have a family, how I took to sex work because I could not really fulfill my desire otherwise, the troubles I faced, how I ran away and spent time at home with my parents. I cried my heart out, as I narrated these events to nani.

'Even those born as women are not happy in their married lives. They get abused and hurt. This, after their families spend thousands of rupees getting them married. What would a pottai like you want with marriage? You ought not have lusted after a man. Didn't I tell you that you must not feel this man-love? Once you're a pottai, it's best that you set yourself up with a chela and others like you, and go and earn money in the market. What's this urge to fly?' Nani went on to say, 'You must be independent inside, you know. In any case, since you now feel this man-love, it is best that you don't go to the shops. I'll send you to another place, where your desire might come true. Will you go?'

I said I would go wherever she wanted to send me.

'I am sending you to my gurubai's parivar. None of our people are there. You must behave and earn a good name with them. You must visit me too, from time to time. And no hanging out with other pottais, loafing around, drinking and fighting. Most importantly, you can't take a husband. If you do, be sure that I'll skin you alive.'

With this advice she sent me on my way. But not before she took me to a naik's house in Byculla and accepted me again as her chela. She then took me to a place from where sex work took place. I was introduced to my gurubai, chelas and others. 'Mind you,' warned my guru, 'no running away! If anyone troubles you here, come and tell me. And also come and see me from time to time.' She handed me my clothes and left. That was how I made my journey to Crane Road.

THE PLACE I went to, which belonged to nani's gurubai, in Crane Road, was next to a place called Blouse. The houses there mostly employed women, but there were also houses run by hijras who hired hijras for sex work and tried to pass them off as women. There were also grocery stores, beer bars, clubs, hospitals, paan-shops, hotels and tea shops. Sex trade was carried out along a lengthy stretch of the road, for almost two kilometres. Outside the buildings, on the road, stood a number of women in modern clothes, soliciting customers, while a stream of people flowed past them, some walking, others in cars and bikes, buses, taxies and horse-carts. The road was always crowded and noisy with the sounds of screeching vehicles, the cries of sex workers as they called out to their clients and the music from radios that blared out of tea shops and hotels. It was carnival time always and every day a market day. Shopkeepers who depended on sex workers, those who ran the sex work trade, were all busy in this market.

Only those hijras who looked like women were allowed to do sex work. For people came to this place looking for women. Hijra sex trade is known as 'danda'. The house where sex work was carried out is called a 'danda kantra'. In the house I was in, there were two hijras besides me. It was small and on the road. There was a small bathroom inside where we bathed. But if we wanted to use the toilet, we had to go to the first floor of the building where there was a common toilet. All the houses in our complex were occupied by hijras. Hijras who carried out danda on the first floor still had to stand on the road to solicit. Only after they got a customer could they take him up the stairs. Often fights broke out between those who did danda on the first floor and those who did it on the ground floor about who ought to get customers first.

The house where I did danda stood close to a grocery shop. On the other side, near the stairs that led to the neighbouring building was a paan-shop, and next to that was another hijra danda kantra. Initially, when I was new to the place, I wore a sari even when soliciting and did not ever attract a customer—not a single first one. The others who stood with me wore jeans, skirts and midis, and they all got clients. My mistress, whose relationship with me was that of a kaalaguru, asked the other hijras in our house to lend me their clothes. 'With the money you earn doing danda, buy yourself some clothes,' she said. 'You can't hope to attract a man dressed like this—village-style in a sari.'

In the area in which I worked, each room was in reality a house in itself. Some of these houses were not only meant for doing danda, families lived there as well. If a room had three large cots, three people lived on the cots, and three below them. Of the cot people, those who did not have kantras of their own rented kantras belonging to those who did danda outside. They took their clients to these kantras, but once business was over, they came back to live on or underneath the cots. Some of these women might even have husbands and children. Owners charged those who lived on the cots fifty rupees a day and those who lived below, twenty-five rupees. They had to use the common facilities for bathing, etc. and they had to keep their things close to where they lived.

I saw, heard and got used to an entirely set of new experiences. I wondered at that time if things could indeed be the way they were! How people suffer to eat and live! The things they do! People reached this place because of poverty, the burden of looking after a family; because they were orphans and did not know how else to live; because they had been abandoned by their husbands, cast away by their lovers; because they had been raped and rendered unchaste. People had left their home, family, hometown, even country. Some came out of choice, others came lacking any choice. My heart melted seeing all these people, with their dreams, tears and troubles.

This was a world I had not known until then. I was witness to other people's sorrows, I came to know them as my own. Women doing sex work; hijras who had been deceived by men who praised their beauty and enslaved them, who stole their hard-earned money and spent it all, leaving the hijras with scarred faces, bruised by knives, who were little better than servants, going to the shops, washing vessels; those who had earned in thousands for their mistresses and were yet cheated by them and had to go to other places for work; those who suffered from sexually transmitted diseases and did not receive proper medical care and therefore died; those who had to put up with the capricious demands of clients who paid them a mere fifteen or fifty rupees and who used them as they wished, brutally, and left them with bite marks on their bodies, as if they had been bitten and abandoned by mad dogs; those young ones with great sorrow in their hearts who yet stood on the streets, with powdered faces and painted lips, smiling at prospective customers; those who were carried away by the police for no fault of their own, who were beaten with whips and lathis and stamped upon by police boots, had electric current run through their bodies, who could only leave after paying the police a hefty bribe. I saw all this and more, all that I had not seen until then.

This was the world to which I had come and one where I had to earn my keep. How was I going to do it? I had no choice, I had to live here. My sorrows were nothing compared to what I saw there. I told myself that I was there to earn for the morrow, for my future. God knows if I would be able to do that, but there I was, determined to journey in this world.

I LEARNT TO dress like a film actress by watching how others did it. I learnt to wear make-up and choose my clothes. I came to know only then that there are such things as beauty parlours that help to make one beautiful. I started going to a parlour—to get a haircut that suited my face, to tweeze my eyebrows just so and to get a facial and bleach to remove blackheads. Initially, my mistress sent my fellow hijras to talk to clients, so that I could learn how to solicit their attention, how to talk to them and in a voice and tone that did not give away that I was a hijra. I saw how they pointed to me and haggled over a price. Gradually I learnt to do this myself.

If I had, say, five clients a day, I'd have to hand over the money earned from them to my mistress that day itself. The next day we would split the earnings. If I had earned 500 rupees, I'd take half and she would take the other half. This was how all those who did danda in that house settled their accounts. Since we did the accounts the day after, one had to remember and report the exact number of clients, and who paid what. All those who did danda would sit with the mistress separately and give details such as the number of times they had to do it and the total amount earned. Only then did they receive their share of the earnings. Since I was new, the others would ask me how many clients I had had and what I had earned. I would give out these details, without attempting to hide anything. If it turned out that I had earned more than the others, they would get jealous and try to pick up a fight with me. They never told me though what they earned in a day. I did not ask either.

The hijras would also catch hold of a client who wanted me and claim that he, in fact, wanted them and not me. Our mistress would intervene on such occasions and ask the client who he wanted, and if he pointed to me, the rest of them would leave peacefully. Sometimes, they would try to entice the client at the very moment he came to me, by making gestures or rolling their eyes at him. In that case a man would go with them, rather than with me. In a sense this is what distinguished the seniors from us juniors. If we were not vigilant, they got wind of the fact and stole the client in front of our eyes. And it was not just those who shared our house, but others too. Those who lived on the first floor would stand on the road and forcibly take away clients who came for me. They would, in fact, grab a man by his shirt and yank him off. If my mistress happened to be around when such things happened, she intervened. If she was not there and I protested, it invariably ended up in a fight.

Once there was this man who kept looking at me. But he appeared too scared to come inside. He was waiting for an opportunity to enter our house. Three other hijras noticed this and just when he was ready to come to my door, they jumped on him and held him by his shirt. Caught by three hijras, he got frightened. When they started dragging him, he slipped, fell down and tore his shirt. He somehow managed to disentangle himself from them and run away.

I told the three hijras that it was wrong of them to do what they did, especially after they had seen him seeking me out. I also pointed out that I did not try to drag away clients who sought them out. 'Also,' I went on, 'now neither you nor I have the fellow.' The three did not heed my words and instead started fighting with me. The hijras in my house watched the fight but did not interfere.

'Had you signed an agreement with the guy? How can you say that he came for you? Think you are Rathi herself? She thinks she's a heroine and that he came specially for her!' They began to rain blows on me. The hijras from my house tried to pull us apart, but actually ended up pulling frenziedly at my hair. Such fights were everyday events. It was not just me who got dragged into fights. Everyone did. A hijra only had to be beautiful or display some weakness—that was enough for people to provoke a fight.

As far as I was concerned, the hijras there were from different parivars, and they had their own gurubais, chelas and naathis. I had none to call my own there. My guru lived elsewhere, my nani in another place. If I were to get into a fight with a hijra, all those who were of her household, from the youngest to the oldest, would take her part, never mind that she was in the wrong. I had to tolerate whatever happened to me, because this was my place of work. There were clients who came for me and me alone. Fights ensued over my clients even before they reached my door. If my guru had a house in this place, and I lived with my gurubais, chelas and naathi, that would be a different story. My current mistress did not really care to see what was happening and spent her time playing cards with older hijras. I could not very well tell her to stay around and not play cards.

People like me who could not fight and often got cheated, ended up going to the bars and drinking our sorrows away. Supposing I had fifteen rupees and another hijra had fifteen rupees as well, we would go to a bar and drink a quarter. We would exchange unhappy stories, but we knew there was really no way out of our misery. At that time younger hijras like us could not really go against whatever the older hijras told us to do. We had to abide by their words. If we failed to do so, we'd be told that we had no respect for our elders. The older ones always looked to control those younger than them. If we younger ones made enemies of the older hijras we could not expect to live there.

I thus began to drink, so that I could share my troubles and forget them temporarily. I began to drink every day. I only had to have fifteen rupees and somebody to share a drink with and I'd run away to a bar. If I had fifty rupees, I would go on my own and drink beer. If my mistress knew that I was not doing danda but had gone to drink, she'd get angry and scold me. I would, therefore, go to the bars without her knowledge. Often I'd gulp my drink down as if it were a cup of poison and come back to stand in front of our house. The hijras in my house would sometimes get wind of this and when we quarrelled, they would use this against me. They'd carry tales to our mistress and get me into trouble.

Even though I drank, I did not trouble others. In fact, I was the loser in the bargain. When I got drunk I would talk—of my troubles, my family, of what hijras endured and so on—to whoever was next to me, and forget to do danda. I would talk incessantly not noticing who was looking at me, or calling out to me. At such times, other hijras would steal my clients. Our mistress got to know of this and warned me, 'You must not drink during the day. You can drink at night but only after the house has shut down. If you don't listen, I'll have to report you to your nani.'

Once, my mistress found out that I was drunk during the day. She dragged me into the house and started to hit me.

Unable to bear the pain of those blows, I asked her what right she had to beat me. She then picked up the wooden plank on which one sits and bathes and hit me on my head and on my back. As she hit me, one of the glass bangles on her wrist broke and the pieces scattered all around us. Unable to return her blows, or shout back at her, I picked up one of the glass shards and slashed my forehead. As my forehead turned bloody, my mistress stopped hitting me. My hurt and anger made me injure myself. The piece of glass I had used was sharp and so the gash on the hairline was deep and a good four inches long. As a result, rivulets of blood ran down my face. Seeing this, one of the hijras in the house took a piece of cloth to the wound and held it tight so that the blood flow would stop. She then took me to a hospital nearby.

The doctor there said, 'If I were to stitch this up, it'd look ugly,' and applied medicine on the wound. He gave me tablets to take as well, and sent me home after an injection. That night, I was in pain and so I took the medicines the doctor had given and fell asleep. The next day, I arranged my hair in such a way that the gash could not be seen, and stood, as usual, on the road, ready for danda.

IF I HAVE to think of happy times, it would be the morning hours—getting up late, at around eleven, putting on make-up and coming out. We also worked out different shifts for ourselves. If two slept during the day, one would be up and standing on the road. Usually they preferred to sleep during the day and put on their make-up and come out at around six in the evening. Therefore, I did not sleep during the day. There was no trouble if some customer came looking for me. Those who usually quarrelled with me over clients were not around during the day.

Whether we did morning or evening shifts, before we put on make-up and stood on the road, ready for danda, we would go to the tea shop and have a cup of tea. A man from Kerala ran the shop. He had an old juke box and you could listen to your favourite song for fifty paise. We listened to songs in the order we asked for them, and I would listen to mine after whoever had chosen her song had heard hers. I usually asked for black tea with lime in it. They called it 'Sulaiman tea'. I heard over and over again a song that went '*Rim jhim...*'

Once I remember that it rained incessantly for two days. Since we lived in a low-lying area, all the houses and shops were flooded. We put away our belongings on top of the cots and literally lived in water for over three days. We tried to swim, and even played, spraying each other liberally with the water that surrounded us. We would also walk for long distances in the water. Often, there was sewage mixed with the water. When we continued to play in the water, older people would scold us. But we didn't care, our attitude was: let whatever disease that may come come!

Those who lived on the ground floor suffered the most. They could not cook or eat, and besides had lost their belongings to the water that flooded their homes, even as they were asleep. In some places, even the cots went under water, and people had to lock up their houses and take shelter on higher floors. Several cars and bikes were submerged in the rain water. People came in horse-carts and took photographs, people came to look, and people thronged tea shops and drank tea, while standing in water—it was an extraordinary time. Those days of rain are among the few pleasant memories I have of that unhappy time.

It was also during my stay there that large-scale Hindu–Muslim riots took place in Mumbai. Everywhere you looked houses, cars and buses were burnt down and many people died. My mistress and the two hijras in my house were not in town and I was alone with a young hijra who had arrived only a few days ago. Mumbai city was under curfew. No one could step out. Grocery shops would be open for an hour, between six and seven in the morning, and we had to buy whatever we wanted within that hour. For eight days we lived indoors, petrified that anything could happen to us any time. As far as hijras are concerned, they go to temples, churches and dargahs. We did not observe religious differences. I never failed to go to my favourite shrines every week—to the Haji Ali dargah on Thursdays and the Mahalakshmi temple on Fridays.

EVERY TWO WEEKS I would go to see my nani and hand over my earnings to her. I took the electric train whenever I went to see her. Usually, hijras do not buy train tickets. When I went to the shops I didn't either. Nor did I sit on the seats. I would sit on the floor of the carriage and travel. After I came to this new place, I felt that I had introduced myself as a woman to the larger world. Besides, I had learnt a great many other niceties. I wore ultra-modern clothes and so, when on a train, I imagined that like other women, I was going to college or to work. Hence I bought tickets and sat in the women's coach with great pride and confidence.

On the days I went to see my nani, I would go for the 10.30 show at Arohara cinema hall in Matunga. I would watch a Tamil film and go to see nani after that. Many Tamils lived in Matunga and you could buy things that you only got in Tamil Nadu. I would buy betel nuts, leaves and tobacco for my nani. For my kaalaguru and gurubai, I would buy Gopuram brand turmeric powder, and strands of needle-thin jasmine, *kanakambram* and *kadambam*. In Matunga are the Murugan, Ayyappan and Perumal temples. I would pray in these temples to do well in my trade and for my heart's peace.

Back then, when I lived in my nani's house and went to the shops, my kaalaguru would feed me leftover rice, old curry and stale chapattis. But not now—whenever I visited I was given hot rice and fish curry that had been made that very day. In the past, I had looked to others to earn my livelihood. Even though I earned money I would hand over all of it to nani and merely take a rupee every morning to start my day. But now I was independent. Though I still gave my income to nani, I did so only after I had retained enough for myself.

When I lived with my nani, I did not get to choose my sari or blouse, nor did I seek out a good tailor of my choice. Nani decided everything. She would buy blouses that did not match and which were baggy and made me look old. But now things were different—I wore churidar-kurta, spoke stylishly and gave money to the household. Therefore, I earned all this respect.

When I saw the spitoon in nani's house and the huge copper vessels that stored water, the mortar and stone used for grinding spices and the scrubber used for washing vessels,

I was overwhelmed by memories. There was yet another young hijra doing, and probably feeling, all that I used to do and feel all those years ago. In this world, it is enough that one has money. Respect and regard follow.

My older gurubai lived with my guru at Byculla and I visited them as well. Byculla is also called Kamatipura. There are many houses for sex work there—houses where hijras employ women to do sex work, houses where women employ other women in this trade. My guru's house in Byculla was a large building, one part of which was used for sex work. Near it were other hijra houses and houses run by women. In the basement of the building were a number of Marwari shops that sold saris, perfume, silver and gold. You could get a loan, pawn your jewels...

My gurubai would chat with me, ask me about my danda, clients, the conditions in which I lived and worked, and the reasons for my beauty. When we were talking about my clients, I once sought her help. If a client came to me, thinking I was a woman, they sometimes got to find out that I did not have breasts. I asked my gurubai how I could acquire breasts as large as hers. She said that I was not to tell anyone, and handed over a bottle of tablets. She asked me to take a tablet a day and said that they were from Singapore. I took those tablets for a month and while my breasts did not ever get as big as hers, they grew to a satisfactory size.

Those were happy days—living as a woman, going shopping, going to the movies, visiting temples, being with my loved ones.

MY LIFE IN Crane Road came to an abrupt end one Sunday.

Our mistress bought mutton and cooked it with palak to make an unusual curry. My mouth started watering and I thought that it would be nice to slip away to the bar for a glass of beer while the food was being cooked. I liked to drink beer before eating meat. Since this was a new sort of dish, I felt I must have my beer. I could say that I was going to my guru's house in Byculla, but if my mistress asked around and found out that I had not gone there, it would lead to a lot of confusion. I racked my brain for an excuse and finally left, saying that I was going to the beauty parlour. I took off for a bar that was somewhat far away.

At the bar, I saw a hijra who was kind of an elder gurubai to me, who lived on the first floor of our building, drinking with some men. I sat at a table where two Pakistani men were already seated. They were rather handsome and soon started talking to me. I too chatted back. They spoke in Urdu and I replied in whatever Urdu-Hindi that I knew. One of them asked me if I wanted beer. I thought to myself that I could save fifty rupees and said yes. When the beers arrived, one of the men challenged me to drink my beer at one go and said he would give me a hundred and fifty rupees if I did so. I agreed and holding my head high, emptied the bottle of beer into my throat all at once and only then put the bottle back on the table. 'Sabash!' said the man and gave me the money.

The other hijra saw this and came over to our table and sat down. She asked the man if he would give her money if she too finished a bottle of beer at one go. The man looked at me, then looked at her and said he wouldn't. The hijra thought that I had told the man not to give her money and so started a fight with me. She cursed me in Tamil and started saying abusive things about my mother. I lost my temper and said that I was the one doing prostitution, why was she dragging my mother into this. Would she like it if I said things that would hurt her?

'Try telling me and you'll see,' said the hijra and, pulling me by my hair, started to hit me. Everyone in the bar turned to look at us, and I felt ashamed. And so in turn I tried to clutch at her hair. Mouthing a string of obscenities, she kicked at me and tore my blouse. I felt humiliated. The bar manager asked us to take our fight outside his premises and pushed us out. As we walked towards where we lived, she continued to shout at me and hit me. Hearing us, all the hijras came rushing out.

The hijra called out to my mistress, 'Look, amma! Look at what your pottai has done! I had gone to the beer bar to pick up a customer. He was drunk and had agreed to pay a thousand rupees. I was ready to bring the fellow home, when she came there, started a fight and even abused my client. She told him that I was not a woman, but a hijra and tried to keep him away from me. And not only that, she dared to hit me!'

She got me into trouble and almost got away with it. My mistress believed her and started an argument, 'You said you were going to the beauty parlour. Why did you go to that bar and pick up a fight?'

I tried to explain what had happened but she said I was a liar. I yelled back at her, 'I know now what it is. You all belong to the same parivar and so will not let down one of your chelas. I too have a guru, gurubai and chelas. I'm going to bring them here!'

I took off in a taxi to Byculla and explained to my guru

what had happened. My entire parivar came back with me—in five taxis. All of us, including my kaalaguru, chelas and gurubai went straight to the house of the hijra who had beaten me. Seeing us arrive in full strength, she got scared and cowered behind her guru. If her guru hadn't been there, my parivar would have got to her and torn her apart.

The elders sat down and conducted peace talks. They said that the pottais in the area were all in the habit of going to bars, getting drunk and beating each other up. But in the evenings, the same pottais could be seen walking hand in hand. So it was best, they went on to say, that the elders stayed out of such quarrels. 'As for these two,' they concluded, 'she pulled at the other's hair, but that one also did the same.' 'Your pottai,' noted the elders, pointing to my parivar, 'is new to town whereas this one has been around for several years. She had no business, therefore, to hit her. It is best we drop matters here.' I was denied justice.

Those who earned money for their mistress were condoned, even when they made mistakes. This was because if their wrongs were pointed out, the wrongdoers could desert the guru and become chelas to another and the guru would lose her income. With me, they could not really stomach my bringing back a few clients and waited for a chance to pick up a fight. I did not have the support of the hijras who shared the house with me because I was a pottai from another parivar. There is rivalry among hijras about parivars though we do not observe caste or religious differences.

When nani came to know of this, she decided that I was not to do danda any more, instead I was to return with my guru to Byculla and stay and look after women who did danda.

Her reasoning was that having seen a bit of cash, I had taught myself to drink—God knows what else I'd do. My guru and I went to collect my clothes. My mistress did not talk to me. I did not speak to her either. I just packed my bags and left. As soon as I sat inside the taxi, I saw her coming out with a pot of water. She poured the water on the steps leading to the house. This is done only when a corpse that has been laid on the threshold of a house is carried away. It seemed to my mistress, I was as good as dead. I decided that I would never ever go back to that place. I left for Byculla with a heavy heart.

IN BYCULLA, A lot of lorry drivers visited my guru's houses as well as other houses in the area. Namakkal in Tamil Nadu is well-known for its lorry business and many drivers who come to Mumbai on work end up coming to Byculla. There are men whom I know from Namakkal, even my own kin, who come and spend a night with sex workers. Every woman in Byculla has a lorry driver as her permanent customer. I did not really like having to attend on the women, but since nani had wanted me to stay, I did. I think she had her own reasons for sending me there. Since men from Namakkal were regular customers to the area, she imagined that they would talk to me, and I could thus arrange for clients to visit the girls in my guru's house.

But I was upset by what I saw there. The way the women suffered, their lack of freedom, the fact that, like jailbirds, they were followed even when they went to the toilet, the pain they experienced when in hospital… Besides, I could not even think of soliciting clients for these women. I too have a mother and sister. I could countenance selling my body to earn a living, but not the bodies of others. I simply did not like it. But I could not talk about this to anyone there. In any case, no one would understand my feelings. It seemed to me that there was only one way out—I had to abide my time and wait for a chance to run away.

fifteen

Nani owned two houses in Byculla. My kaalaguru carried out business on the ground floor of one house and my guru did hers on the first floor. I lived on the first floor. There were ten women sex workers there. They were not allowed to go out. If one of them fell sick, I played security and escorted her to the hospital. I was the one who was sent out to buy beer, brandy, cigarettes and food for the clients who came to that house. My guru gave me five rupees every day.

Most of the time, we did not cook in the mornings. There were some people from Tamil Nadu who made idli, dosai and vadai and sold them from house to house. The women and I would buy our breakfast from them. My five rupees was never enough for me to buy the food I needed. I was afraid to ask for more money from my guru and so ended up being hungry in the mornings. Our afternoon meals were cooked at home, and leftovers eaten at night.

The women called me 'pinjamma'. Women here did not ever call hijras by their names, instead they referred to them as 'amma'. Since I was little, I was called 'pinju amma' (little mother). Around five o'clock in the evening, the women would comb their hair, wear flowers and put on make-up. If some of them had fallen asleep it fell to me to wake them up.

'Girls, get up! It's five and you're still sleeping!' I would yell and try to wake them up. Often, I would be told, 'Pinjamma, last night I had to be with two men, one after another. I am so sleepy. Can't I sleep a bit longer and then get up? Please, don't tell on me!' This happened sometimes, that two men wanted the same woman, and she had to sleep with both of them in the same night. She also had to make sure that neither knew about the other. If either of them came to know, he would abuse her, since he had paid for the entire night.

It was common for clients to spend the night. Those who came during the day were usually men from north India. From seven in the evening to nine in the night, the clients who arrived were usually lorry drivers from Tamil Nadu, who booked the women they were used to or desired. They paid for their night with that woman and usually handed the money over to my guru. The women were tipped by the customers directly. Using that money, the women bought whatever they needed for themselves.

My guru would entreat me to go and stand on the road. 'Wear make-up and go! Make sure that clients coming here are not whisked away by other hijras.' I, too, would comb my hair, like the other women did, wear flowers and go and stand on the road. My neighbours would pick their clients and take them into their houses to the women of their choice. Then they would return to station themselves on roadside to get more clients. The hijras were really my gurubais. We often went to the hotel together to drink tea and buy beeda for the elders.

One day, when I was drinking tea with my fellow hijras, seven men came in a taxi. They turned out to be lorry drivers from my village. They immediately identified me, 'Dai, Doraisamy! You're here!'

'I'm fine. I've come to visit my guru and spend some time with her.'

'Then where do you live?'

I felt bad that they called me 'dai' and used my village name. And so my replies were mostly murmurs. The hijras who were with me began to tease me, 'Di! Is your name Doraisamy? Why do they do call you "dai"?'

Just then a voice thundered out from one of the houses, 'Where the hell have you all gone? These are our clients. Come on! Take them!'

The seven asked me where my house was and wanted to be taken there. Barely had I started to lead them, when the other hijras pulled the men by their shirts and shouted at me. 'Ay! These are our clients. How dare you take them away?'

The men indicated that they would like to go with me, whereupon the hijras started to fight with me. The hijras from my house came down and joined the fight. Finally, it was decided that the men would go to the house to which they went habitually.

'He may be your future husband, but all that's in your village, all right? These chaps always come to our house. You can't claim so-and-so is from my village or her hometown. You have to know whose client he is, only that is of significance. In future, if you come here claiming that person is from my village, we'll strip your head off its hair! Be careful!' Having warned me, they took the men away to their house.

'What sort of a pottai are you? Of those seven, three are new fellows. They have come here for the first time. You could've brought them here!' This was my guru's complaint.

'How am I to know they are new? I've been here only a few days. I don't know the system here. Especially who's come here before and who is whose client. I don't even know the clients that come here regularly that well. What am I to do?'

'You know nothing, except to gobble a plateful of rice!' My guru was exasperated. 'Call yourself a pottai, and you can't talk to a fellow nicely and entice him here! And you dare stand here in front of me. Get out, go back to the road. Your gurubai will point out our clients and you go and bring them here.'

That was my life in Byculla—some fighting and a bit of happiness. Sometimes, if there were several clients, there would be no room to sleep. I had to sleep on the road. Not just me, but other hijras had to as well. On such nights, I found it difficult to buy whatever it was the client needed. 'Pinjamma, Pinjamma!' As soon as the call came from the first floor, I had to rush up. My guru would give me money and say, 'Go and buy biryani!' And I would be told to get it from the Delhi Bar Hotel. That place was at least one and a half kilometres away. A packet of biryani cost thirty-five rupees. The client would hand out a fifty-rupee note for it and I would run all the way and get the stuff. My guru would pocket the remaining fifteen rupees. Could she not let me at least keep the change? Up and down I had walked a distance of three kilometres. I could have used the money to take a taxi. Why must I be made to walk? Surely I could be given a bit of money for my troubles? I often reasoned to myself.

Whether it was the girls, or my guru, whenever any of them asked me to do things for them, I wondered why they could not all pool together their requests. It never happened that way and sometimes I would make five or even seven trips to Delhi Bar Hotel. I often wept on the nights I had to do this. There was no one to share my troubles. I felt that even the street dogs were mocking me with their barks. I felt as though a sharp needle had pierced my laden heart. I would think that in my previous workplace I had a bit of freedom. In the new place, I had to work harder and there was never enough money. I could not buy nice clothes or even a nice pair of sandals for myself. They even calculated the amount of water I used for bathing!

MY NANI FOUND a chela for me. Her name was Mya, and she lived with my kaalaguru on the ground floor and did sex work along with the rest of the women there. I was proud that I had a chela of my own. She would secretly buy brandy for me at night. The booze was a salve for my wounded heart. But I made sure that my guru did not know I drank.

One day Mya sought me out when I was alone and started to cry. I asked her what the matter was. She said that she felt very trapped in that house and asked me if I could send her away to some other place. I told her that she appeared to be better off than me, and asked her what was bothering her.

'See, I take money from the clients, like the others. I have enough for my food and clothes. But nani is refusing to send me home! She's saying that I'll have to earn for her for three years, and then she'd send me home. I want to see my village again.'

I told her that I was not in a position to help her. In fact, I wanted to leave this place myself, I added, but did not know how and when. 'How can I help you? Wherever you go, wherever you are, even if you become another's chela, you'll continue to be my daughter. You are my first daughter. I'll never ever forget you. Wherever you go, I'm willing to follow you there.'

Mya said that she would go first and I could join her later. She left eventually, I don't know to what place. In that short span of time I had known her, I felt in my heart that she was my daughter. Often I thought of her and wished her well, wherever she might be.

My guru spoke to me about my runaway chela. She cautioned me against running away. 'Don't you dare run away! Only if you stick it out here, however difficult it is, will your nani give you jewels and money and send you home.' I wanted to tell her, 'Who cares for your money or jewels, when all I want to do is run away?' I never gave voice to my response; instead, I nodded to whatever she said.

The women sex workers did not share their woes with me. They were scared that I would report them to my guru. The women were treated more or less like prisoners. They had to do sex work for three years, earn money and only then would they be sent home. They were also not paid much. And like I said before, even when they went to the toilet, they were watched. Going to the shops for them, keeping vigil, fighting over clients, not having enough money, not getting enough to eat in the mornings—all of this corroded my spirit. I did not how I was going to get the money to run away from this place.

Without my guru and the hijras in my house knowing, I started doing sex work with clients who fancied me. I took them to houses run by women, where I rented a space for something like five rupees and got into the trade. Whenever my guru noticed my absence and asked me where I'd been, I lied, saying, I'd been downstairs, or that I had gone to the tea shop. Like this, I earned around five hundred rupees. Now that I had sufficient money, I could make plans to leave. I thought that I would be caught if I took the train, and so decided to go to Sion, and from there take a bus home.

I CAME TO know of Sharma Travels when I used to visit the shops. One morning I left Byculla and went to Sharma Travels in Sion and asked if there was a bus going to Salem. I was told that I had to go to Bangalore and take the bus to Salem and it would cost me three hundred and fifty rupees. I handed the money over and got my ticket. The bus was leaving at four in the afternoon, so I went to Matunga and watched a movie that morning. I watched an afternoon show as well and left before it ended to catch the bus. I got on the bus, but until it started, I felt that my life was not in my hands.

My seat was in the first row. A woman sat next to me, by the window. The bus had two drivers. One of them drove the bus. The other lay on a cot that was behind the driver's seat and in front of mine. There was a glass partition which separated that area from where we were sitting, and it could be opened and shut. There was also a cloth screen drawn over the partition. I found the driver on the cot eyeing me while pretending to sleep.

At around 9 o'clock, the bus stopped at a hotel for dinner. Everyone got off the bus, but I did not. I was not hungry. The passengers finished their dinner, boarded the bus and we took off. Many fell asleep. The girl next to me slept. I could not sleep, and my mind went over all that had happened to me. I thought to myself that I should perhaps wait till I got home and then think about what to do with my life. I had no money, clothes, jewels, nothing. I had nothing whatsoever to take home to my father and mother. If my mother were to ask, where is your money girl, after all you've worked for so long, what was I going to say? Mourning my fate, I too fell asleep, leaning back on my seat.

I woke up, feeling something touch me. The driver on the cot had opened the glass door and his hand was sliding up my leg. I did not know what to do. He looked rough, big, with a large moustache. I was scared that if I were to ask him to remove his hand, he would get me into trouble. Afraid that if I spoke my voice would give me away as a hijra, I slowly pushed his hand away from my leg. He did not stop though; he kept pushing his hand up my thigh. The girl next to me was fast asleep and I wondered what she would think if she woke up and saw what was happening. A thirty-year-old man, who was on the seat behind me had obviously noticed this.

He got up and confronted the driver. 'Why are you doing this? That poor girl! How you're troubling her! She is silently suffering! She is unable to even speak. Don't you have sisters? What kind of a driver are you? You're supposed to protect us, and here you are behaving badly!'

The driver immediately withdrew his hand, but yelled back, 'Mind your business. Is she your sister or what? I haven't done anything. While sleeping, my hand must have slipped onto her leg. And here you're screaming as if she's been raped! Get back to your seat, will you?'

Everyone in the bus woke up. So did the girl next to me. But no one said a word and neither did they ask what happened.

'Ay! You! Did I put my hand on your leg?'

His rough tone frightened me and I did not dare reply. I was scared too that he would do something to me, once we got to Bangalore. This was going to be my first time in Bangalore and I did not have a soul to help me there. Ashamed, I put my head down. The man who had got up to defend me returned to his seat. The driver closed the glass door and drew the cloth screen across it, taking his hand with him.

Around two in the morning, the bus stopped at a tea shop. Only a few people got off the bus, while others remained on board. The man who spoke up for me got off. The driver who had troubled me also got off. He had a lever, the kind used for changing tyres, in his hand. He rushed to attack the other man, hitting him on his back and on his legs. The other man defended himself and soon they were both on the ground, pummelling each other. Those who were off the bus moved in to separate them.

I was more frightened than ever. All this was happening on my account, and God knows what would come of it all. I saw the two returning to the bus and take their seats. The bus started. I sat quietly, expressionless, as if I knew nothing of what was going on. My face felt tight. I did not even dare move.

At nine in the morning the bus stopped again. I was petrified about stepping off the bus, but I had to, to use the toilet. Once that was over, I hopped back on. I did not eat anything. Looking out of the bus window, I saw the man who had spoken up for me limping. Poor man, I did not have the courage to say even a few consoling words.

It was seven in the evening when the bus got to the Bangalore office of Sharma Travels. I went in and showed them my ticket. They said that the Madurai bus, which I was to take, would leave only at 9 o' clock. I said that I was new to the city and had no place to go. They pointed out a room that was meant for passengers and said that I could wait there. They would call me when the bus was ready to leave. I went and sat down in that room.

I wondered if I should report what had happened on the bus. But my cowardice kept me silent. The man who was beaten up had alighted from the bus earlier. I felt bad, thinking of him. What would he have thought of me?

After this incident, I grew afraid each time I saw a stoutly built man, or one who spoke in a bullying tone. There was no safety for women who travelled alone. I wondered how I was going to survive as a woman in this world.

sixteen

For the second time, I entered my village in a sari. On my way home, I was greeted rather warmly by people from the neighbourhood who did not know me very well. 'Revathi, you arrived just now? Are you well?' I smiled, acknowledging their goodwill. As soon as I reached home, the women from houses nearby called out, 'Look, Revathi's here.' They sounded happy to see me.

I went into my house, and my mother exclaimed, 'Why, it's Revathi!' I felt as if I had been healed from the horrible experience on the bus.

Soon I was in the middle of women—my mother and our neighbours. 'Revathi, ever since you left, you've been in your mother's memories! "Doraisamy's gone, God knows when he'll return" was your mother's constant refrain. Why, even yesterday, we were talking about you, and here you're today. Sister! Your daughter is here! Cook something nice for her.'

'Dai, couldn't you have at least written a letter?' said my mother.

My father was watching television. As soon as he saw me, he smiled and said, 'Dear one, how're you?'

'Appa, how're you keeping? And you, Amma?'

'We're fine, we only worry about you. You went away, and your brothers fought with us—picked a quarrel with your father. Seems they want to drive long distance, so they are now driving other people's lorries to Mumbai and Delhi. As if that's not enough, your middle brother wants his share of property. Your father thought that he should let these illiterate donkeys make a living driving lorries and so made them drivers, and taught them a trade. He showed them a way. He did good, there's no doubting that. They could drive the milk-lorries locally, come home every evening and be content. But they don't want to drive locally any more, they say. And so they've gone their ways, driving the long-distance routes. Each wants his share of the property. They want to buy their own lorries.' My mother narrated a long tale. I had a long tale of my own to tell, but could not.

We still had our four lorries and employed three drivers and four cleaners. My father drove one of the lorries himself. He had obtained yet another tender for delivering milk. He wanted to fulfill the contract and not reapply for the tender. His lament was that his sons were not all right, and so it was best that he sold all his lorries and held on to the money. I could not very well interfere in these family matters. What did I know, anyway? Let my parents and brothers decide. I was bruised, I had very nearly destroyed myself. If I were to narrate my woes, I'd be told that I had brought it all on myself. Saying nothing, I went to the bathroom.

In the bathroom, I wondered: on my way home, the villagers had referred to me as Revathi. In front of them, my mother too addressed me as Revathi, but once in the house, she said 'dai'. Had she accepted me as Revathi? Was the 'dai' merely a matter of habit, something she had used for a long time and could not shake off easily? I did not understand. I also asked myself if those who called me Revathi did so truly, from their hearts, or were they actually mocking me. Whatever it is, I concluded, I am glad they called me Revathi. I was going to be this way. Slowly, gradually, they're bound to understand my womanly feelings. There's perhaps a legitimate reason for my mother calling me 'dai'. I told myself that I ought not be angry with her.

As far as my village was concerned, they did not look at me as before, as if I were a strange creature. They appeared to have accepted who I was. Also, they had told and retold stories about me till they grew tired. What was there to talk about me any more? Some of the older people still called me Doraisamy, while others addressed me as Revathi. But all of them were affectionate and treated me as a mother would treat her child. I felt abashed going about in a sari in front of them.

I could not however get over the drinking habit I had picked up in Mumbai. Who'd give me money to drink? And how would I drink? I thought that if I remained stuck at home, I'd want to drink. Perhaps if I found a job, I'd not be troubled by that thought. And so I went into town, looking for work, in STD booths, in grocery stores, textile shops… But no one wanted to give me work. Their responses hurt me, as if they were so many spears aimed at my heart.

'If we're to employ you, you'd be the ruin of all the boys here.' 'If you worked for us, we'd have to shut shop, and steal away, a towel on our heads!' 'We can't employ people like you. What do you know, anyway? Get lost, go to Mumbai or Delhi and be with those like you. You're all fit only for dancing on the roads, and having cheap, riotous fun!'

Each stated a reason for not giving me a job. Heart-broken, I returned home. I sat down on the steps of my house, sad that I could not find work. Just then, a moped rushed down the road but stopped suddenly outside my doorstep, almost colliding into me. I looked up and saw that it was my middle brother.

'Dai, pottaiya, when did you come?'

'Fifteen days ago.'

'I've just got off the lorry. I'm waiting for our brothers to return. I've a case in court, asking for the family property to be divided. After the others return, we're going to have the property divided through the court. You'd better agree to not demand your share! Make sure that you sign a statement saying you don't want any of it! Do that and then go back to Mumbai or wherever to your community of number nines and continue to clap your hands.' He said this aloud, so that his words could be heard by my mother and father, and then sped off on his bike. My father and mother, however, advised me to insist on my share of the property.

By now my three brothers lived in houses of their own. My third brother had married a woman he loved. My middle brother was not married, but lived with a woman. They worked for different employers, and were drivers. My eldest brother wanted to become a driver for the state transport corporation and had registered himself as an applicant. Since my brothers did not live with my parents, I did not have to deal with their abuse.

IT WAS TIME for the Mariamman temple festival. My sister, her husband and their children had come for the occasion. They greeted me warmly and were affectionate towards me.

Each household had to contribute two hundred rupees for the festivities. As always, every household began to get ready its share of rice flour to hold the lamps that would be lit at the temple during festival time. Rice was pounded and mixed with coconut, bananas and sugar syrup until it formed a thick paste. The paste was then carved into square blocks. Lamps filled with ghee were placed on these squares and taken to the temple. This is an offering dear to Mariamman. My mother and sister were busy decorating a plate with camphor, betel-nut and agarbathis.

'Let Revathi carry the rice lamps. I won't go this time,' said my sister.

'No, you go. If he goes, everyone will stare at him,' replied my mother.

'Who is going to stare and why? There's nothing new for them to stare at. As if anyone does not know about Revathi! Why, she's gone about the whole world in a sari. And if they stare, let them! And if there's talk, that's fine too. It's not wrong for her to carry lamps to the temple.' My sister was adamant.

'Do what you will. It's your business, yours and your brother's!' replied my mother and remained silent thereafter.

My sister turned to me, 'So, will you bring the lamp to the temple, Revathi?'

'I will, but you must go with me, I need support.'

'My, aren't you a virgin? And won't the fellows make eyes at you?' My sister laughed and agreed to go with me to the temple.

My nephew had grown. My sister pointed me out to him and said, 'Dai, that's your mother's sister. Call her aunty!' It felt so nice when the child started addressing me as his aunt. How much my sister loved me! She had accepted me, wearing a sari and being the way I am, and she called me her sister! I was thrilled. I asked her what sari I should wear to the temple. She said that I'd look very nice in my eldest sister-in-law's wedding sari. 'It would suit your complexion,' she added. 'Go and get it from her.' My mother made a face—perhaps she did not like any of this.

I went running to my eldest brother's house. My sister-in-law was breast-feeding her son. 'Revathi, welcome!' she said. I was hesitant to enter the room, seeing that she was feeding the child. She adjusted her sari, put the child down and started talking to me.

'Just a small thing. My sister wants me to carry the rice lamp to the temple. So, if you can lend me your silk sari...' I paused. My sister-in-law went in to get the sari. I picked up my nephew and told him, 'Look here, baby, this is not your uncle, but your aunt! Say "aunty"!'

My sister-in-law came into the room with the sari, and seeing me with the child, said, 'Yes, baby, that's not your uncle any more, but your aunt! And if you call her uncle, she's going to get angry and she won't play with you any more.'

She gave her sari to me and asked if I had a matching blouse. I said I didn't, but would wear a white blouse instead. Now that I had the silk sari, I wanted to run home. But my sister-in-law did not let me go, 'Revathi, your brother's bathing. He just got off the lorry. Wait for him to come out and have lunch with us.'

My eldest brother entered the room as she was talking, 'Dai, Doraisamy! When did you come from Mumbai?'

'It's been twenty days.'

'Look at you,' he said, turning to his wife, 'and look at him. See how he's wearing his sari! So stylish. And you look like a woman working in the fields, wearing your sari so high!'

'That's enough. Take a look at yourself! With a face like that, be glad I am there for you!' my sister-in-law replied, grimacing. I excused myself saying I was going home and added that I'd return the sari the next day.

Ours was the only Mariamman temple in three villages. Women from all three villages, holding rice lamps, stood in the temple corridor in parallel lines which extended outside the temple premises. They stood in such a manner so as not to obstruct the view of the goddess. My sister and I had reached early and so stood very close to the inner sanctum. According to custom, everyone waited for all the lamps to arrive and only then was the coconut broken and worship offered by all present in unison.

Only women carry the plates with rice lamps on them. Everyone there looked at me in surprise and talked amongst themselves. The women from my village who stood opposite me, both the married and unmarried ones, said to me, 'Super, Revathi! You look very beautiful. In the silk sari and with all that jewellery you look like a real woman. We have to beg for attention, with you looking like that!' They also asked me if I was wearing my sister's jewels. As soon as all the lamps were in place, they commenced the ceremony. It lasted for an hour and a half. It was airless inside the temple, with the lamps burning, and I felt my silk sari become wet with sweat. Sweat poured like water down my body.

Everyone jostled their way out of the temple, eager to get home. On the way I saw that men had gathered in hordes and were stumbling over each other to catch a glimpse of me. Those who could claim kin relations commented, 'Revathi, so you brought a lamp! How nice!'

My sister teased them, 'Will you guys marry her?'

'How much gold will you put on her, how many boxes of cash will she fetch?' they said in response.

To which my sister said, 'We're giving away such a lovely girl! You tell us how much you're willing to give when you take her away as a bride!'

I wasn't sure if they were all teasing me, merely saying things. But I felt a sort of happiness in my heart. I understood their interest as a victory for my femininity. We came back home and ate up the offerings from the temple. Then I went next door and showed the girl—who had let me wear her clothes when I was a boy—my sari and jewels. She said, as if partaking of my happiness, 'Super, Revathi! You've got what you wanted.' She also introduced me to the guests who had come for the festival. I felt happy that for the first time in my life I had gone as a woman, with other women, to the temple, carrying a lamp. All the women were certain that the year's Mariamman's festival would be known for Revathi's presence.

'How is this Revathi so like a woman? Do you think she has breasts like us? God alone knows, but it is surely God's will that she should turn female in the middle of her life…' So the women spoke about me.

That year too, there was to be a play at night. I wanted to dance just as I once did, when I was still wearing a man's clothes and had to dress like a woman. I asked the manager, 'Brother, give me a chance to dance before your play starts.' He agreed to let me dance to a devotional song and called the make-up man to help me dress me up. The make-up man helped me tie my silk sari with folds at the back. He applied powder on my face, streaked my eyes with kohl, tied a band across my forehead, placed a garland around my neck and handed me a bunch of neem flowers. I looked like the goddess Mariamman herself.

They announced on the mike: 'As part of the Mariamman festival, a play called *Vasantham* produced by a group of friends will be performed in a while. Before that we have a dance performance by the daughter of (here he mentioned my father's name), Revathi. We request everyone to come closer to the stage.'

They say that dancing feet don't ever stop. I did not learn dancing formally, but as a hijra I have seen other hijras dance and learned to dance. Without any practice, knowing only the song to which I was supposed to dance, I came on stage. The director whistled, lights came on stage, the song started playing and I danced.

I danced to the song 'Chellaatha, Mariaatha'. After I was done, everyone clapped and roared. Those who had come for the evening from outside our village thought I was one of the girls in the theatre group. Later on they came to know from their friends that I was not a girl, but a man. For several days after the festival ended, people came to visit me and praise my dancing skills. Whether they came on this account, or merely to talk to me, and chose to talk about my dance since they could not bring themselves to talk about me—I don't know. In any case, I was happy that I was not heckled by the local lads.

SIX MONTHS HAD gone by since I came from Mumbai. My middle brother had taken to troubling my parents frequently. For instance, by locking up the pumpset room in our fields and once even locking my parents in their own home.

'Here I'm on the streets and why should you alone have a house and sleep comfortably in it? Divide your property and we'll each go our own way!'

I found this rather amusing. My father felt that his property was his own, and that he did not have to give it away. He also said that as a matter of right, his sons could only lay claim to what their grandfather had left behind. 'I bought land and the lorry with my earnings. It is only this house that is from your grandfather's time. The rest of the old man's property was divided among my first wife's children. If I wish, I could sell my property to whoever I want to. What can this fellow do?'

It went on, my brother abusing my father, my father abusing my brother. They talked about property all the time, but they never talked face to face. My brother would say his bit to my mother at a time when my father was not there. Caught in the middle, what could my poor mother do? She could only cry, conveying to my father what my brother said, and reporting to my brother what my father said.

When my father's first wife's children took away grandfather's property, we were all very young and did not know anything. If it had happened now, we wouldn't have given in easily. My brother was very clear, 'You married a second time and had all of us. So divide your property among us. After all, we did not go to school—we worked and earned for you!'

'If I am to divide the property right now, these fellows will fritter it all away. That's why I want it to happen when I'm dead. But this fellow, he comes and creates trouble when I'm not there! What do I care if all of you end up losing out in the long term? You fellows divide up the property without fighting!'

My father arranged to divide up all he had with a lawyer's help and through the court: five acres of land, four lorries, a large single-storeyed house. My brothers came home when my father was not there and threatened me, 'You pottai motherfucker! Be glad that we've let you be in a sari! Think you can hang around with those number nines, with your cock chopped off, and still demand your share of property? We can throw you out and deprive you of an address if we want! On your own and with due respect to us, sign a statement saying that you do not want anything and that you have no claims on this property. If you do this, you can return to Mumbai alive. If not, we'll finish you off and there'll only be charred ash the morning after!'

They added that when it was time for the court to intervene, they would all say that their brother Doraisamy was a man, whereas I was not. Dressed as a woman, and without a cock, they could disown me, saying that I was not their brother, but a pottai, who, having heard of this property dispute, had come to lay claims on it.

'We'll make you flee the village! So think and decide wisely.'

I reported what my brothers had said to my father. He listened and then took me to the lawyer. Having heard us out, the lawyer said, 'They can do nothing. When you are summoned to court and the judge calls out "Doraisamy" they'll look at you and ask if you are indeed him—they'll want proof. It is best that you come to court in a man's dress.'

'I desperately wanted to be a woman. I put up with a lot for that, got beaten by all sorts of people, got abused, grew my hair—and today I am a woman. I even agreed to have my cock cut off. I felt that even if I am to die, let me die after having been a woman for a day at least. Now, for property's sake, I'm not about to become a man, or cut my hair. None of that please!'

'Listen, I'm not telling you should be in a man's clothes forever. Your father could say in court, this is my last son, but he's become an 'Ali'. But if someone objects to that, then the property can't be immediately divided, and the case could be endlessly adjourned. Why risk that? Why can't you be a man for a day?'

It was easy for the lawyer—as though what he wanted of me was merely like the story of a man who had to shave his moustache to act in a play. Would the lawyer like it, if I tell him to appear in court, wearing women's clothes? I remained silent.

My father looked crestfallen and sat with his hands on his

head. He then looked up and asked the lawyer if there was another way out. The lawyer looked thoughtful. He then asked me to step out for a bit, while he talked to my father. After some time they called me in.

'There's just one other way out. But for that, you must trust your father. Do you trust your father?' The lawyer's voice was loud. I said I did trust my father.

'You don't have to come to court. You sign a statement saying that due to unavoidable circumstances related to your work, you are not in station, and so in the eventuality of the property having to be divided, you have authorized your father to sign on your behalf and accept whatever is due to you. We'll provide your father with the power of attorney to act on your behalf. Do you agree?' asked the lawyer.

I agreed.

'I'll have the document ready tomorrow, so come and sign. You must not sign as Revathi, but as Doraisamy. You must sign as you did when you were in school,' the lawyer warned me, and my father and I returned home.

Well, my destiny changed mid-way, I thought, and so who knows how I signed my name back then? I searched and found my school marksheet. I had signed, 'Doraisamy' in Tamil. The next day, my father and I went to meet the lawyer, and I signed whatever needed to be signed.

I don't know what my brothers, father and the lawyer discussed, but they told me that I had to pay forty thousand rupees towards expenses incurred in preparing documents. I did not even have four paise, so where was I to go for forty thousand rupees?

'Ay! You say you want property, then you've got to pay for it—pay the lawyer, pay for the documents. You can't say you don't have money. Listen, why you do need this property? Hand over forty thousand rupees, or accept whatever money we're willing to give you, and sign a statement saying you have no more claims on this property.' My brothers were firm in their demand.

And so, each of them contributed thirty-five thousand rupees and gave me a lakh and five thousand as my share of the property. I also signed the document they wanted me to sign.

I wanted to live as a woman. My father, mother, brothers and sister, and their children, were all the family I had. After they had decided this was the thing to do, I could not really go against their decision. If I did, who would be there for me? Besides, I consoled myself, I was not giving my money away to strangers, but to my brothers.

When my sister was married, she was given jewels and dowry, so she was not given a share of the property. But each of us, including me, set aside ten thousand rupees for her. My brothers divided the land amongst themselves equally. My father and brothers each got their share from the sale of the lorries. The house in which my parents lived was given to them. We gave up our claims on that house. My father made it clear that once the property had been divided, my brothers had no right to come to his house and make trouble.

My brothers did not like me staying with my parents and wanted me out of the house. My parents too felt that my presence could cause trouble. They asked me to move out. Unable to counter them, I looked for a place and finally rented a room in an old woman's house for two hundred rupees a month.

After having given away ten thousand to my sister, and spent five thousand to buy things for the house, I had ninety thousand rupees left. I deposited this amount in a cooperative bank in our village and took to living off the interest. (I could make a deposit only in the name of Doraisamy.)

Namakkal town, as I've mentioned, is about three kilometres from my village. If I needed to buy anything for the house, or wanted to go to the cinema, I had to go to town. I had to pay a bus charge of one rupee fifty paise to get there, and then pay again to get around the town by local bus. The bus was always crowded. People leaned on each other, were squashed up against each other—it was unpleasant. Through that three-kilometre stretch, I had to endure teasing, laughter and people grazing against me. I felt heart-broken when these things happened.

Once, when the bus was empty, I sat down on a seat next to a girl. She got up, smiling, and found another seat. In my part of the world, women don't sit next to men. I, too, don't sit next to a man, even if there's an empty seat. Whenever the bus driver used his brake and halted suddenly, the men sitting behind would deliberately lean over and fall all over my back. Younger men, little more than boys would call out: 'Macchan! Bus'll reach at nine o'clock!' Or 'Mapillai! What's the time?' And the reply invariably would be 'Nine da!' Such teasing upset me.

Sometimes, unable to hold back my rage, I would yell back, 'Why call out "Number 9" in such a roundabout way? So, I am that Number 9! What do you care? Have I come to you for a sari? Or begged for food from you? Watch out! I'll get you with my slippers—hit you till they fall apart!'

'Oh my! What a voice! A man's voice, da!' they'd retort and laugh.

Could not God have given me a woman's voice at least? When I was dressed like a man, they said I spoke like a woman, and now after I've changed into a woman, they say my voice is like a man's! Ashamed and frustrated, I would not be able to respond.

Not wanting to deal with all this, I asked my brother if I could borrow his moped to go into town. As payment each time, I had to put in a litre of petrol or else buy him a quarter litre of whisky. If I went into town two days in a row, I had to fill a litre of petrol on both days. Unable to do anything about it, I ended up buying whisky for him instead. I was living off the interest on my capital and I couldn't go on spending money on petrol and whisky. Caught between a public that considered me odd, and my brothers who were willing to be affectionate for a price, I had to live in the midst of people who did not understand me. I wondered if there would ever be someone who understands me. Would I ever find such a person?

I had to get water from the public tap every morning. Some of the women spoke nicely to me, even affectionately. 'So what've you cooked today, Revathi?' someone would ask. 'Peerkangai with paruppu and rasam,' I'd reply. There would also be questions such as, 'You take so much water! Where'd you pour all that?' 'I do the same as you do,' I'd reply and walk away, holding the pot of water on my hip. I'd hear the women saying, 'How nicely Revathi carries the pot on her hip, just like us women!'

Whenever the old woman whose room I'd rented asked

me, 'Ay Doraisamy! Have you paid this month's rent?' people hearing her would laugh.

I would patiently tell her, 'Aaya, how many times I've told you to call me Revathi?'

'Revathi or Thevati, I don't know, can't get my tongue to pronounce the name. Isn't your name Doraisamy?' the old woman would ask. When I explained that back then I was Doraisamy, but now I was Revathi, she'd say, 'Look, just because you decide to change like this in the middle of your life, you can't expect us to forget what we used to call you! I am used to calling your Doraisamy and that's what my tongue finds easy!'

Those who understood what this was all about, those who were educated, even if they mocked me or gossiped about, addressed me as Revathi.

seventeen

The temple of our family goddess was at a distance of twenty kilometres from my village. I remembered going there as a child with the rest of my family, and playing in the temple grounds. The memory inspired a desire in me to visit the temple, this time as a woman.

I asked my brother for his moped to go to the temple. Because of the distance, he wanted me to take the bus. I tried to convince him by arguing that I'd have to walk at least two kilometres from the bus stop to the temple. I bought him his whisky and somehow managed to get the moped.

I was nervous about the long ride, but also exhilarated. I was leaving my village to go to another—no one there would know me as a hijra. It felt wonderful riding the moped as a woman. I stopped in front of the temple, parked the moped outside and went in. The temple priest welcomed me and asked where I was from. I gave him my village name, but did not give out my father's name, or my mother's. If I had, he'd have identified me. Our family goddess is a virgin goddess. Women don't go into her shrine. They are not supposed to see her or be in her proximity. Only women who have stopped menstruating can go in. But men could go into the shrine. That day there were around twenty people, both men and women, in the temple. The priest began a common pujai for all of us. The pujai started at the Vinayakar temple and he moved towards the shrine of the goddess. The women stayed back, while the men followed the priest. I thought that since there was no question of me menstruating I could go to the shrine of the goddess. I started walking in that direction.

The priest and some of the women shouted, 'Amma, amma, you're not supposed to go there!'

A woman muttered, 'What kind of a woman are you! Don't even know this!'

To which, I replied, 'But I can go!'

Everyone looked perplexed. Just then one of the men in the crowd recognized me. He said, 'Yes, she can go. There's nothing wrong in that.' He then mentioned the names of my parents to the priest.

The priest understood immediately. 'Ayya Doraisamy! They said you were somewhere in Mumbai! When did you return, dear? Are you well? Come to the shrine of the virgin goddess and pray!'

Some in the crowd understood what was going on, others did not. Those who did whispered to those who did not and explained who I was. Everyone's eyes were fixed on me. After the pujai was over, some of the devotees wanted to do the flower choice. It works like this: if a person wants to know whether something would work in his favour, he would bring two flowers, red and white, and wrap each of them in a piece of paper. The two paper packets would be juggled and then placed in front of the goddess. The priest would open one of the two, and going by the colour he'd picked, he would pronounce whether or not the proposed deed would end in victory for the person.

That day, the priest wanted me to pick the flower. I hesitated. Whereupon he said, 'Come on, do it. You and that goddess are the same.' I looked around me, looked at everyone, and wondered.

I heard someone say, 'Come, pick a flower. Nothing wrong in that. You're not like us, you're like the goddess, unblemished, unlike us who've done wrong. Go ahead. Don't hesitate to pick a flower for us.'

Around ten people did the flower choice that day and I picked flowers for all of them. Everyone sat around in the temple for some time and then left. I remained behind, went to each and every shrine to offer worship, and after pressing a fifty-rupee note into the priest's hands, I left. I climbed on my moped and soon reached the main road leading to my village.

Along the way, I stopped at a petrol bunk to fill petrol. There was a man filling petrol for a vehicle just like mine. He was dark-skinned, but something about him filled me with longing and made me want to look at him again and again. He returned my gaze but we did not speak. I took off on the moped on the road leading to my village. He followed me on the road. I could see him behind me in the right-hand mirror and I accelerated. He accelerated too. I slowed down so that he could go ahead, but he too slowed down and kept behind me. I got a little scared. So I stopped, got off the moped and pretended I was searching for something in the side-pouch.

He stopped behind me and asked, 'What happened?'

'Nothing, the moped engine got warm. So I stopped.'

'I've seen you before. Are you from Namakkal?'

'Yes, I am. Where are you from?'

'From a village near the petrol bunk. Going somewhere?'

I said I was returning from the temple of my family goddess. Now that I was talking to him, I felt less afraid. I asked him his name.

'Babu. And yours?'

'Revathi.' I took courage and asked him, 'Where do you work?'

'I am a film operator in a cinema hall in Namakkal.'

'You go there every day on this moped?'

'Yes. I could take the bus, but in the night, after the late show, there are no buses.' He asked a question in return, 'Are you married?'

'No. Are you?'

'No.'

We got on our mopeds and drove silently. As soon we reached the turn to Namakkal town, he stopped.

'If you're ever in Namakkal, come to the cinema hall.'

'Okay.'

I GAVE MY brothers and mother sacred ash from the temple. I also returned my brother's moped.

'How much petrol did you put?'

'Two litres on the way up and two litres on the way down.'

He opened the hub-cap and rocked the vehicle. He did not say anything.

For a week I could only think of that man. Did he speak with me thinking I was a woman? What would he have thought of me? I wondered if I should go and visit him in Namakkal. The kind words he spoke, his respectful manner, his courteous behaviour—all these made me want to see him again.

I went to the cinema hall that he worked in. They had not started issuing tickets. People had gathered at the counter. People were also standing around in clumps. I was alone, and I did not have anyone to talk to. I felt uneasy and sad. I was also scared that someone would recognize me. I couldn't really ask for Babu, I felt. I thought that even if he did work there, if I were to ask his colleagues about him, they would think ill of him. So I stood alone in a corner, my arms folded, and trained my gaze on the building. The women's counter only gave out tickets for the bench and floor seats. There was a queue of women in front of it. Only if I got a balcony ticket would I be near the operator's room. I joined the mixed queue of men and women standing in front of the balcony counter. It moved slowly and I moved ahead with it. I finally got a balcony ticket, climbed the stairs and sat in a balcony seat. I sat alone, next to an empty seat. Suddenly I found Babu sitting on it.

'Hello madam, come to watch the movie?'

'Yes.'

'You've come alone or is there—'

I interrupted hastily, 'I've come alone,' before he could even finish asking his question.

'The film will start now, I have to go. Come to the operator's room during the interval. We'll have something to drink.'

We had not spoken much and no one could therefore suspect that there was anything between us.

I went looking for the operator's room during the interval. He was alone. He opened a bottle of something cool and handed it to me.

I learnt that he was a Muslim, that he had been working in this cinema hall for three years. That he lived with his parents, a brother and a younger sister. I told him about my family and added that I had been a Bharatanatyam teacher in Delhi and was at present living alone because of family problems. I did not tell him I was a hijra.

'Can I visit you at home?'

'Oh, yes. You can come as a guest.'

'When should I come?'

I said something vague and said goodbye, 'I'm going home.'

'Why? Is the film boring?'

'No. But I came only to see you. I've seen you, so I'm going home.' I left the cinema and caught an auto home.

In my heart of hearts I was not sure if he should visit me at home. Yet I'd asked him to visit. Clearly, one part of me wanted him to come to my house. But if the old woman who is my house-owner asked who he was, what could I say? If he were to come into the village, what would people think? If and when he did come, what if the old woman addressed me as Doraisamy? Would he not get suspicious and think ill of me? I decided that I should tell him who I was and only then invite him home. I was beset by the fear that if I told him I was a hijra he might not want to meet me.

I must have gone to the theatre at least a dozen times in the next few months. I made it a habit to sit with him in his room and talk. I could not bring myself to tell him I was not a woman. Neither did he ask me why my voice sounded the way it did. Sometimes I would bring him a dish I had cooked at home. One day, having made a resolution, I gave him my address and the name of my village. He said that he would come after the show ended at night.

That suited me. At around ten that night, everyone in the house retired to their rooms to sleep. Lights were on in the room of the college students who shared that house with me. They were studying. The main compound gate was bolted and the old woman had gone to bed. I was anxious. The night show would end at one in the morning and he would come after that. Around that time I opened the compound gate, locked it after me and stood waiting for him outside on the road. He came on his moped. I had to caution him to be quiet, and to park the moped inside the compound. I shut the gate after us and took him to my room.

I felt that he was not as scared as I was about the visit. I did not sense fear, either in his eyes, or his words. I did not say anything at first. I gave him food and he started to eat.

'Have you eaten?'

'Not yet.'

'Why don't you eat too?'

I took a plate, sat down, heaped food on it and started eating.

'Where's your parents' house?'

'Nearby.'

'Do your parents come here?'

'So far they haven't come. I visit them once in a while. What about you? If you don't go home for the night, won't your parents be up, waiting for you?'

'No. Sometimes I stay back in the cinema hall. So no one is up expecting me.'

After we finished eating, I put the plates away, returned all the vessels to where they belonged and got ready to sleep. I showed him the cot and spread a mat for myself on the floor.

'You can sleep on the cot too…'

'It's all right. Let me sleep on the floor.'

He did not respond. We both lay separately.

'Why haven't you got married?' he asked me.

I was caught off guard and did not know what to say. I managed though. 'I haven't attained puberty yet. Doctors tell me my womb hasn't developed. I am not fit for conjugal life.'

I lied to him. I could not bring myself to say that I was born a man and had become a woman. I don't know what he made of my answer.

'Why haven't you got married?'

'I am only twenty-one, there's a younger sister. Only after she gets married will I marry.'

Deep down in my heart I began to fall in love with him. I felt a desire to lie with him, hold him tight. But I was scared that he would know what I was, and I did not dare tell him what I longed to do. I could only consider this relationship a friendship.

That night both of us fell asleep.

In the morning I got tiffin ready. I went and filled water for him to bathe and then saw him off. The old woman asked me who he was. A friend who studied with me, I said.

'Friend? Dai, you appear to serve him as you would a husband? Then you say he's a friend from school?'

'Nothing like that, grandma. He studied with me and came to visit, that's all.'

He started to come often. I did serve him, did all that a woman does for her husband. Since he visited regularly, the women next door and those I met while fetching water started talking of all that I did for my visitor. Some were surprised, others teased me, and spoke of this to each other and to me.

At the water tap, a woman asked me smiling, 'Revathi, is he your husband? Seen him off to work? What does he do?'

'He *is* my husband.' I lifted the pot of water to my hip and walked off.

'See, how she looks after him. Why, even we don't do for our husbands all that she does.' So the women spoke.

This news reached my brothers. It was a Sunday and around eleven in the morning. I had fried meat, made rasam and had just put the rice pot on the stove. Babu had gone to the town, saying he had some work. My three brothers arrived. They came in and sat on the cot. The college students were in their rooms. The three said, 'Seems there's a man who visits you here. In the village they claim he's your husband. You're a man, so is he. Why do you need a husband?'

They yelled these questions out and I felt very ashamed and upset about what my neighbours would think. I was also frightened that he would return while they were there.

Anything could happen. The three started talking amongst themselves.

One said, 'Dai, they say he's her husband. But how will these two sleep together at night?'

Another replied, 'You don't know how they do it? All these number nines, like the one here, take a man's cock into their mouth and suck at it. Seems the ooze is a balm for their parched and hairy throats! These number nines have hair in their throats and that's what they do, and that's what he probably does too!'

When I heard the sound of Babu's moped, I went out and requested him to stay for a while in the college students' rooms. I returned to mine. My brothers did not know that he had come. In any case, they would not have recognized him.

My brothers started again. 'See, she's cooked meat for her husband,' one of them said and opened one of the vessels.

'Only if she does that will he give her his cock to suck!' said another brother.

'You pottai motherfucker. You're a man, after all. We did not mind you traipsing around in a sari. But how dare you want a husband? If we hear that he's visiting you again, be sure that we'll tear his guts out and make a garland out of them! We'll finish you off as well...' He said many other awful things about him and me—things that I can't find words for.

Unable to hold back my fury and disgust, I yelled back, 'Yes, a man does come here. He comes for me, and yes, he is my husband. I am not sleeping around. I am a woman and I do what any woman does. I have feelings too. What did you ask? What could a man and man do? Well, I do exactly what you do with your wives. Do you understand now? What is your business here in my house? Do I come to yours and ask what you do with your wives or how you sleep with them? How dare you talk of me like this? Aren't you ashamed?' A storm was brewing inside me and it made me talk.

'Shame? Why should we feel any? We are men and we have married women. We've made families. How can you claim to be a woman, you who have gone and chopped off your cock and worn a sari? Do you want to dishonour our name, the respect we enjoy?' Saying this, one of my brothers came towards me, as if to hit me.

The house-owner burst into the room and stopped him, 'Get out all of you! I don't want anyone fighting in my house!'

My brothers tried to argue with her, but she chased them out.

'If we see that fellow here tomorrow, we'll kill him.' With that my brothers left.

Hurt, angry and ashamed, I called him into the room. He came in and sat on the cot. For a while neither of us spoke. After some time, I started speaking. 'Now you've understood what I am. I could not say it to you. You don't have to suffer on my account. Please don't visit me again!'

He did not respond, and after some time he said he was leaving. I did not stop him, nor did I tell him not to come back. I was in a daze. The pain in my heart was as if a spear was twisting in it. I felt a flutter inside, as if a bird were beating its wings in alarm. I wondered if I should continue to stay in the village. I did not remember until nightfall that I had cooked and the food was lying uneaten. I recalled, over and over again, all that my brothers had said. I was intrigued by their references to hair in the throat. It was their imagination, yet I kept turning that idea round and round in mind, saying to myself, 'I don't have hair in my throat, why would they say so?'

If society scorns us, then we turn to our families, if we have a family. But if family scorns us, who do we turn to? Is this why people like me do not stay in touch with their families? Could not God have created me as a man or a woman? Why did He make me this way? Why is He savouring this spectacle that He created? In a rage, hitting my head against the wall, I began to cry.

Families respect you only if you have money, you look modern, wear nice clothes and jewels. If you are a hijra and poor, you must expect to be abused and humiliated. It is best I be with others like me, only that would ensure me of dignity. As I thought about returning to Mumbai or going to Delhi, I remembered what a hijra told me when I was in Kamatipura—that there was a *hamam* (bath house) run by hijras in Bangalore. I decided to go there.

I slept that night in my room. In the morning, I cleared my room and deposited my belongings at my parents' place. I told them that I was off to earn a living, since I was not given respect in the house and the village where I'd been born.

I left for Bangalore.

eighteen

I got off at Majestic bus stand in Bangalore and got into an auto. I asked the auto-driver in Tamil if he knew where the hamam was and if he would take me there. He knew the place and the auto had run up a meter charge of fifty rupees by the time he dropped me at my destination. From inside the auto I saw that there were people like me—sitting around, combing their hair. I felt immense relief on seeing them. I paid the auto charge, got off the main road and walked into a side street.

I saw the woman I'd seen in Mumbai. I approached her and said, 'Paampaduthi amma.'

'Jiyo beta! Where're you coming from?'

'From my village.'

'Di! Aren't you Revathi and haven't I seen you in Byculla?

Don't you recognize me?'

'I do, amma.'

'Di, your chela, Mya, is here. Mya! Mya!'

Mya stepped out of a house. When she spotted me, she came running.

'Are you well?'

'I'm fine. And you?'

'I'm well too. Now that I'm here, I have become her chela,' she said, pointing to the woman who had greeted me. Mya had become my gurubai, she was no longer my chela.

'After that Mumbai house where I earned for everyone else, I came here with practically nothing. But after I've become her chela, things have got better.'

Mya's guru interrupted us: 'Take her in, give her a cup of coffee, give her breakfast, and then chat.'

After we went into the house, I filled in Mya on what had happened to me. I told her that I wanted to find work in the hamam and live in peace.

'Here? No, don't do that. Rowdies come here every day, threaten us with knives and things. They knock on our doors at night, they don't let us sleep. They even throw huge stones at our doors. I don't know if you can put up with all these problems. It is best that you go back to your village. If you like, I'll send you two thousand rupees every month.'

The situation Mya described was daunting. But then there were about seven hijras there—Mya, her guru, the guru's gurubais (Mya's kaalaguru) and some others. Surely they too faced these problems. Why would Mya want me to return to my village? Did she not put up with rowdies and other problems? I thought that I should stay for a while. 'Let me see. If I don't like it, I'll go back,' I said.

I was eager to see what a hamam looked like and Mya said we were in a portion that's called God's House. I noticed images of Hindu gods on one wall and there were Islamic inscriptions framed on another. There were Christian figurines too. The hamam was next door and it had its own entrance. I was eager to see what a hamam looked like, so I asked Mya to show me around.

In the hamam, there was a huge iron tank that had been cemented up. There were facilities for burning firewood and heating water. Next to the iron tank stood another tank made of cement that stored cold water. There were six or seven bathrooms past the tanks, and at the very end was a toilet. A bucket of hot water cost five rupees; a bucket of cold water, two rupees; and a piece of soap, one rupee. Mya pointed to a board on which all these details were written. Only then did I understand what a hamam was.

'Come, let's eat,' she said and took me into a room where we sat down to eat dosais.

'So when did you become a chela here?'

'It's been some months.'

'Did you have to go to Mumbai for the reeth?'

'No. This is a Hyderabad house and the naik lives here. We went to her for the reeth.'

Mya's guru, gurubais and kaalaguru were all part of the parivar that owned the house where I'd done sex work. From what Mya said, it appeared that as chelas of a Hyderabad house they had become a parivar themselves.

At seven in the evening, Mya bathed, wore a sari, applied make-up and, bag in hand, seemed ready to go somewhere.

'Where're you off to?' I asked.

'I'll tell you after I return.'

Mya's guru told me that Mya went out to do sex work.

'Out? Where?'

'Wherever. She'll stand on the roads, and if she finds a client, they'll go to a lodge or some other place. This is how Mya earns a living.'

'Won't Mya have problems, standing on the roads like that?'

'People like us always have problems. If you go out to do sex work, you get into trouble with rowdies, you bribe the police… Of course Mya's scared, but she has to deal with all these problems. Some days she comes running because rowdies are after her. Some days it is the police who are shooing her off. If she doesn't get a client, then she returns home. What can we do? The money we earn at the hamam is just about enough to pay rent and for all of us to eat. Mya looks like a woman and passes off as one in the outside world. If you can't pass for a woman, not a chap will look at you. Now only Mya goes out. The others, chelas and naathis, help out in the hamam, pour water for the clients, give them oil massages and so on. They get tipped for this. They use the money to buy powder, face cream, clothes… If at times they don't earn enough, they go to the shops and beg. What to do? People like us have no choice but to beg or do sex work. This is how we've lived our lives…'

'How long has this hamam been here?'

'It's ten years since I came here. Another woman, not from our parivar, ran it for twenty years. I've been here since her time. I worked here, pouring water for the clients and doing odd jobs. That woman's now dead.' She continued, 'Listen, your chela has become my chela. Do you want to become a chela in this house?'

'No, amma. How many times is one to change gurus? I'll remain a chela to my Mumbai house. Maybe I could work and stay here with you?'

'You too look like a woman. You could go out with Mya and do sex work.'

'Will Mya take me?'

'Let me talk to her when she returns. All she has to do is to show you where to go and tell you how to get home. Apart from that, you know what to do—how to talk to a client, how to return to the hamam. Di, I want to ask you something. I've made Mya my chela. So she's become your gurubai. Does this make you sad?'

'No, it happens all the time amongst us, doesn't it?'

'Look, if you don't want to become my chela, you could become a chela to my gurubai. Perhaps you think that your chela has become my chela and you don't want to become a chela along with her? If so, there's my gurubai...'

'No, amma. Let me remain a guest in your house. I don't want to become a chela. In any case, whether I'm your chela or not, you and your gurubai are my gurus!'

I WAS NEW to Bangalore. Those who lived in this house were veterans, they had worked in the hamam for years, performing many different tasks. Essentially I was a junior, which is why I helped around the hamam voluntarily. I helped to clean and wash the place; got warm water for customers, transacted business with them; attended to the gods in the house, both in the morning and evening; helped pump water from the bore well and fill the bathtubs; and fetched stuff for the elders from nearby shops. I learnt to think of them as my own family and I worked tirelessly.

If at night someone threw a stone at our door or yelled at us, Mya's guru counselled us to keep quiet. This happened regularly, this throwing of stones and knocking on the door. Initially when this happened, I would get quite fearful. But these incidents took place with such regularity that I slowly got over my fear.

We feared other things though. That our neighbours would get wind of this stone-throwing and disapprove of our presence. That the stones might break the old tiles that made up the roof. That a rowdy might get in easily—he only had to remove some tiles on the roof to do so. When a tile did break, in order to prevent rain water from getting in, we patched the hole with tarpaulin and fastened it to the roof with tar. We lived in an old house built of mud. It had withstood time miraculously, as if in fealty to some unuttered truth. We did not have the resources to mend things around the house. Those who lived in it led lives on a razor's edge.

The hamam was a sort of small town inside Bangalore city. It was located at the corner of a main road. Whoever went on that road, in their vehicles or sometimes in a procession, never failed to take note of the hamam. Young lads would yell as they passed by and sing film songs. Sometimes they teased us. This happened often and was actually funny. Bangalore has its tourist attractions—Cubbon Park, Lal Bagh, many temples, Vidan Soudha, the museum, etc. Our part of town had also become one such attraction.

The hamam was pointed out with incredulity, as if we spelt danger, as if we were oddities. So much so that husbands and wives, friends and others, pointed us out to their ignorant companions, as if we were a spectacle, something to be gawked at.

When I went to buy groceries and vegetables in the vegetable market, people sometimes threw rotten tomatoes at me. They hit me on my back, or even aimed for my head. When I turned back to identify the culprit, all the shopkeepers kept their gaze averted, and would fuss around their vegetables, arranging them in neat piles—as if they had had nothing to do with the tomatoes.

Sometimes I'd see a person laugh and think that he had thrown the tomato at me. I'd then harangue him, 'What do you think I am? A waste bin? You think pottais are nothing, that we are like waste? I've come here to buy vegetables. I pay for what I purchase. I am dressed as others are. What have I done that you should pelt tomatoes at me? Am I walking around naked or did I come and ask you for money or did I call you to me? Why did you throw those tomatoes at me, then?'

That person would then say, 'Why do you ask me? Ask the person who threw the tomato at you! Do you know who I am? I could prevent your mother from coming to the market!'

People smirked at me, but would deny doing so when I confronted them. I'd then curse the one that had thrown a tomato at me—pray for him to suffer, for a pottai to be born in his family...

Once I complained to the vegetable-seller we frequented. He advised me not to take note of the trouble-makers—

those child-fuckers, as he called them. He said they were mere bullies who had grown fat on their own bullying. 'Look, we've seen people like you for years. We speak to you with civility, always address you as amma... Are you new around here?'

'Yes, I am.'

'Your people come here regularly. They're not here today.'

'No, they are not.'

'These men tease you with those tomatoes because you're new. They are scared of the regulars. They say whatever slides off their tongues. The lads speak nonsense, and these people retaliate... Leave that aside, there's a god that'll account for all such talk. What vegetables do you want today?

'One kilo onions, quarter kilo tomatoes, and how much does a drumstick cost?'

'Two rupees for one, amma.'

'Two rupees for one! In my village you get a bundle of six or seven for one rupee. The place is awash with drumsticks and here you charge so much for it!'

'Amma, this is Bangalore. I bought them for one rupee and seventy-five paise. I make a profit of only a quarter of a rupee.'

'All right, give me five of those.'

Even as I was bundling up the drumsticks, he asked me, 'Amma, did you have an operation, and those'—he pointed to my breasts—'are they real?'

'How does it matter to you?' I glared at him. And so I discovered he was like the rest of them. He seemed different, spoke nicely, and yet he asked such a question.

Why was I born a pottai, I asked myself, as I returned to the hamam from the vegetable market. It was a clear case of the dog barking at the sun. The dog's bark did not hurt the sun, but only itself. I did not ever report the things that happened in the market to the elders in the hamam. What if they came to the market and kicked up a ruckus? Besides, when I go alone, I'd have to face all those shopkeepers all over again.

One of the flower-sellers at the market was different. Often she would entreat me to buy flowers from her. 'Akka,' she'd say, 'buy a string of flowers from me. Be my first buyer for the day!' Her calling me sister and asking me to be her first buyer—for I was thought to bring luck—made me glow inside. Even when I did not really want flowers, I bought them, because I did not want to hurt those who had faith in me and who obviously respected me.

Not all flower-sellers were like that. Some teased me, some were nice to me, others did not care about me one way or another—they merely wanted to sell flowers and were nice to me therefore! It was not so much that I couldn't tell who was playing true and really liked me, and who spoke nicely merely to sell me things; neither could it be said that I was ready to be beguiled by sweet and affectionate words. My heart melted only when someone thought of me as a woman and spoke to me as they would to other women.

ONE NIGHT, ALL of us—Mya, her gurubais and I—were eating. We had locked up the hamam. Both the gurus had gone to Mya's village. God knows how or why, Mya and I got into a fight over something minor. Mya addressed me as if I was a man, called me 'vaada' and so on. I asked her if she had forgotten that she had been my chela in Mumbai—how dare she address me disrespectfully?

'Mumbai's story ends with Mumbai. This is a Hyderabad house. Here, I am above you. Here, your laws mean nothing. You're a guest in this house, you eat for free! You've come here to earn a living. But if you want to work here, become a chela of this house. Or else remain a guest and take each day as it comes.'

It was as though the calf had chosen to turn against the cow. Here was my chela, someone I had nurtured, humiliating me. Her gurubais did not say anything in my defence either. What could I do though? I'd come to the hamam to find work. I knew that without money even a dog doesn't care for you. And I had found out that even among pottais, only if you had your own chela and naathis were you accorded respect.

I went to sleep thinking of all that Mya had said. She had spoken the truth. If my guru had looked after me and helped me with money, my predicament would have been different. I decided that what I needed at the moment was to earn money and have a place to live with gurubais who were fond of me and a guru who was affectionate. I did not want to return to Mumbai. Perhaps it was best that I became a chela of the Hyderabad house.

My seniors in the hamam visited their families from time to time. They bought clothes and household things for their brothers, sisters-in-law, nieces, nephews, mother, father, aunts, uncles... When I saw them pack their bags with goodies, I told myself that I too must return home one day, with a bagful of things for my folks. But I did not have money, not much anyway. Perhaps if I did sex work I could earn and buy things for home and family. In fact, I wanted to.

Here, sex workers were not kept imprisoned, like in my guru's house in Kamatipura. Here, I would not have to rush to get biryani packets, without a tip and without money to take a taxi. Here, I wouldn't be given five rupees and asked to buy food with it. Besides I could go home whenever I wanted. If I fetched warm water for a customer, and rubbed his back, I was given a tip. I had to hand over only five rupees to the hamam owner, the rest was mine. For the water I would be paid five rupees and ten for the back massage.

I was expected to eat my morning tiffin from what I earned. But unlike in Mumbai, both seniors and the younger hijras in Bangalore would buy food for those that did not have money and were nice to them besides. I was also surprised to be fed lunch and supper—the hamam owner cooked these meals for us.

I decided that it was best that I did not pine for a guru who was not there for me, and choose one who showed me affection. That would be the intelligent thing to do, I told myself. To earn a living I would do well to become a chela here. And so I asked to be made a chela to Mya's guru's gurubai. Mya's guru agreed and a date was fixed to make me a chela the Hyderabad way.

My guru—my third guru—was happy to receive me as her chela.

nineteen

A few days later, we decided to go to Hyderabad for the chela ceremony. Apart from me, a few other hijras were also to undergo the ceremony.

We spent the morning cooking the meal we would eat on the train. My new guru had given me the money to buy the things we needed to make tamarind rice, and I bought just what was needed. My kaalaguru asked to us to clean the tamarind thoroughly till it was free of stone and dust, and to remove the seeds and stalks from the dried chillies, so that the rice did not end up too hot when we mixed it with the sauce. My gurubai began to cook, and soon I was handing her the chillies, while my guru poured out sesame oil, even as she instructed us to squeeze the tamarind for juice to make a rich, thick sauce.

We finished cooking, and around five in the evening left for the station to catch the train to Hyderabad. For the first time, we were travelling as a family—guru and chelas on a train.

In Hyderabad, before I could become a chela, the naiks of our community asked me if I had been a chela before, and if so, in what house, and when did I have my nirvaanam done. I identified the house in Mumbai that had arranged for my nirvaanam, and said that I had later become a chela to someone in Matunga and then again returned to my first guru.

'So, in effect, you've spent time in three houses, and this will be your fourth,' said the elders on hearing my account. 'Beta, do you owe money to anyone in those houses or to any house? Money or jewels?'

'No, amma. The nose-ring, anklets and lajja which my first guru gave me, I returned to the jamaat when I became a chela the second time. In my second house, they gave me nothing. Neither do I owe them anything. When I returned to my first house, I received nothing. It was I who earned for all of them. But today I stand before you, with empty hands and an empty purse.'

'Our accounting does not concern itself with what you earned, only with what you might owe. So tell the truth—you are sure you owe nothing? For, if we come to know, or are told that you've brought things from your previous gurus' houses here, we become complicit, you see. If there is anything you owe them, tell us now, so we can settle it right away. Do you understand?'

'I do, amma. I have brought nothing with me and that's the truth.'

My new guru had to pay to our jamaat twice the fine on my behalf. She had to pay my former guru, to the one who arranged for my nirvaanam, and also make up for the danda money my old guru paid to make me her chela. The elders accepted the money; they would make sure that it reached whoever it was meant for. Only after the fine was paid did they perform the chela ceremony for me. Four rupees was paid to the jamaat and they called out the names of my new house, the naik of that house and the concerned parivar; they also called out my name and the name of my guru.

'Beta, for good or bad, stay with your guru and don't leave her for other gurus. Be a good chela and in time may you have your own chelas and nathis! Till the very end, please respect the honour of Hyderabad, our house, and make sure that you are respectful to your elders.' My gurubais also became chelas in front of the jamaat. We did paampaduthi to the elders, after which we all shared a meal. We left after bidding farewell to the naik of our house. She gave all the new chelas new saris and asked us to visit her often.

ON REACHING BANGALORE, I fell at my guru's feet and did paampaduthi. She responded with the customary 'Jiyo beta', and asked me to be a good chela, earn my keep and not take up with a man or find a husband, and honour her name. She too gifted me new clothes and said that she had no objection to me going out and doing sex work, if I wanted to. Whereupon my gurubais exclaimed, 'Why right away? She can't go just like that! She does not know the city or its streets, or how to take an auto to go anywhere. What if she loses her way and lands up with the police or rowdies? Let her learn about the city a bit more before she goes for danda.'

For a while, I observed how the others spoke, how they left and returned, the roads they took, the way they solicited clients, their ways of talking to them… I learnt by watching and making note of whatever they did.

I was petrified about going out to do sex work. What if a policeman or a rowdy was to accost me? What would I do? If the policeman was in khaki, then I would be able to identify him and run for cover. But if he was not, how would I know? As for rowdies, they could come in any number of guises. Every day I anguished over these things, as I wandered the streets, skulking like a dog. If people on motorbikes or cars stopped in front of me, I'd be afraid to talk to them or go with them. They could be the police, I would tell myself, or rowdies. I did not go with the men who obviously liked me, those men on bikes or in cars, and instead walked the streets aimlessly till I found myself back at the hamam.

When I returned without having found a customer, my friends in the hamam would laugh at me.

'How foolish you are! You can easily identify a rowdy or a policeman by how they talk. If you shy away from men who look at you, who obviously like you, thinking they could be the police or rowdies, if you're this afraid, then what can be done? How are you going to make a living? If we were like you, if we were only as pretty, as feminine, we'd earn plenty of money, just like that. All you have done is waste money on an auto! How do you think you're going to find work in Bangalore?'

My guru called me aside, 'If a chap stops his bike on seeing you, go and talk to him. You'll get to know whether or not he is a good fellow. After you're sure, you can talk business with him. Supposing a client asks you how much you charge, tell him that you'd go with him for two or three hundred rupees. If he agrees to pay that much, then ask him if he's got a place. If you're scared to even go up to him in the first place, then there isn't much help for you. You'll end up doing the sort of work you do at the hamam, and making do with an earning of few rupees. Go tomorrow, get hold of a client, talk to him like a woman. Come on, you should know by now how to do this. After all, you have done danda before! When pottais who don't know anything go and get clients and make money, what's your problem? You look like a woman!'

Despite my guru's encouragement, I found sex work difficult. It was quite a task, getting hold of a fellow, talking to him, taking him to a place and making sure he paid. On some days I found people, on others I returned home empty-handed. Sometimes I waited, as if I was going to catch a bus or an auto. But I did not ever stand in one place, for that would make people suspicious. Instead I kept walking, I went wherever my feet took me. Initially, neither the police nor the rowdies knew that I was walking in order to solicit. So I did not face any trouble from them in the early days. Also, the police are not suspicious of women who walk on the roads, at least not immediately. They identify us eventually when they notice us walking the same streets often, and because we stop and talk to people on bikes and cars. Then they catch hold of us. How many times they've caught me thus, beaten me in full view of the road, snatched money from me as a bribe and sent me off!

The first time it happened, it was a man in civilian clothes, around forty years of age and well-built. He forced me to get into an auto with him and said that he was taking me to the police station. I soon registered that we were going down dark alleys with almost no people. He then attempted to force me into having sex with him.

'Samy! Let me go! I'm not a woman. I'm a pottai! I got into to this for my stomach's sake. Please let me go!' I held my hands together in supplication.

He replied in Kannada, 'So you're a khoja? But you don't look like one!'

'But I am,' I said.

'Okay, okay, now hand over whatever you have with you.'

He checked my purse and took away the two hundred and fifty rupees that I had. Not content with that, he snatched the copper chain I wore around my neck, thinking it was gold. I had copper bangles on my wrists. He wanted those as well, but I could not get them off easily. He would not believe my protests that they were copper bangles until he finally struck a match and examined them in the light of its flame. He then left in the same auto, and I found myself alone in that dark neighbourhood.

'Cursed fellow! He's taken my money, my copper chain and worse, left me here. May bad things happen to him! If he had a pottai like me in his own house, would he do this to me? Thank God, I was not wearing a gold chain. I wore this because it looked nice and it cost me a hundred and fifty rupees, and the fellow has snatched that away! Why did he not snatch the chain on his wife's neck? Why me?' I bemoaned my fate.

I was all alone and it was dark and I did not know the way home. I was also terribly scared that someone else would come along and beat me up. God, I thought, I know no one here, and don't have anyone to help me out. I started walking, letting my feet carry me wherever. I tried unsuccessfully to stop the autos that sped past me. Finally, a man on a bike stopped and asked me if I was lost. He helped me find an auto. 'Bless you,' I said, as I headed home.

I narrated all that had happened to my guru. One of my gurubais, who was listening to my tale, asked me how the man looked.

'About forty years of age and tall.'

'Was he balding in front?'

When I nodded, she said, 'Same chap. He did the same to me once and today he caught hold of you. He does other things too: he keeps a watch on us, who we speak to and so on. He then walks over, takes away the keys of the bike or car, shoos us off and blackmails the client into giving him money. You should watch out next time. Clients shouldn't think that we've set up people to take money from them. They might even try and harm us the day after.'

'What a thing to do and how dare he!'

When I went in to change my clothes, another gurubai asked me, 'So, good money today?'

'I got caught by a policeman and you're asking me if I made good money? He took off with my money and my chain.'

'Don't take it so hard. You get both laddus and lathis when you go out to work,' replied my gurubai, smiling.

At night, when I was getting ready to sleep, my guru called me to her. 'Look, beta, when you go out to do danda, whether or not you earn, whether you eat a laddu or get hit with a lathi, you have to hand over a hundred rupees every day. Pottais who are in the hamam don't earn. We have to pay the rent, and we need money for water, food, worship and other things. Whatever you may earn out there, make sure that you give me a hundred rupees, okay?'

'Of course, it's a chela's duty to help the guru in times of need,' I said.

The days when I did not get clients, I'd come home and try out new saris, stitch stylish blouses with plunging necklines, try out a new perfume…

ONCE, WHEN I was walking on St Marks Road at around seven in the evening, a police van stopped in my path, picked me up and took me to the Cubbon Park police station.

One of the policemen asked, 'Hey khoja, where're you from, son?'

'I am from Tamil Nadu.' (The whole conversation was in Kannada.)

'Why did you come here?'

'We're pottais. No one is willing to give us work. My family does not want me, and so I came here to earn for my stomach.'

'Why the hell can't you do that in Tamil Nadu? Why come here?' A policeman brought his lathi down on my legs and hands. Another kicked me with a booted foot.

'Samy, samy! Let me go! I won't ever come this side again!' I cried out.

'Let you go? Not a chance! Go and sit in that corner. Our senior officer will come and after that we'll shave off your head and send you to jail!'

I was made to sweep the station and swab its premises—all this while I was waiting for the superintendent to come.

There was no response to my plea: 'Sir, I've done all you've asked me to. Let me go, my people will be looking out for me!'

I wanted to run away, but there were men with guns standing guard, and what if one of those men shot at me? Also, if I tried to get away, they'd probably beat me and torture me more. I could do nothing but wait. It was well past eleven in the night and there was no sight of the higher official. Around midnight, a policeman with two stars pinned on his shirt came to me. 'Our saheb won't come tonight. He'll be here only tomorrow. He's asked me to take a statement from you.'

He took me to another room. Adjacent to it was a small cell and there was a man behind bars. He had chains on his feet. The policeman said, 'Why don't I put you in the cell along with him? In there, you can be as you want with that fellow!'

I screamed that I did not want to go into the cell. I fell at the policeman's feet. He kicked me with his boots. He then asked me to take my clothes off—right there, while the prisoner was watching. I pleaded with him and wept, but he forcibly stripped me. When I was standing naked, he stuck his lathi where I'd had my operation and demanded that I stand with my legs apart, like a woman would. He repeatedly struck at that part with his lathi and said, 'So, can it go in there? Or is it a field one can't enter? How do you have sex then?'

I felt heart-broken and could not speak. The policeman then shouted at the prisoner. 'Dai! Have you seen enough? Want to see more?'

The prisoner smiled uneasily and covered his face with his hands. My heart beat very fast—I was petrified that he'd throw me to the prisoner and ask him to do as he wished with me. The policeman then threw his lathi at the prisoner. It hit the bars of the cell and clattered down. Bending to pick up his lathi, he yelled at the prisoner, 'Dai! Turn away! Don't look!'

Picking up a sheet of paper, the policeman scribbled something on it, and asked me, 'Where did those breasts come from? They grew on their own?'

'No, not on their own. I took hormone tablets to grow them.'

'Open your mouth wide.'

I obliged him.

'Bend down. I've got to inspect your back.'

I bent and showed him my back. He then asked me to hold my buttocks apart so that he could see my anal passage.

When I did, he thrust his lathi in there and asked, 'So you get it there?'

I straightened up, yelling with the pain of it. He then handed me my clothes and asked me to sit in a corner as before. I spent that entire night there, shivering in the cold. I did not sleep at all.

At around one o'clock, a man handed me a parcel of food and asked me to eat. I spread the paper packet on the floor and began to eat. Since the paper was soggy, some of the food spilled onto the floor. The man forced me to eat that as well and watched me as I did so.

That night I cried silently to myself, thinking of all that I had to go through. There was not a soul there to take pity on me. I felt intensely ashamed and enraged. I even thought that I should perhaps grab one of the guns there and shoot myself. But I did not know how to shoot and besides, I was afraid to even go near one of them.

The next morning, at 10 o'clock, the higher official finally arrived. He asked me into his room. 'Dai? Do you chaps have no other work? Why do you walk the streets? What're we supposed to do with you guys? We beat you, arrest you, and yet you return to the streets. So many people complain about you—vendors, college students, restaurant owners... If I am to see you fellows again on the road, you'll be permanently put in jail!' He then called out to another policeman and asked him to put me in a van.

On the way to court, they told me that I must not speak of how I was beaten or humiliated. Instead, I was to accept responsibility for my crime, pay the requisite fine and leave. I agreed to do what they asked of me. Once we reached the court, they said that they'd rather I paid them two hundred rupees. In which case I could go straight home, and they would pay the fine on my behalf. I gave them the money I had hidden inside my petticoat and left, glad to exit that scene forever. I went straight to the hamam.

My people were looking out for me and greeted me with exclamations. They had been worried on my behalf. When I told them what had happened, my guru asked me if I had told the police I was from the hamam.

'No, amma, I said I'd come from Hosur.'

'All right, all right. Now go and pour water over your head and wash off the memory of the night. May all the sins of that place be washed away from you!'

twenty

Some of the hijras from the hamam had gone to the Koothandavar temple in Villupuram. I had long wanted to visit that temple, but did not travel much when I lived in Mumbai. When I was living at home, I wanted to go the Koothandavar festival, but did not have the money to make the trip. I could go from Bangalore, but I missed my parents and wanted to visit them instead. I asked my guru if I could go for about five days. She gave me permission to leave after those who had gone to Villupuram returned.

Though my brothers had treated me badly and hurt me often, I continued to feel fondness for them. I bought clothes for everyone, toys for the children and also took with me the money I'd managed to save. I was received with love and warmth. Everyone was happy with the clothes I'd bought them. I gave all the money I had to my father, keeping back only a little for my expenses. The day after I arrived, my father came home with rabbit meat and asked me to fry it. After lunch my father and mother asked me if I continued to dance for a living, if I was comfortable wherever I was and if I was with my own kind. They advised me not to fight with my people, but to behave well and make a proper living. My mother then said that they wished to carry out alterations in their house and wondered if I could send money from time to time. I agreed to help out.

Thereafter, I sent money home and often bought things for the house. My father, with difficulty re-built the house, while I, with as much difficulty, did sex work in Bangalore to help him. As I have said repeatedly, my work was hard. I faced all sorts of problems, I endured physical violence and torture of the mind. I had to fight every day with police and rowdies. The police took bribes from us all the time, and yet at the end of the month we were taken to the police station, beaten, hurt and sent back. If ever I saw a rowdy on the road, I fled the scene swiftly in an auto.

Sometimes, I wondered if I should continue to do sex work at all. But what else was I to do? I had no choice but to suffer it. I had to get used to living thus, not knowing what the day would bring or what the morrow held for me. I'd been born a pottai and if I wanted to live as a woman, I had to endure this life. Sex work was considered a crime, which is why if a rowdy grabbed one of us on the streets, or bundled us into an auto, there was no one to take our side. In fact, from our perspective there was no difference between a police and a rowdy. They both behaved in a similar way.

I GOT SOME respite from sex work around the time of Ganesh Chaturthi. We were asked to dance in villages and small towns at weddings and at temple festivals. We would be booked for particular days and I could put off walking the streets.

The village elders would do this: they'd come, look at us and choose whoever they wanted to come and dance that year. My guru showed me off the year I was there. 'Look how lovely she is! She must dance in your village. You must pay all you can to get her to come. She is not like the others.'

'Oh, so you've got an Urvashi or a Ramba here? What about breasts? Does she have to stuff her chest with cotton or...'

'No, no, all real. If you wish, you can inspect her.' My guru then asked me to show them my breasts. Rates were discussed afterwards.

It is like shopping at the vegetable market. You pinch, squeeze and satisfy yourself of the vegetable's quality before you buy. We were inspected likewise. One's self-respect had to be hawked thus to feed one's stomach. Imagine, they actually grab your breast to make sure it is real!

My guru would demand that each of the five members in the dance troupe be paid five hundred rupees. Whereupon, the visitors would gasp, 'Five hundred rupees!'

My guru would not relent. 'Yes, five hundred rupees. It has to cover everything, from the clothes we wear to our make-up costs. We need three hundred rupees to just cover the expenses. In the end we'd be left with only two hundred rupees.'

And so she would bargain, offering them breasts, blessing them by laying her hands on their heads, at times very nearly falling at their feet. In the middle of all this, the visitors would be fed tea, coffee or cold drinks. We would bargain until we were tired and exhausted.

'Look here, amma! We spend lakhs of rupees on these festivals. You should dance your best. Give us a super dance, okay? And make sure you wear super clothes. And you must send these girls, the ones you've shown us. Don't do what you did the last time, when you showed us one set and sent us another useless lot of people.' With these words, they'd leave after paying an advance.

I did not want to go. But I went and danced, for my guru's sake.

WHEN WE WENT to dance at these places, we stayed in schools or in the rooms of village officials. We'd eat there, apply make-up in those rooms. When we did this, the entire village, including the children, would stand and watch. We'd behave as if we were women, and not let out that we were pottais. Even so, we'd hear people whisper to each other, 'Are they men or women?'

The dancing would happen at night. On the day that the Ganesh idol was taken in a procession around the village or town and immersed in the pond, things would get very festive. Huge lights were lugged around, accompanying the idol that was carried in a flower-bedecked palanquin around the village, down every street. We'd be asked to dance as this happened, as part of the procession.

I remember once when five of us went to dance in a large village in Karnataka. We were asked to stay in a school classroom. As always, people came to gawk at us. Someone exclaimed, 'They look like real women! But when they speak, they sound masculine!' The village elders who had booked us for the show shooed them off and shut the windows. These men then proceeded to harass us. We were forced to submit to their wants, because we were afraid not to, scared that something would happen to us if we opposed them. We were strangers in that village, who would take our side? These men were respected, and they abused us in a school where their children studied!

We had to dance alongside the villagers. They often fought with each other and this scared me. What if such fights exploded and caused trouble for us? We managed to survive the night because the five us were together and united. We danced from ten in the night to six in the morning, as the god wound his way through the village's many streets and finally reached the water tank. After that, we removed our make-up, collected the money owed to us and left for Bangalore.

You imagine that you can make a living by dancing, but here, too, you have to sell your body. It would then seem to me that the other life was better, that it was easier to sell yourself, put up with police and rowdy trouble. You pull yourself together and do what had to be done. For better or for worse, I had do what I had to, calling on God to help me bear my burden. Working thus, suffering thus, unable to talk about what I endured, and feeling as if I was no one's child, I'd send to my father the money I earned.

The old house actually belonged to my mother, and my parents were converting it into a bigger place. My father did not know that I did sex work to earn the money that I sent him. I would tell my parents that I danced, that I did small comedy roles in films, that I posed for advertisements, as if I were chasing the hero after a music show, as if I was asking for ice-cream... In the end, I never had much money. After I'd handed over money to my guru and spent some on the parties that we were invited to, I'd have about five hundred rupees left. I could not afford even to buy a sari with that amount. My poor father must have attended to restoring the house, thinking his son was earning and that all would be well. But I am sure that the money I sent home was not enough.

WHEN I DID walk the streets again after that terrible time at the police station, I was listless. One day I walked for miles on end, until my feet hurt, yet I did not find a single client. There was no one to ask me if I was doing all right. I felt depressed. Even if I could make two hundred rupees that would do, I'd get a hundred after turning over a hundred to my guru. It was past 8 o'clock. I feared I'd be spotted by the police and rowdies if I hung out on the road. I decided to stay in the shadows.

A car stopped and picked me up, only to drop me off. This happened a few times. God knows whose face I happened to see when I woke up that morning, for though these men in cars gave me lifts, I could not make any of them my client. I felt desperate. When a white Maruti stopped in front of me, I put my head into the car to see if there was anyone in there besides the driver. There was no one. The man said, 'Five hundred rupees?'

'Do you have a room?' I asked.

'We'll go out of the city, to the outskirts. We can park somewhere and do it in the car.'

I agreed and got into the car.

'Your voice is somewhat rough? You a woman or a khoja? Get down, motherfucker!' Yelling, he stopped the car.

'Why shout like that? You asked me to get in! In a single day, if ten chaps behave like you, how am I supposed to make a living? You chaps waste my time! You call yourself human?'

The man hopped out of his car.

'Khoja! Fucker! Do you know who you're talking to? Asking me if I am a man, are you?' Shouting, he pulled me by my hair, threw me down and kicked me. He beat me again and again, and then rushed to his car and took out a knife. He came at me with it, ready to scar my face with the instrument. I hit at his hand and the knife dropped, but not before it slashed at my left hand. I tried to run, but he pulled at my sari. He kept pulling until he had stripped me of it, and I was down to my petticoat and blouse. There were people on the road, quite a number of them; there were motorcycles and cars that whizzed past; there were shops, hotels, offices on that road, but not a soul came to my rescue, to ask what was happening.

I ran until I found myself in front of a large building. I decided to hide in there and so ran headlong into the gate. The watchman of the building tried to stop me, but I pushed him aside, ashamed and desperate to save myself. I went into the basement, found a place where a large number of cars were parked and hid there. The man who beat me had flung my sari on the gate. The watchman picked it up with a stick and dropped it next to me. The sari was torn, but I hurriedly wound it around myself, rushed out, found an auto and returned to the hamam.

I felt wounded. So many people had watched the man beat me, stared at the spectacle. No one had done anything to help. What sort of a world was I living in?

ON ONE OCCASION the police used me just so that they could show a case on their records at the end of the month. I was out walking when all of a sudden five men surrounded me. They looked squat and tough. They held me down, like they would a chicken, and lugged me off. I was not sure who they were—I thought they were rowdies and so yelled for the police.

'Hey! We're the police! Why are you here? We've received reports about you. You cause us so much headache. Our officers have warned us, and asked us to lock up people like you. We've been watching you for several days now. Think you can throw chilli powder in our eyes and escape? You've been caught today. We're going to file a case against you. You'll learn your lesson if we lock you up for six months.'

'Aiyo samy! Forgive me for coming here. I didn't know I must not. I've got to earn for my stomach! Please don't do anything to me. Please let me go and you'll be blessed forever.'

'Shut up! We've heard these lies before, and from many others like you! Why can't you feed your stomach doing honest labour? Why walk the roads and cause us endless headache? VIPS come on this road often! How dare people like you wander around? You are nothing but trouble! Do you know how may people call us, complaining about you? And we get yelled at by our bosses who ask us, what the fuck are we doing, not attending to all this?'

I was not sure if they were indeed the police, but what could I do? I was trapped and could not escape. I was deeply afraid of what would happen.

'Look, if you help us catch ten of your regular guys, we'll let you off,' they told me.

'Get you ten fellows? How is that?'

'You hang around the road, as you usually do. If someone comes up to you and talks, speak with him. Answer as you would normally. We'll get him. Mind you, we'll be around, watching. Don't think you can signal to your clients and warn them. We'll hang you upside down, beat your buttocks off your back and skin you alive.'

They hid themselves behind trees and within buildings as I walked up to the road. Whoever it was—whether they were walking, or were on bikes or in cars—they only had to stop and talk to me, and they were carted off. The police who closed in on these men, first relieved them of their keys before they dragged them by their shirtfronts to the van. Their vehicles were parked in a underground car park nearby.

Neither I nor the police knew why people stopped to talk to me: whether they wanted to take me some place and have sex with me, whether they were merely asking for directions, whether they were concerned if I was lost. They could have come to me for any of these things. But the police did not care about reasons.

I could not tell those who stopped not to talk to me or look at me. I kept praying that no one would approach me, but unfortunately that day, many actually did. There are times when not a soul is around to ask why I was standing thus. 'But today's not such a day,' I lamented to myself. Poor fellows, God knows what sort of men they were, what they wanted from me, and why had they even stopped to talk to me in the first place!

When the police surround a man like that and take away his keys, he cannot but shudder with fear and anxiety. A few thought that I had set up rowdies to catch them and take away their money. Only when they were pushed into the police van did they realize what had happened. That day the police made me stand around for two hours and arrested around fifteen people.

The police finally asked me to climb into the van along with the men who had been rounded up.

'Samy! I stood on the road as you wanted me to. You got the men you wanted. Please, now let me go!' I cried, falling at their feet.

They brought down their lathis heavily on my back. 'Get lost! And don't you dare come this side again!'

I could barely walk, but I managed to run till I found an auto-rickshaw.

I don't know what they did with the men they took away, or where they took them. They must have taken money from them and let them go. Whatever happened, all those who were caught that evening were bound to think ill of me. They must have thought I was a police spy. If they chanced to see me some place, they'd surely beat me, or even throw acid on my face. I decided not to go back to that road, not go out at all, or do sex work. The pain I felt, the hurt I suffered—my entire being shudders when I recall what happened to me that evening.

However, I could not stay back at the hamam and expect the money I earned there to feed or clothe me. I had to somehow continue to make a living. I decided to go home for a few days.

IF YOU HAVE a government job, you have to work on all days except holidays. Whatever problems there were at work, you could at least tell the world that you worked, that you had a job. But my profession is considered unacceptable by society and law. Besides, I was born a man and had become a woman—that meant more trouble, more problems. A man sometimes has to struggle to live; but for people like me, to live was to struggle and fight.

Things happen and sometimes you forget them. There are times when you know what is in store and you endure the problems and the pain. I want to write about all of that, but I have to protect myself. I certainly don't want to cause pain to others by writing things that might hurt them. So I can only write about things selectively.

The world looks askance at me. It holds me wrong for having turned into a woman after being born a man. God has given me these feelings, and I have to live in a world that does not respect my feelings. The world considers it wrong of me to beg, wrong of me to want to get married... It is not as if I have killed or cheated or committed theft.

If someone beats me, pinches me, scolds me, I hurt. I feel hungry, I have to eat, I have to cover my shame with clothes. I too need to be with my loved ones. I want their affection. I want to experience pleasure. I long for respect. I want to live a life of dignity. I want to go to work as many women do.

But who gives people like me love? Or respect? Who offers us clothes to hide our shame? When I am hungry who feeds me? If I want all of this, what am I to do? Did I come with a mission at birth, wanting to be a pottai? Did my parents imagine I would be one, when I was born? I did not imagine that I would walk endlessly on several roads, begging, doing sex work. Who is responsible for what has happened to me? Did I take to this profession, because I wanted to? I did not choose this profession on my own. I wanted to live with a man. I did not get all that I needed for my everyday life. Men use me only for sex, they are unconcerned about all else. I do not desire to do sex work, but I had come to accept it as my destiny.

There are many who want to become doctors, but they do not get the opportunity, or they lack the resources. They end up doing something else. It's like I wanted to become a doctor, instead became a teacher. What could I have done? One needs a job. I may not like being a teacher, but I cannot become a doctor after having been trained to be a teacher. The law will not permit a teacher to function as a doctor. I continue to be a teacher, because I've got to earn a living.

I thought I could get money by tying up parcels in a grocery store. That too was not to be. This world that exploits my youth and beauty does not know how to bring out the talent there is in me. If I have to live in this world, I've got to adjust to its demands. So I live as I do. The situation is such that I can only make a living thus. As far as I am concerned, it is society and law—indifferent as they are to me—that have brought me to where I am today, where many of us are today. It is not so much that we are abducted into sex work, rather we are the reasons for the very existence of sex work and that is no exaggeration. Society and law not only think we are doing wrong, but are violent towards us.

For the sake of money, I have put aside my honour and have taken to the roads. I'm called a hooker. What should the police be called then—they who use us and snatch money from us?

Chapter 21

I visited my parents often, and while I stayed with them, if I wanted to visit Namakkal I had to go by bus. The heat, the crowd, the sweat running down my body—I disliked all of it. I was often the largest woman on the bus. I looked big and so people stared at me. Some pressed themselves against me, some even blew air down my back. The bus ride to town was always unpleasant. I began to think about buying myself a Kinetic Honda, a scooter that had just been launched.

My father wasn't pleased. 'You live in Bangalore. Why do you need a scooter here? When you're gone, it'll languish in the yard. Surely you don't need a scooter for the two days you're here? You could take my motor bike to go to the town.'

He owned a large bike which could be heard over a radius

of a kilometre. Women did not ride such bikes in this part of the country. If I were to ride it to town, people would stare and might even laugh.

'I want a scooter—that's the kind of vehicle women drive.' I was firm in my resolve and took my father to a local scooter showroom.

My father did not like the idea of buying a scooter, especially the one that I wanted, which would give only thirty miles per litre of petrol. Also, the days I was in Bangalore, the scooter would be lying idle, and that would affect the battery. My father tried to convince me to buy a TVS 50. He said that it would give me eighty miles per litre. But I did not like that vehicle. Besides I felt the Honda suited me, it suited my body. It had an automatic gear, the vehicle could be started with a turn of the wrist, and I was convinced that if I were to ride it, my prestige would increase. I was therefore adamant. Even as my father and I discussed the matter of buying the Honda, I was scared that the staff in the shop would hear us.

Finally I chose a black and grey Honda. With extra fittings and insurance, it cost forty thousand rupees. I gave them the money I had brought with me and requested that the vehicle be registered in my name. I was told that I had to provide proof of address, and they asked me to fetch our ration card. But I was Doraisamy in the ration card. The staff had so far thought I was a woman. If they came to know that I was in fact the Doraisamy mentioned in the card, what would they think?

My father asked me to stay back in the shop and went home to get the card. When he returned with the card, flushing with shame, I approached the shop owner. I informed him that I was a woman now, though I was Doraisamy in the ration card. I asked if the RC book could be issued in the name of Revathi. The shop owner was taken aback. He looked at me carefully, from head to toe. Since I wanted to get the matter over with, I decided to remain calm.

'We can't do that. Whatever is your name is in the ration card, we'll have duplicate that in the RC book.'

Unable to find a solution, I agreed to have the RC book issued in the name of Doraisamy.

THE FIRST TIME I rode the Honda I was scared. But since I had used my brother's TVS several times, I soon felt confident on the scooter. The first trip I made was to the shrine of our family goddess to offer worship.

Like everybody else, I wanted to be law-abiding, so I decided to obtain a driving licence. I went to a private driving school and asked them if I could get a licence in the name of Revathi. They said that I'd have to change my name in the ration card and get a life insurance policy in that name. My father helped me with the ration card. He took it to the tahsildar's office, where they struck out my original name and wrote Revathi on top of it. The tahsildar signed on it and affixed his seal of office. Meanwhile I paid a hundred and fifty rupees and got an insurance policy and went to the driving school with copies of both documents. They gave me forms to fill and asked me to reach the brake inspector's office by ten the next morning.

The next day I joined the queue that extended from the inspector's office to the road. The driving school instructor gave me the papers I needed to get a licence and took two thousand rupees from me. He asked me to remain standing in the queue, and said that he would join me when it was my turn to appear before the inspector. I stood in line for two hours. The inspector observed each person carefully. When it was my turn, I approached him with my papers and handed them over. The driving school instructor too appeared at that moment and gave the inspector some money.

I don't know if the money given was not enough, but after looking through my papers, the inspector said, 'We've never had such a case before. I can't grant a licence to this person,' and flung the papers at me.

I was angered by his action. 'Sir! Why throw the papers at me? I haven't done anything wrong. I respect the law, and so I want to get a licence before I started driving my scooter. Why fling these papers and show so little respect? Doesn't your law allow you to give licences to people like me? I haven't cheated you or anyone, I have produced the papers you asked for and yet you say you won't give me my licence?'

'Look here, we've never had a person like you come here and ask for a licence. I don't have the powers to grant you one. I'll discuss this with my superiors. After that, we'll see.'

'Your superiors? Who is above you who can do this? What have you found wrong with me that you won't give me a licence? You say you've not encountered this sort of "case" before. Well, I was born a man and I became a woman. I have taken an insurance policy in my name, that is, Revathi. My name has been changed in the ration card. What more do you need to issue a licence? You think I'm going to commit acts of terror or violence once I have a driving licence? I've come here to get one, because like everyone else I want to live by the law. If you don't give me a licence, I'll drive without one. And if someone stops me and asks for my licence, I'll say that you refused to give me one. I'll even go to the papers and appear on television, I'll tell people that the government only issues licences to men or women, not to people like me.'

The driving school instructor entreated me not to shout and said that I would get the licence eventually. He pressed five hundred rupees into the inspector's hand and coaxed him to take back the papers.

'Go and get a letter from the village officer saying that you are Doraisamy who has become Revathi,' said the inspector.

I went to the inspector's office the next day armed with a letter from the village officer. I also demonstrated my driving skills to him. He then sent me off to get my photograph taken and said I should return in a week's time. When I did, I finally had my driving licence. The licence did not specify whether I was male or female. Instead it referred to me as 'Revathi who is Doraisamy'.

To get a licence under the name of Revathi, I had to go through all of this. It was exhausting, and worse, what ought to have cost me a hundred fifty rupees set me back by two thousand rupees. However, I had my licence, and I was happy to have it.

AFTER I STARTED going about on my scooter, many strangers appeared to somehow know me. I am not sure what they made of me, whether they knew I was a hijra or thought I was just another woman. Whenever I went to town, to the vegetable shop, the grocery store, whenever I stopped to buy cosmetics or medicine, several people came up to speak to me. 'You're Revathi, aren't you? I've seen you in Mumbai. I'm sure you've seen me…' Others would address me intimately, as if they were my kin.

I would mumble in response, 'Where have I seen you before? When…'

'What's this Revathi? I'm saying your name right, am I not? And aren't you from…?'

And if they got my village name right, I had no choice but to agree I was indeed from that village. 'I don't remember where we met…'

'I am your brother's friend. I've come to your house several times…' And they would go on to identify my house right.

But I did not know these men who knew me, my name, the name of my village, my house. I was bewildered that they knew so much and I did not know them.

I was also baffled when people called out to me, 'Dai, Doraisamy! New scooter, is it? How much did you pay for it? Your mother keeping well?'

When I wore my churidar-kurta and perfume, and rode the scooter into town, there were all these people who knew me and insisted on talking to me. This did not happen when I was on a bus, or merely walking on the road. So I was mystified when people came up to me and introduced themselves. I was afraid that if I was seen chatting with these strange men there would be talk later. I was also scared that these men would harm me and use me. I did not therefore encourage conversation, and often left the place right away, after the briefest of exchanges.

Some men looked at me in astonishment as I sped by on my scooter. They would slow down and stop by the side of the road. I knew that they did so to take a better look at me. On my way home from town, some would follow me, to find out where I was going, where I lived. I found a few of them attractive, but I hid my desire and behaved exactly as women do. I never let a man get a hold on me. I did not so much as look a man in the eye. I behaved as a woman is expected to in our society.

Whenever this happened—when men spoke to me, said suggestive words, followed me—I wondered why none of this happened when I was in male attire yet felt that I was a woman.

A ROW OF autorickshaws can usually be found in front of the bus stand in Namakkal. Buses entering the bus stand usually do so one after another, and anyone trying to get past the bus stand at that point of time has to wait till the road is clear. One day, when I was on my scooter, waiting, I heard the auto-rickshaw drivers talking amongst themselves about me. One group was sure I was a man, the other group insisted I was a woman. One of the men in the first group said that I was big-built and no woman is that large, and no woman would wear the kind of clothes I wore or cut their hair as I had done. I felt great anger when I heard this. I got off my scooter, parked it by the wayside and went up to the drivers.

'So you want to know whether I am male or female? Should I tell you or should I show you that I am not a woman, but a man? Have you got nothing else to do, but speculate who is a man, and who's a woman? Seems like this is what you do for a living!'

Some of the drivers said, 'Who told you that we are talking about you? What is your business with us? Go on! Get on with your work!'

I felt that if I let them get away this time, they would talk about me whenever they saw me. I stood in the middle of the road and yelled out: 'Dai! So you want to lay bets on who's fat, who's thin, who's a man, who's a woman? What do you fellows get out of talking like this? Listen! I am a pottai! I was a man who changed into a woman. If you had one like me in your family, would you place bets on a person like me?'

As soon as I started shouting, the drivers slunk off. By this time a huge crowd, comprising both men and women, had gathered around me.

'Call the police to come and get these guys! They have got into this habit of teasing women. It looks like soon no woman can walk safely on the road. These fellows need to be given a good beating.'

Many in the crowd supported me. I was moved that there were at least a few who did not look upon people like me with disgust, that they felt sympathy for us. I realized that I was merely going through all that a woman does, all the time. At least I had taken to the middle of the road and yelled back at my tormentors. Which woman would dare do so?

There is this power in me, this urge to fight wrong. I don't know if it's because I was born a man and became a woman. I am not sure I'd have thus stood on a road and shouted had I been born a woman.

AFTER A FEW days I returned to Bangalore. I could not spend long periods of time in the village. My brothers were ashamed to be seen with me. Other people too appeared afraid to talk to me in public places. I think this is why God makes sure that people like me seek out others of my own kind. It seemed to me that I was perhaps better off with them.

Chapter 22

Some time after I got back to Bangalore, three people came to see me. All of them wore men's clothes, but had pottu on the forehead and their eyes were streaked with kohl. I understood at once that they were like me. I was sitting outside the hamam, on a block of stone near the entrance. They came up to me and said, 'Mummy, paampaduthi.' When I heard them say 'Mummy' I knew they were educated.

'Come women, where are you from?'

'We're from here, from Bangalore,' replied one of them and mentioned the area where she lived. It turned out that the three them were from different parts of the city. I noticed that they spoke to each other in English.

'Mummy, we're friends. We've seen you on this road many times and we've always wanted to talk to you. But we were scared to approach you. Today we decided that somehow we must talk to you. You are very beautiful. We feel like gazing at you… all the time…'

'Tell me, you've applied kohl to your eyes. What if someone you know sees you? Won't they go and tell your families?'

'That's what we are afraid of. We seek out parks, bathrooms, apply kohl, wear pottu. And we go to places where no one knows us. On our way home, we rub off all this. But we don't want to lead this sort of life—a life that is neither this nor that. We want to be like you, have the operation and live as women. Will you accept us, Mummy?'

I was reminded of my past. Of the time that I left home for Delhi. My journey from Delhi to Mumbai.

'Well, like you, I too wanted to become a woman. I underwent much in that process and I continue to suffer even now! You all look like you're educated. You should study well, get good jobs.

'I do understand your feelings. I'm not saying that you shouldn't spend time with us, sing and dance and have a good time. But I don't know if you should give up your studies, get this operation done and suffer like the rest of us. Do you know how difficult this life is? If you want to, stay with us, wear saris, and after you've experienced all of that, get back into men's clothes and return home. If you become like us, then life is not going to be easy.'

'Mummy, we're sure people said the same thing to you when you were like us. Our feelings and desires are not different from what you experienced back then. Even if you tell us not to, we want to have this operation. Please tell us where we should go. We'll be grateful for that information.'

I did not want them to endure all that I had suffered. So I desisted from giving them that information and sent them off with more advice. But they sought another hijra's help and all three underwent the operation with the money that one of them had brought from her house. They came to see me a couple of weeks later.

'Amma, mata...'

I knew as I saw them walk, their steps hesitant, that they had indeed had the operation.

'I can see that you've had the operation. In whose house are you now that you've had it done?'

They gave me the name of the hijra and details of where she lived.

'So why did you not stay there?'

'She told us that the money we gave her barely covered the costs of the operation. She wanted more to look after us. We did not have the money, so she would not take care of us. We've come to you, please don't send us away!'

My gurubais in the hamam warned me against them. 'Look, they are from this city, and educated too. If you take them in, their families are going to blame you for what happened. Also, they are not like us—they did not want to live with us, learn right from wrong. They went off on their own and got this operation done. What do they know about our culture or our customs? If you are a pottai, you have to know all that is there to know about a pottai's life. You have to respect your gurus and nanis and earn for them, and only when the guru allows it, does a chela undergo nirvaanam. These three have done all this on their own.'

I was in a quandary. 'Why did you have to go and do this? Didn't I tell you three repeatedly not to have the operation? But you do exactly that, and in such a rush!'

'Amma, we're in pain. Please accept us as your daughters and teach us right from wrong. If you don't take us in, we have no choice but to die. If our families come and ask us, we'll tell them that we did this of our own volition.' They were in tears.

I felt their pain and hurt, and recalled my own operation. They were probably in great pain, similar to what I had experienced. I decided to take them in, come what may. Since the three were friends, they all wanted to become my chelas. Since my gurubais might resent that, I decided that one could become my chela and the other two could become chelas of my gurubais. But the three were firm, insisting that they wanted to be my daughters. So my gurubais gave in.

I gave them a place to stay in the hamam and decided to wait for forty days to pass before I took them to Hyderabad to my naik's house in order to accept them as chelas in her presence. But all three left the hamam before the forty-day period was over. Mayuri, the eldest, healed first, even when she was with me in the hamam. She decided to go home in male attire, as if she had not had an operation. The second, Famila, called her parents on the phone and told them that she had had this operation and returned home in male attire. The third, Rithu, went away with her lover. According to hijra custom, as I've described earlier, those who had undergone the operation could not go out or look a man in the face till forty days are over and all the rites have been done. But these three left saying that if their families started looking for them, they did not want to land me in trouble. They assured me that they would come back in time for the ceremony.

My gurubais spoke to me of the rituals that had to be done for my three chelas. 'All of us pottais have been obedient to our gurus. We did not mind the beatings and kicks we got from them—we learned from them, earned for them and only then did we undergo nirvaanam. But these three spent their own money and got the nirvaanam done. Be that as it may, you've got to spend money now to take them to Hyderabad. What if they run away after the rites are done? What is the guarantee that they'll earn for you?'

'If they have truly accepted me as their mother, they won't leave me. I don't intend to do these rites with the expectation that they've got to earn and recompense all that I've spent on them. I'll do for them what a mother would do for her daughters.'

'You are a mad woman! You had to earn for your guru in Mumbai and only then did she allow you have your nirvaanam done. And why did she agree to your nirvaanam? She and the other elders knew you by then, you had earned for them, you had done all that you were asked to do—and so they allowed you to have that operation. Isn't that the custom amongst us?'

'Look! These pottais have gone and done it. They want to be my daughters and are on their knees before me. I can't talk now about all that is due to a guru. I have to fulfil a guru's responsibility and I wish to do it wholeheartedly. It's fine if they decide to stay with me, it is also fine if they go and live some place else. I am happy I have these three daughters.'

I bought all that was needed for the mata puja for all three of them—saris, nose-rings and anklets. They arrived a day before the puja. I could not afford to hire a mandapam, so I performed the rites in the hamam, in the presence of my gurubais and gurus. I then took my three chelas to Hyderabad, adopted them as my own, and did what tradition and custom demanded.

Of the three, two left the hamam, unable to live there, and set up house on their own. Famila alone stayed with me for some time. She too did not like the restrictions that we observed in the hamam. She smoked, she read an English newspaper in the mornings, and she did not take to hijra custom. So she too left to join her gurubais.

In the course of time, they called their parents to visit them and talk matters over. Famila's parents asked her to return home, but insisted she wear male clothes. When she refused, her father cut off relations, but her mother and younger brother continued to visit her. Like me, the three of them did sex work. I continued to live in the hamam, as always, knowing that wherever they lived, they would be my daughters. We visited each other often.

I WAS CLEAR that my chelas should not encounter the difficulties that I did in Delhi and Mumbai. As their guru, I did not wish to stand in the way of their freedom. Let them live as they wish and if they miss their guru, let them visit, I told myself. I did not want my chelas to earn for me, nor did I wish to use my authority to extract money from them. I had lived by hijra rules and tenets in Mumbai and Delhi, and continued to do so in Bangalore. I lived in the world of the hijra community, with all its particular sorrows and joys. My chelas wanted to live in the wider world, and I wanted them to live as they wished.

My chelas took lovers, had their own homes and lived as they wished—demonstrating to the world that they were women. Whenever I visited them, I felt fear: what if the neighbours came to know I was a hijra? They too were uneasy about this. They had probably passed themselves off as women when they rented these houses, and had perhaps described their partners as their husbands. The hamam was different—the entire world knew that we were hijras. I liked the way my chelas lived, but I also liked living in the hamam with my own kind. I had spent the better part of my adult life living with my gurus, kaalagurus, gurubais, chelas—as part of a large joint family.

My three chelas had been born, raised and educated in Bangalore, and they had a number of educated friends. Among them were some kothis and also educated homosexuals. They would go to bars and pubs, dressed like college girls, in jeans, sometimes in skirts… I had not heard of or seen hijras doing this sort of thing. You would not see such clothes in a hijra neighbourhood or in hijra houses. Hijras in Bangalore wear only saris. In the north, they wear salwar-kurtas. Whenever I saw my chelas dressed fashionably, at home or when we went out, I longed to wear such clothes myself. When they addressed me as 'Mummy' and when I went out with them, I felt I was indeed their mother. In hijra society, they were my chelas, but to the outside world, they were my daughters and I was their mother. I had never felt sad or troubled because I could not bear a child. But the affection my chelas expressed warmed my heart. It had a healing effect. I never ceased to be surprised by their friendship.

MY CHELAS TOOK me to a place that was meant to help people like us. My chelas had been there before and had known about it even before they had their nirvaanam. The place was known as Sangama and the organization was celebrating its first anniversary in a modest fashion. The organization collected information on people like us—kothis, hijras. I'm not sure of the month or day that I went there. I only remember that it was 1999.

The welcome was warm. I met people who expressed their love by hugging even those they did not know. They all spoke very good English too. Initially, I felt rather shy. I did not know English and could not talk to any of them. I watched in astonishment as my chelas spoke to everyone there in English, and shook hands with them. When I was sure no one was looking, I drew Famila aside, 'Are they people like us?'

'No, some of them are gay.'

'Gay? What is gay?'

'They are homosexuals.'

Famila introduced me to the people there, who immediately said 'Hi!' I greeted them in Tamil, 'Vanakkam.'

We were given coffee and snacks. The people who had come for the occasion did not behave like guests, rather, each of them was busy with a task. Some were washing up, others handed around plates of food, yet others carried the used plates to the garbage bin. Each washed his or her own coffee cup. I thought about the division of duties between the young and old in a hijra household.

'Famila, do all these people work in this office?'

'No, one of them started this place. He set it up using his fellowship money, and then two others joined him. Come, let me introduce you to him.'

She took me to the person who started it all and after we greeted each other, I asked, 'What sort of work do you do here?'

'We are collecting and documenting information about homosexuals from newspapers, weeklies, the internet. We extract what we need and file it under different heads. This documentation will be useful for posterity. At present there is nothing available on homosexuals, and our files will help those who do research on the subject. People can come here, leaf through the files, read...'

'What sort of news do you file away?'

'Well, instances of violence against homosexuals, the consequences they face when their families find out they are gay; also, of how they are denied their rights, of how society disregards their feelings, refuses to accept them for what they are... there are some who do not understand their sexuality and so end up committing suicide...'

'What'll you do with all this information?'

'Homosexuality is not abnormal, it is natural. Yet Indian law considers it a crime. Indian customs too criminalize it. Homosexuals cannot be open about their sexual orientation and cannot express their feelings in public. Sangama provides a space for them to be who they are. Here, they can ask questions, address anxieties about their sexuality.'

'Do hijras, people like me, come too?'

'Famila used to come, while she was in male attire. Now she's brought you. We collect and document information on hijras as well—on the changes they undergo when they opt for a change of sex, the violence they endure at the hands of the police…'

'It seems like there is nothing for us hijras to do but sex work. We lack the education to do much else, and there's no one to offer us work. Sex work brings with it all kinds of problems—we suffer at the hands of both the police and rowdies. We are not accepted by our families. Initially my family didn't accept me, but today I can visit them in a sari. However, there are many others whose desires and dreams lie buried deep within them. I wish to help people like me. Do you think I can get a job here?' I asked.

'We've in fact been discussing this for some time now and putting aside money. Once we have things in place, we'll be in a position to take in more people and we'll surely employ you. It is very important that people like you who understand, who are enthusiastic and who can shoulder responsibility come into this kind of work. Please leave your address with us.'

'If you get in touch with Famila, she'll find a way to let me know.'

FOR SEVERAL DAYS I kept thinking of my visit to Sangama. If I could indeed get a job there, I'd have found a way to work for my community.

twenty-three

Three months after I had visited them, I heard from Sangama. I was given a job as an office assistant with a pay of two thousand five hundred rupees. My parents were not particularly thrilled about my new job. The salary would be barely enough for me to get by in Bangalore and they were not sure if I would be able to send them any money at all.

For me, money was not everything, and it did not matter that my salary was modest. I wanted to be like other women—go to work, do something for society. The man who started Sangama had, with the support of his friends, got together some money to pay my salary. I knew that when Sangama had more money, there'd be more work to do, and I'd be paid better.

I said farewell to sex work and joined Sangama even as I continued to live in the hamam. My guru did not approve of my decision. 'What does a pottai have to do with work? And what sort of work is this that fetches you only two thousand five hundred rupees? If you go and do danda in MG Road or Brigade Road, you'll earn more!'

'Amma, people like us have done this forever. For generations all we have been able to do is begging or sex work. How much longer should we have to do this? If our elders, at least some amongst them, had gone out into the wider world and found other work, then younger hijras would have followed their example. You taught us your way of life, but hijras of my generation want more. We want to acquaint the world with our lives, and we wish to live like others. That's why I am going to work.'

My guru gave up. 'Do as you will. It's your life.'

IN MY EARLY days in Sangama, I was prompt and punctilious, and did all the work that was asked of me. This endeared me to all the senior staff. I opened the office, made tea, went out and bought things that were needed for the office. I would cut out the portions marked for filing in newspapers and magazines and stick them on white sheets, jotting down the date and the name of the publication. I learnt a lot from the seniors in Sangama about sexual minorities, and about minorities in general; about violations against dalits and adivasis; Hindu-Muslim differences and conflicts; the effects of wars waged by the large nations ... I learnt of these matters in workshops, where they taught us in a manner that helped us understand. I was beginning to understand what Sangama work was all about.

Five others had been taken on as staff along with me. Famila was not a staff member, but she helped with Sangama work on the rights of sexual minorities and was paid for it. Eventually Famila was appointed the Hijra Outreach Coordinator. Though she was my chela, I learnt much from her. Soon we shifted to a new place and more people joined the staff. All of us were paid a bit more than before.

I was able to rent a place of my own near the hamam. My guru bought me things needed for the house. I knew the house owner, and he agreed to rent his house to me when he found out that I was working in an office and not doing sex work. But he would not allow me to have hijra visitors, for, he reasoned, if hijras are seen visiting, then men would follow in due course. Neighbourhood families would object if hijras or men came to the homes of young women, or so I was told by my house owner. I agreed to his condition because I felt the need to have my own place. In any case, the hamam was close by and I could visit my guru and gurubais any time.

I lived in an apartment, one among many women, with some of whom I forged friendships. I rather liked the life I was leading—cooking for myself, packing lunch, going to work. My house owner and his family and my neighbours thought of me as a woman. They did not discriminate against me or set me apart. They called me over to their homes on festive occasions, gave me kumkum and shared their food with me, as I did mine.

SANGAMA BEGAN A campaign for the rights of sexual minorities through seminars, workshops, film screenings and public meetings. Our aim was to challenge stereotypical and incorrect perceptions of sexual minorities. I participated in these events and spoke about hijra culture, hijra ways of living, and the violence and discrimination that we faced. I also spoke about hijras and property rights, and the stakes involved for someone like me who had opted to change their sex. As a spokesperson for hijra rights, I also gave interviews to newspapers and spoke at public meetings. And I worked in tandem with those involved in other rights issues.

Before I joined Sangama, I was scared to admit that I did sex work, or even that I was a hijra. Initially in Sangama too, I would decline to speak when people asked me to talk about myself for their articles. I was afraid that if the world knew I was a hijra, I would be isolated. I was afraid that if my family or people in my neighbourhood came to know that I had done sex work, they would consider me a bad person. I felt that it was wrong to be a hijra, and to do sex work. However, working in Sangama I was beginning to realize that none of it was my fault—the way the world perceived me and refused to accept me, the manner in which it snatched away my rights and made it difficult for me to earn a living except through begging and sex work, the violence it contemptuously inflicted on me. The realization increased my desire to work for the rights of those in my community who had faced as much or more violence and difficulties than me. It was not enough for me to merely challenge the violations suffered by sexual minorities—I wanted to fight against sexual violence as such.

I worked in tandem with those involved in struggles for the rights of male and female homosexuals, dalit women, child workers; and those working against dowry-related violence and communal violence. Sangama enabled me continue my struggle, even as it gave me the opportunity to realize my vocation as a social worker. It literally lent its shoulders to my efforts. Initially, before I got involved in these struggles, I used to assist with documentation. That helped me comprehend issues related to the rights of women and children.

AS SANGAMA GREW as an organization, more and more people joined us to work for sexual minorities. In the early days, my chela, Famila, and I were in the forefront of those who identified themselves as hijras and asserted their sexual rights. It took us about two years to explain Sangama's work to the community. In the beginning no one understood what we were doing. They did not come forward to learn about their rights and to extend their understanding. We found that fear and suspicion lurked large among hijras. It was only when they faced violence because they were hijras and Sangama helped them get out of the false cases foisted on them, that they began to come to us.

In the course of doing Sangama work, I realized that some things had changed. There was less violence now than when I had done sex work. I found that the general public was less inclined to harass us. The police too were not as ready to accept bribes or resort to violence against us. When Sangama began this work with the hijra community, there were many who told me that I ought not to be doing such work, as there was no other hijra who spoke out in public about the violence we endured. They said, 'What if someone tries to harm you? Perhaps you should give up this work…'

My argument was: 'How much longer can we continue to live in fear? Don't we deserve to live free? Do we not want people to think differently about us? Don't we all want the violence to end, or least decrease? If each one of us is to think that this is none of my business, then how are we going to get people to understand hijras?'

Some of my male friends, including those in my village who read about my consciousness-raising efforts in the papers, asked me how could I bear to give such interviews. Apparently they felt shamed! I replied that I did what I did not to shame myself, but to uproot the notions that people like them held about us, hijras.

I COULD SEE that my thoughts, feelings and behaviour were changing. People were moved by my testimony when I wrote about it or spoke in public. Sometimes I felt a glow of pride. I had wanted to study, get a degree and go to work, like other people. Of course, none of that happened. But today, I was going to various colleges and universities to conduct classes for students on sexuality, identity and culture. I challenged the police on the atrocities they commited. I was speaking up for my community, doing workshops for hijras, conscientizing doctors. I was able to respond to questions and clarify doubts. There were so many things that I could be proud of, but I felt that this was about more than an individual hijra's success—it was a matter of pride for all hijras.

Every hijra has a talent, but the talent requires the right opportunity and context to find expression. In my case, Sangama had enabled me find my talent, and I wanted to be able to do that for my fellow hijras. Indeed, it was my duty to do so.

I tried to make people understand our predicament. Everyone knows about the violence we suffer, but we do not speak of this in public out of fear. Don't different groups of people have their own sangams which fight for their rights? Do we hijras have such a sangam? How many of us are even conscious that there is a social group called hijra? Since people are not even aware of our existence, they think ill of us. It is our duty to dispel such ignorance. Just as how dalits have come to oppose the violence inflicted on them, why cannot we hijras get together and fight for our rights? Do we not have the right to change our sex? Aren't we human too, born of mothers, as others are? We have not descended from the sky, have we? We have rights, just like the others. We are citizens of this nation. Don't we want all those rights that are granted to other citizens: the right to have a ration card, to hold property, to have a passport, the right to work, to marry, adopt or raise a child?

In the early days of my work, hijras would tell me, 'You've got a job and a salary that goes with it. You are brave. But us? We don't have jobs, we have to do sex work to feed ourselves. It is easy for you to say "come to a meeting", "come to our office", "come to this programme"... But if we come, will you give us money? Give us food to eat? If we come for a day, then we lose a day's work. If we go to a few shops, we'll at least earn something.'

They were right in thinking the way they did. I had a job and an income and so could ask them to come for a meeting. They had a point when they said they'd lose their income for the day. I agreed with them, but I also explained that it was important they know of their rights, that they come together to fight for what was due to them. Alone, I could achieve nothing, we *had to* somehow pull together.

twenty-four

My salary from Sangama just about covered my rent and living expenses, and I had stopped sending money to my father. And because of the changes wrought in me by my experiences as an activist, I had become more assertive. Unlike before, I had started to challenge my father occasionally when we disagreed on something. This angered him and he began to tell people that I did not send him money anymore, and that each time I visited, I picked up a fight with him. According to the will he had drafted, I was to inherit a portion of his house. But he began to threaten to rewrite the will.

My eldest brother had been given his share when the family land was divided, but my father continued to take care of the property. I think it suited my brother that my father worked on his land. Because he felt comfortable with his oldest son, my father invited him to come and live in that portion of the house he had set aside for me. He did not want his other sons living with him. This caused resentment and my other brothers decided to use me as a weapon to settle scores and cause confusion.

My father felt that since he had already settled his sons' share of the property, he had the right to ask whoever he wanted to come and live in his house. My father indeed had the right to do what he wanted, but I did not want him to treat me unfairly. Listening to the advice of others, I asked him not to let my elder brother stay in the house. If he did, then my other brothers would also have to be allowed to live there. 'And what about me?' I demanded, 'Am I not your son?'

Because of these fights, my eldest brother moved into a rented house. My father blamed me for this and threatened to settle my portion of the house on my brother's son. I kept insisting that he ought to register the property in my name. My brothers felt that I did not deserve the house as I had no wife or children. To my father, they said, 'We live in rented houses. We work hard to look after our families. He has no family! Don't give him the house.'

Around that time, the death of his wife caused my second brother to take to drinking. He managed to gamble away his portion of the land to fuel his habits. Though my brother had hit me in the past and heaped insults on me, I assisted him in whatever ways I could, especially where his children were concerned. My father did not like that. So there were enough causes for my father to dislike what I said and did. Perhaps he also feared that once the house was mine, I would sell his ancestral property to outsiders or give it to hijras like me.

I ended up getting drunk and having a particularly bitter fight with my father over the will. At that time my eldest brother was also present. My mother took the part of my father and brother. It was clear that their combined objective was to somehow not let me have the house. Resolving to stay strong, I spoke somewhat hard-heartedly, 'I believe you tell others often that you want to rewrite your will. Therefore I don't think that a will is sufficient security. I want you to register this place in my name.'

'That can't happen, not while your mother and I are alive,' said my father. 'I'll make a will, I'll do nothing more. I dare you to take the case wherever—to the government, the courts, to lawyers. But while we are alive, I will not register the house in your name. After our time, you can enjoy the property.'

'But you have the authority to rewrite your will. You want to do that, just as you've been telling everyone.'

'What do you expect me to do, especially when you come home drunk and create trouble? I say I'll change my will only to scare you into your senses. But I haven't done it yet, see for yourself.'

'If I insist on my rights, you say I'm creating trouble. Please imagine my plight if you actually change your will! You kept saying this house was mine, was for me, and now it looks like you want to cheat me! You've betrayed my trust…'

'What betrayal are you talking about? You don't trust me! When you don't trust me, how can you expect me to trust you? And what if you throw us both out, saying it's your house, after I've given it to you? What will become of the two of us? Where are we to go in our old age? How am I to trust you? If you continue to create trouble, then I will give the house to whoever I like.'

My brother added, 'Yes, tomorrow, in a drunken state, you might settle the house on your fellow pottais or one of those vagabonds on the road, on anyone at all—any man who smiles at you and talks to you.'

'Look, I'm not asking for a share of anything settled on you. Have I asked you what you've done with your property? It's yours to do as you want; likewise, what is mine is mine. I'll sell it or destroy it, you have no business asking me what I'll do with it.'

'Yours? What's yours? Had we not settled money on you? This house belongs to our parents, and we have a stake in it. Think you alone will be allowed to cock-suck, pottai bastard?'

All my brothers joined the chorus—all of them claimed a share in the house.

'You have your families and you divided up the land into three parts. You gave me one lakh rupees and got me to sign that I would not claim anything more. In the years to come, only if I have a house will you give me any respect. If I have nothing, not even a dog will acknowledge me!'

My brothers retorted: 'Who asked you not to shell out money to register the land when the chance was offered? You said you did not have any. So we gave you money instead of your share and divided the land amongst ourselves. What's to be done now?'

My mother cut in, 'Look, we divided the property and gave it to all of you—none of you should come here and shout and scream. Your father and I will decide what's to be done with the house after our time. Why, we might even sell it! We are not going to partition this and be at your doorstep for a place to stay. I've got high blood pressure and diabetes. Leave me in peace in my old age!'

My father turned to me and said, 'It's painful to have you come here and create trouble. If you continue to argue, I might have to call the police. It's only because of your behaviour that I threaten to rewrite my will. If you listen to others and come here to pick up a fight with me, then I'll really write a new will. Do what you can!'

'What about the money that I gave you?'

'What money did you give me and when? Where is the proof that you ever gave me money? What'll you do if I were to say you did not give me any money? You did not give me any money, that's it. Just get out! Do your worst!'

That was my breaking point—when my father claimed there was no proof that I had given him the money. I alone knew all that I had to go through to earn that money. Filled with rage, I shouted, 'You want proof, do you? God is my witness! How dare you ask me for proof after taking money from these very hands! Never mind that I sometimes arrived late at night, before I did anything else, I would hand over bundles of notes to you. And you ask me for proof? The proof is in your heart, in your conscience. Every brick of this house bears witness to how I struggled and slaved to earn that money...

'To earn that, I suffered at the hands of all sorts of men. I did not mind climbing the steps of the police station several times. I got beaten, tortured. I earned even when I had to sell my body, become a prostitute! I earned by dancing in all sorts of places till my feet bled... I actually danced up and down streets to earn that money. I went out every day to earn, and was never sure when I left my house in the morning if I would come back in one piece. I knew I would have to deal with rowdies, with the police, with all their kicks and beatings. And for all my pains, I got called a prostitute, whore, number nine, hijra, pottai...

'After all that, after taking from me the money I earned, you ask for proof? What am I to make of you? What title shall I confer on you? I thought you to be rock-like, dependable! I have been served well for my trust. You won't prosper if you claim you never took my money! You'll be destroyed!' In that moment of anger and anguish, all that I had kept within myself burst forth. It broke my heart to let them know what I had done, nevertheless it happened.

I picked up a can of kerosene and rushed out of the house to the road. I poured kerosene over my head and demanded a matchstick from the crowd of onlookers who had by then gathered on our street. They must have been scared, for they held back, and kept staring at me. My parents and brothers remained inside. Perhaps they wanted me to set myself on fire and die. They remained quiet, as if they did not know what I was going to do. For about fifteen minutes, I stood there, kerosene in my hair, screaming and sobbing in agony. I recalled all that I had endured, how I had thought myself part of a family, as a person who mattered to my parents, my brothers and their children, how I had spent my earnings on them. Now not one of them was willing to support me or take my side.

No one came forward to console me or help me. If I had access to a matchbox I would have surely set myself on fire.

But it so happened there was no matchbox and after a while, I changed my mind. I decided that I must show them—these people who did not care about me—that I would endure. I was the one that would lose by my death, I reasoned. I went to the backyard, put my head under the tap, and stayed there until I felt my anger subside. It was not the money as such that bothered me, but all that I had suffered to earn it.

News about my behaviour spread in the village and I left for Bangalore.

UNABLE TO FORGET what had happened, I began to drink heavily. I would bring up the subject with my fellow hijras. I cried, recounting that day to my colleagues in office. I did not have the heart though to fight for what was due to me—I could have counted on my office to support me and find me a lawyer. But I thought no matter what, I could not furnish proof, and the house would be mine only if my parents willed it so. I felt cheated, and emotionally drained. I lost faith in the world.

On the one hand, there was office work with its attendant tensions, and on the other, my family troubles. It was an unhappy time for me. Besides, I lived alone and had nothing to distract me. I kept mulling over my predicament. I somehow managed to feed myself, but what of the heart's hunger, the body's needs? I had neither a husband, nor a partner, nor a friend who could assuage that longing.

A week later, my mother called me. She said that my father wanted to return the money I had given him. He had got the amount from my elder sister and in return, was going to register the house in her name. I went home once again. My sister too had been called. In front of my brothers and my mother, my father made ready to hand over the money to me. But I could not bring myself to take it from him. My heart was not in it. I was afraid that once I accepted the money, I might lose my family forever. I was scared that if my family abandoned me, I would be rendered an orphan. I was deeply fearful of losing my family's affection.

I did not want to be left alone, separated from them. So I said, 'I did not give you the money for you to keep it for me. I gave it to you because I thought you'd register the house in my name. As if I don't know how to put money away in a bank. Have you decided to will the house to my sister just because I am a pottai with no spouse or children to call my own? The law allows you to settle the house on her, but not on me, on this pottai! How you've managed to cheat me! You don't trust me, not to the extent you do my sister. Haven't I trusted you all this time? I asked you for the house because I felt that my brothers would do their worst, after your time. At least all of them have a family, they have children who would look after them. But I, who do I have apart from you all? So you want me to take the money and be isolated forever from all of you, as if I were an orphan? Amma, akka, what about you? Where is your conscience? Fine! Keep the money. Let it be my gift to my parents. I'll go away and you can all enjoy being together!'

I wept even as I spoke.

My mother and sister entreated my father, 'Why don't you do as he wants? Register the house in his name—surely he is not going to throw us out or destroy the house!' My mother added: 'If we are to settle this on our daughter, it becomes hers, and therefore her in-laws' home. When we die, even our bodies won't find a place here. It's best you register the house in Doraisamy's name. Do it in such a way that till our time comes, we can continue to live here.'

My father agreed. 'All right, but he has to pay for the registration. He can sell or enjoy this property only after our time. That's how it's going to be put down!'

I met the man who prepares the registration deeds and documents. He said that if the property was to be willed to me, then it would cost sixty thousand rupees to register, but if my father were to settle it on me as a gift then it would cost less, around thirty thousand rupees. I discussed this with a couple of lawyers as I wanted to know if there would be problems in the future if the house was to be made over to me as a gift. I was told that a gift settlement was not different from a willed one, but as a precaution I should arrange to receive all bills and receipts, for electricity, telephone etc. in my name. After my parents' death my brothers could very well claim that while my parents had gifted me the house, I had not accepted it and that my father had all along maintained the house. They could then produce bills and receipts in court and snatch the house away from me.

I managed to get the deed written in such a manner that it would not create problems either for my parents or me. In it my father said: 'Since I am growing old and my son, who has since become a woman, needs security and protection, and in the belief that he will continue to look after me and my wife, as he has done so far, I gift this house to him. No one, including my wife, my other heirs and I, henceforth can break this settlement or take a loan against the house so settled.

Doraisamy cannot, by this deed, sell, pledge the house as security against a loan or ask my wife and me to leave the house until the time of our death. After our time, Doraisamy has the right of enjoyment to this property. Until then, my wife and I have usufruct rights to the house, that is, we have the right to live here and use it. Whatever will or document exists with respect to this house stands cancelled from now on. Though Doraisamy is my son, he will sign as "Revathi".'

Thereafter, I made sure that all bills and receipts were issued in the name of Revathi. I had to spend quite a lot of money to get all this done, largely as bribes to government officials. They still took their time and dragged the matter for over three months, despite of my having paid the village officer a hefty bribe to get the patta for the house in my name. That officer got transferred and left without doing a thing! But the man who came in his place issued the patta in my name, without taking a single paisa from me.

My father continued to have complaints. 'Why does this fellow want the bills in his name? Clearly he does not trust me. The electricity bill for his eldest brother's land continues to be issued in my name. He has not asked to change it, but this chap has. He has no faith in me...' I let him be, since he did not seem to know better. In any case, I could not do anything with the house, till my parents were alive. If I were to die before my parents did, God knows who'd inherit the house. My second brother, the one whose wife died leaving behind two girls, had been diagnosed as HIV positive. I thought that I would assign the house to his children in my will. They had all plotted to prevent me from owning property, from letting me be part of the household. But here I was planning to ensure that legally I am able to give the house to my nieces!

I was confident that whatever the law, my love for my family would triumph over its demands. If it seemed that a family member was in crisis, then I suffered too. I wanted the affection of my parents, brothers and sister. I didn't want them to isolate and ostracize me. My parents continued to live in my house—my mother has since passed away, but that's another story.

I spend as much as I can on my second brother's family. I know what it is like, to be afflicted. It's not only that, there are the children—I don't want them to suffer and I want to ensure that their rights are not violated. Though the children have not contracted HIV, this world will look at them with suspicious eyes. If my brother were to die suddenly, the children will become my responsibility. I don't how the children will fare, given their father's condition, and if they were to be raised by a hijra. I therefore pray and hope that my brother lives long.

twenty-five

The Koothandavar temple is in Koovagam in Villupuram district in Tamil Nadu. A festival is held there every year on the day of the full moon in the month of Chitirai (mid-April to mid-May) and thousands of people congregate for the celebrations. Men and hijras—women do not participate in this ritual—make a vow to tie a *thali* to Aravan in the temple. After the temple chariot is drawn through the streets the next day and the ritual sacrifice carried out, they break their bangles and rip off their thalis.

The origins of the festival can be traced to the events of the Mahabharata. To ensure that they win the great war, the

Pandavas have to sacrifice a young man who is perfect in every way. Only three men were considered perfect: Arjuna, Krishna and Aravan, the son of Arjuna and a Naga princess. Since Arjuna and Krishna needed to play their part in the Kurukshetra war, Aravan agrees to be the sacrifice. As his last wish, before he steps on the sacrificial altar, he wants to marry a woman and enjoy, however fleetingly, conjugal bliss. Since no woman would come forward to marry Aravan, Krishna assumes the form of a woman, Mohini, and marries Aravan. After a day of conjugal happiness, Aravan enters the sacrificial space. After he is sacrificed, his wife Mohini (Krishna) laments his death and assumes the garb of a widow.

Hijras from all over start assembling in Koovagam a week before the festival, and take up rooms in the lodges and hotels in and around Villupuram. Some of us from Sangama also attended the festival.

Hijras meeting, exchanging affectionate hugs, wearing new clothes, showing off in public, walking tall—one needs a thousand eyes to take in all these sights. On the day before the thali-tying ritual, a few NGOs had organized beauty contests, singing and dancing contests, and oratorical contests. You could see how people had saved up for the occasion so that they could buy the clothes they wore to take part in these contests. And as the beauty queens came up on stage, their friends, gurus and gurubais would call out in support enthusiastically. Watching them walk and being cheered I realized that the event perhaps bore witness to all that they desired deep inside themselves. Then there were those who had flocked to document all of this—journalists from newspapers and television channels, researchers from foreign countries, and many others. It was quite a sight to see them vying for space, as if they were trying to get a glimpse of famous film stars.

The contest area in Villupuram was overflowing with people. I participated in an oratorical contest and I won a prize for my speech. I started it by reciting a poem I had written:

In the garden of love
was planted the seed of grace.
Watered with goodness
a plant sprouted
a tender, caring flower—a flower
that does not adorn
sacred sites and prayer rooms.

Every year we gather here. We sing, dance and enjoy ourselves. But is this enough? Should we not organize ourselves and insist that the state address our demands? The feelings I have are natural and they should be recognized as such. We want those like us, born as men, but with feminine feelings to have the right to sex-change surgery.

All I ask is that you accept as worthy of respect what you've all along considered unnatural and illegal. If you have an unnaturally long finger, do you therefore cut it off? If there is something wrong with a woman's uterus, you don't hesitate to surgically remove it. If you happen to know that your child to be is a girl, you don't mind destroying the foetus. Thus, each one of your acts falls foul of the law, of nature. But you bring up issues of nature and law only where certain things are concerned.

Listen, I am not diseased. I consider myself a woman. But I possessed the form of a man. I wanted to rid myself of that form and live as a complete woman. How can that be wrong? In some countries, government-run hospitals counsel people like me, put us on a course of hormones, carry out sex reassignment surgery and acknowledge our right to change our sex. Such women go to work, get married, do as other women do.

We want the Indian state to do the same: provide us with counselling, put us on a course of hormones and assist with sex-change surgeries. Since law and society in this country do not acknowledge our right to live as we wish, we are forced to beg, take up sex work, and suffer as a consequence. Today, sex-change operations are carried out in a few private clinics, where surgical procedures are seldom followed, and which do not extend the sort of care we require afterwards. Many of us end up suffering all sorts of infections.

We want to live as women, and if we are granted the facilities that will enable us do so, we'll live as other women do. We were not born to beg or do sex work. Circumstances, faulty laws and social hatred have left us with no course but to beg and do sex work. Our parents begot us like they did other children. We are also human.

On behalf of everyone here, I request the state to grant us ration cards and housing rights, to ensure employment for us and to provide us medical care. That time has long gone, when we lived in fear, in the shadows. That day when our rights will be fulfilled is very near. If we come together and struggle we shall avail of those rights.

A senior police office who appeared on stage afterwards assured us that strict action would be taken against those who referred to us as 'ali' or 'number nine'. He also suggested that since we get married to Aravan, we could perhaps call ourselves aravanis. This label stuck and today in Tamil Nadu all of us hijras are referred to as aravanis.

That evening everyone took buses from Villupuram to Koovagam. My group and I joined the party. Like everyone else, I wore a silk sari, dressing up as a bride would. I bought bangles from the shop outside the temple and things needed for the puja, including the yellow thali, and joined the others in the long queue that waited outside the shrine. After the ritual I felt that I had indeed married Aravan, that I had actually married a man.

We left the crowded temple and stepped out into the night, which proved to be very festive. Aravanis appeared particularly happy. There was a large crowd of outsiders, people who had come to see us, and there was no room to even park bikes and cycles. The harvest had just concluded in the fields adjoining the temple and so we could actually sit there on the grounds. I felt light inside, it was as if my wounds had been healed.

Of those who had tied thalis, several remained in Koovagam village until dawn. Others returned to their lodges in Villupuram. We too returned to our lodge. The next day, early in the morning, Aravan was borne into the village on a chariot. As it started rolling down the street, people threw flowers, vegetables and fruits at it. A group of aravanis lit camphor and took it around the chariot. They then gathered in a circle and did the kummi, praising Aravan through song and dance. Like the previous day, they were in shimmering silk saris, their yellow thalis flashing proudly. As soon as the chariot reached the sacrificial pit, the aravanis started plucking out the flowers that adorned their hair. They threw them away, rubbed off the pottu on the forehead, and keening loudly, gathered at the spot where they would eventually tear the thali away from the neck. I too went along with them.

I felt tears gathering when I heard the keening. They cried just as a woman who had lost her husband would. The priests of Aravan were gathered at the spot where the thalis were to be removed. They broke the bangles that the aravanis wore on their wrists and tore off their thalis and threw them up on the branches of a nearby tree. Some aravanis brought their two wrists together and broke their bangles themselves. All the aravanis then took a ritual bath. After that, they discarded their silk saris and wore white saris, and once more sang and danced. Then they all began to melt away, with sorrow in their hearts, to their various towns and villages.

I, too, wore a white sari, and returned to the lodge. I learnt that usually aravanis remain in white for three days, after which they feed at least ten poor people, partake of that food themselves and only then change into a coloured sari. That evening I went to a nearby Mariamman temple, accepted the holy kumkum and changed into a coloured sari. Then we caught the bus to Bangalore.

twenty-six

One tends to get involved with the people one works with, especially in a place like Sangama, where people are deeply committed to what they do and spend long hours working. I had grown particularly devoted to a person who was one of the most active members of Sangama. He too had a good opinion of me. We had travelled to many places and even stayed together. During a trip to Mysore, I ended up sharing a room with him. That night, we went out for drinks and dinner and returned to our room. Unexpectedly, I found myself in an intimate situation with my roommate.

I felt uneasy about what had happened. He was a senior staff member, a person I respected and treated with deference. What would the other staff members say, should they come to know of it? Yet, I was loath to forget that night I had spent with him. Until then I had not known what it was to be intimate. That night I discovered how every nerve in the body is sexually charged. I thought of him as a devotee would think of a god. My memories of us together combined with my regard for him resulted in my falling in love with him. It was as if I had no choice in the matter.

How could I declare my love to a senior colleague, my superior? It was like a lame man trying to reach for a honeycomb. I wanted to surrender myself to him. His devotion to work, the concern he exhibited towards society at large, the persistence he displayed in whatever he did, the fact that he did not consider himself superior and others inferior, and the way in which he understood me—everything he did filled me with fervent longing. Unable to express my love to him, I went about like a mad person, till the day when I finally went up to him and asked if I could speak to him alone.

'What about?'

'About myself…'

'We can talk right here, in the office.'

'No, let's go out and talk.'

'All right, we'll go to a restaurant after work.'

At the restaurant, we ordered food and sat facing each other. I did not know how to begin or what to say.

'Revathi, you said you wanted to say something. What is it?'

I could not bring myself to say that I loved him. Gathering all the courage I was capable of, I said hesitantly, 'I cannot forget what happened between us. After that night I am afraid to stand in front of you, to talk to you. Even now I find it hard to say what I want to say.'

'Whatever it is, please tell me. I too wanted to speak to you, but there was so much work to be taken care of that I did not seek you out.'

'I love you with all my heart.'

'I don't like the word "love". I desire you very much. I like you very much. The intimacy we shared, we both assented to it. That was a natural thing. You needn't be confused about it, or be afraid of what happened.'

'I keep thinking of you, I find it hard to sleep. I feel haunted... I have become a mad woman. I want to be able to talk to you, be with you, even if it's only for a short while.'

'Why don't you then? You can visit me at my house whenever you want. I'll come to you when you want me to.'

'The place I live in, the house-owner has made it clear that I cannot to receive men. Unless I tell him about us, you cannot visit me in my house. Also, my place is close to the hamam where my guru and gurubais live. If my house-owner knows about you, sooner or later my guru and gurubais will come to know. If you are to visit me at home, I would prefer to tell everyone about us.'

'No problem. Please tell whoever you wish to tell. You may also tell your colleagues. Make sure that you don't get into trouble, though.'

He added, 'I used to be close to another person in our staff. But I am not any more. Please don't ask me who it was.'

I was confused and wondered who it was. I was also a little afraid.

'You say you are not in that relationship any more. Were there problems between you?'

At this, he held my hand tight and his eyes filled with tears. I assumed that the other person had not understood his feelings and, therefore, he could not continue with the relationship. I decided that I must do all that I could for him and give him all my love.

WHEN I INFORMED my house-owner, he said,'I don't mind him visiting you. But you must keep silent about this to my wife and children and everyone else in the neighbourhood. All they need to know is that a colleague from work is visiting you.'

And so he began to visit me, whenever he had time. He took me to the cinema on some days. I was not sure what he thought of our relationship, I mean what he really thought of it deep inside his heart. I was sure of myself. I was in love with him, I was happy, I imagined myself leading a life with him. I thought of him as the man I was married to.

I made my feelings known, on the phone and when we met. If I messaged him 'I love you', he would return the sentiment. If he had to travel on work, I would call him. If he was busy he would not be able to talk to me. He would then message me 'I miss you'. I assumed he was in love with me.

One day, I told one of my friends in the office, someone who was close to me, about our relationship. I showed her the message he had sent me and asked her to read it out to me. That woman, who had been my close friend, stopped talking to me afterwards. And worse, she became sullen if I was in her presence. If I touched her hair to say how nice it was, she would slap my hand away.

Whenever I asked her 'Why are you behaving like this?

Have I done anything wrong?' she said she wanted to be left alone.

During staff meetings, my friend would get into fights with the man I loved. This caused a great deal of confusion among the rest of the staff members. If he supported me on any account, some of the staff members were not too happy. I figured that all this had nothing to do with office work, but could be traced to personal tensions. Finally, another senior staff member called me aside and told me that my woman friend and the man I loved had been in a relationship earlier. I was deeply disturbed and I felt that I had unwittingly betrayed someone.

I sought out my friend and tried to speak to her. But she did not respond. I persisted. 'When I told you about my love, I did not know that you two had been in a relationship. I realize now how difficult it must have been for you when I asked you to read out the message he sent me. Please, you must forgive me, I know I have betrayed your trust.'

'Please don't speak to me about him. I don't like him at all. I have no interest in him. In fact, I hate the man. But you don't have to give him up on my account. It is your business, whether you love him or leave him.'

Some other staff members came to know about us three—me, my friend and him. They could not speak of it openly, but discussed the matter amongst themselves. This created further discomfort.

I could not forget him, at the same time I was beset with guilt that I had wronged my friend. My chela, Famila, consoled me and even counselled me. She helped reinstate the relationship I had with my friend. Soon my friend began to speak to me as before, with affection. I thought then that I should move away from him, and perhaps resign my job. But my friend reiterated that I need not break up with him because of her.

He did not move away from me. But he did not bring up the problem that had cropped up between me and my friend. He was hurt and perhaps upset by all that was happening. I did not know then why he and my friend had parted, or what had transpired between them. I only knew that their relationship had ended. Who knows who was in the wrong?

I was confused, but he was kind and there for me during this time. Once when he came to stay with me, he suggested, 'Perhaps one of us should give up working in Sangama. Our relationship is creating problems in the office. I'll be accused of supporting you because we're in a relationship. And I think I should resign because you won't find it easy to get a job. I am educated, and wherever I go I'll find a job.'

'You are very important to Sangama. I don't want you to give up your job. I will resign,' I said.

'Maybe you should. Whatever I earn should do for both of us.'

'Should I resign right away?'

'Wait a while. The Sangama board wants to discuss this matter.'

HOWEVER, I FELT that if I were to leave Sangama and had to depend on his salary, it might be a problem for him. I began to think about ways to ease my financial burdens. I got a small amount from the money I'd put away under fixed deposits and thought I could use that to lease a house. That way I wouldn't have to pay rent every month. So I found a place on the third floor of an independent house in Shivaji Nagar. I used my deposits, along with the interest, which amounted a lakh and a half rupees, to lease this house. I thought I would not be leased a house if I came out as an aravani, so I requested my sister's mother-in-law to come from the village and pass off as my own mother-in-law, and likewise presented the man I loved as my husband, with his permission. I signed a lease for two years.

My sister's mother-in-law helped me move to the new house. I had warned her not to tell people that I was an aravani. One evening, after I got back from work, she reported a conversation she had with the woman on the second floor. 'She wanted to know how long you've been married to my son. When I said, "Two years," she had a question, "No children yet?" To my reply "God's grace hasn't yet come her way," she had another question! "Taken her to a doctor?" When I nodded in assent, she commented, "It'll happen when it has to."'

I was glad of the support from my sister's mother-in-law. She told me then, 'Oh, the things the world thinks if a woman is alone! People look askance at you. See how a woman has respect only if she has the protection of a man.' Soon she went back home, agreeing to my request to not mention my relationship to my parents or my sister. A few days after she left, he gave up his house and moved in with me. I was very happy that he would be with me all the time.

In the meanwhile the board met and decided that if staff members had relationships with each other, that was their business and it was for them to make sure that the relationship did not get in the way of work. They did not think I needed to give up my job. However, I thought I should. He did not agree though, as he felt that I must continue to work for my community.

'I could do so voluntarily. I'll continue to support Sangama's work.'

'It's best if neither you nor I end up being dependent on the other. Please continue to come to work.'

WE WOULD LEAVE for work together, and it was as if I was leading a normal family life, much like other women. He often worked late and returned home only at night. I'd get dinner ready and wait for him. Even if I was hungry I'd wait and eat with him. He'd tell me not to wait for him and eat if I was hungry. I'd protest, 'But I like eating with you.'

If it got very late and he was still at work, I'd phone him. He'd assure me that he'd come in half an hour's time, and when he did not, I'd call again. He'd say, 'Sorry, ma, I am starting now.'

Sometimes he chided me, 'Am I a child that I can't come home safely? Why call so often?'

'But you said you'd be home in half an hour. I was worried…'

'Idiot,' he would say fondly, running his fingers gently over my head.

On holidays, he would come into the kitchen and kiss me on my back. When we lay down together, he'd make a pillow of his arm and if, thinking that it might hurt him, I tried to take his hand off, he'd ask, 'Don't you like it?' I'd go to sleep with his arm cradling my head.

Often at night he would tell me ghost stories and horror

stories. The nights he was not there, I'd recall his stories and grow afraid. When he told me these stories, I would feign anger and turn away from him. 'Come, come, I'll stop,' he would say and make me go back to him, whereupon he would hug me.

Watching television, cooking, the times I spent with him, the life we led, all of it filled me with great happiness. I felt my heart melt at all that I experienced, all that I had not known until then.

Since he did not want to be dependent on me, he would insist that I don't wash his clothes. Whenever I had the time, I would gather all his clothes and take the lot to the laundry. I would have liked to wash them for him, but since he did not like me doing so, I ended up taking my clothes to the laundry as well!

He liked my cooking. He liked the way I cared for him. And I liked the way he was. I often wondered why I should not marry him. Sometimes I asked him this question. But he did not like the idea. He thought marriage was a prison. 'I consider you my partner,' he'd say. Eventually I stopped bringing up the subject.

However, I felt that we would be happier if we got married. I heard him say in many places that if he did get married, he would only marry someone who is a sexual minority. I asked myself why I could not be that person. For me, marriage would confirm that I was living a womanly life, and I also believed that it would free my life of fear. Since we lived as man and wife in that house, people in the building would stare intently at my neck, to see if I was wearing a thali.

Of course, a thali is something that we have adopted as a

symbol of marriage, but it is nevertheless something that validates a relationship in the eyes of society. If you are born a woman it is believed that is how one ought to live. Some NGOs have tried to work against these beliefs, and I too have thought of such symbols critically. But in the course of everyday life, the thali can become a source of small yet persistent difficulties. I therefore decided that I would wear a thali. I made one and asked him to tie it around my neck, but he refused. So I tied it around my neck, in front of him.

Since he held an important post in Sangama, he had a lot to do, indeed more than anyone else. In the life that I led with him, our everyday life, he did not always seem to be present. So I had to take care of him. I did all that a woman normally does for her husband. I cooked our meals and made sure he ate on time. I cleaned the house, took care of the clothes, and all other chores. If he had to go away to Mumbai or Delhi for work, and decided to leave from the office, he would phone me and ask me to bring his clothes. I did not think I was serving him, I thought that I was serving Sangama since he was an important part of the organization, and therefore could not attend to his personal work. I was there for him while he worked to improve Sangama, to create the facilities that would bring about the realization of the rights for sexual minorities. I wanted to assist him in all that he did, stand by him, lend my shoulders to his effort, just as I supported him in his personal life.

In his heart of hearts he liked what I did for him. I was his mother, companion, office assistant, lover and good wife.

twenty-seven

We had been living together for three months when he suddenly brought up the issue of marriage. One night, around ten o'clock, as we were getting ready for bed, he turned to me and said, 'I'll marry you.'

I could not believe my ears. 'Really, you really mean it?'

'I do.'

I pinched myself just to make sure that I was not dreaming. I was incredibly happy! Hugging him, I asked when, where and how we would get married.

'We could get married tomorrow.'

'Tomorrow?' I was taken aback.

'But we must talk before that.'

'Let's talk,' I said.

'You know I am a bisexual. Won't this upset you or your aravani community?'

'I don't see why anyone should feel upset. So what if you're a bisexual? Haven't I learnt from Sangama that two people who love each other have the right to be together?'

'Will you treat me in the future as you treat me now?'

'There's no need for you to doubt that. You know that you're my very life.'

'Well, tomorrow I may lose interest in having a conjugal relationship with you. Will that cause you much sadness?'

'Is it possible to dislike a person you love, whatever that person's frame of mind? As far as we are concerned, a marriage bond is not only about conjugality. It also means understanding each other and caring for each other. It means love and so many other things. So that'll do for me,' I assured him.

'What if we fight? Will we fight, do you think?'

'There are bound to be fights and disagreements. These things happen in a relationship, in a family. We should sit down and talk, agree to give up certain things for each other, and work at resolving our disagreements. There's no way around any of that.'

'I believe that it is a person's right to do or not do sex work. Supposing you quit Sangama, you might want to take up sex work for a living. But I don't want my partner to engage in sex work.'

'I am not interested in taking up sex work. I don't want to, in fact. When we get to a stage where it seems there's no way out, we'll deal with it then.'

'After you marry me, you must not turn your back on your aravani community.'

'As if I will or I can. I am what I am because they showed me the way.'

'There ought to be no hierarchy between us, as man and wife.'

'Certainly not.'

'I won't be able to spend too much time on housework.'

'So what? You're educated, and you've got to do Sangama work. If you're going to be doing that, I have no problems taking on housework for your sake, for our sake.'

'You musn't consider me your husband, you must refer to me as your partner.'

'I know this English word only in the context of business relationships. We love each other and want to live together, so I don't want to call you my partner. If you want, I'll refer to you as my partner in the presence of your educated friends from NGOs. To aravanis I'll introduce you as my husband.'

He agreed to that and tapping me lightly on the head, he said, 'You're mad.' He added, 'Well then, everything's okay, but mind you, I won't tie a thali. Or if you want me to, we'll need two thalis. I tie one around your neck and you do the same for me.'

'A wedding without a thali? Nobody will accept that,' I argued.

'You garland me, I'll garland you. That should do.'

I gave in and he said, 'So that's settled. But how are we going to get married?'

'Both of us are Hindus. Let's go to a temple and exchange garlands.'

'So tomorrow is our wedding. We'll invite four people on your side, and four on my mine. I'm going to phone my friends.'

'It's eleven now, let's go to sleep. We'll get up early in the morning and call people.'

We decided that our wedding would take place in the presence of my guru and gurubais at the Ellamman temple next to the hamam.

I WAS IN A state of pleasant shock. My life's dream was about to be fulfilled. The person who understood me was going to be my companion for life. I felt that I was indeed blessed.

Setting the alarm for five o'clock the next morning, I held him in my embrace and tried to get some sleep. But I could not—tears kept pouring down my cheeks.

'Why're you crying, amma?' He wiped my tears, and with a smile, ran his fingers through my hair, saying, 'Mad woman!' After some time I heard him snore. He had gone off to sleep. I was wide awake, my thoughts focused on my impending marriage. I tossed and turned, wondering what my guru would say when I landed up at her doorstep. I was not sure what her reaction would be. I also wondered if the marriage would cause problems at work, especially for him. I thought of the sari I would wear tomorrow, of how I would adorn myself. My aravani family, his friends and our office staff—only these people would know of our marriage and so there should be no trouble, I reasoned.

I passed the night waiting for the alarm to go off. As soon as it did, I got up as though I'd been sleeping through the night. I went and looked at the images of gods and then tore away the previous day's date from the daily-sheet calendar. This day is an important day for me, I told myself. A dream that I had nurtured since I was sixteen-years-old was to be fulfilled now in my thirty-third year. Aglow with happiness, and feeling shy like a sixteen-year-old, I tried to wake him up. He asked me to get ready and went back to sleep. I bathed and then he got up and started calling his friends, his colleagues actually, and asked them to assemble at my guru's house. He asked me to call my friends as well. I said that they would all be at the hamam with my guru.

When I asked him about the sari I should wear, he said, 'Don't deck up like a bride, dress as you would when you go to work.'

We had to be in the hamam at nine o'clock, so I pushed him to bathe and got dressed. Then I lit lamps for the images of gods that I had at home.

WHEN WE REACHED the hamam, my guru greeted the man I loved and asked the aravanis there to buy tea and coffee and so on.

'What's up that you've come here early in the morning?'

He looked at me enquiringly as if to ask, 'Haven't you told her yet?' I felt rather shy, having to tell my guru that I was shortly going to get married to this man. I called her out, and rather fearfully told her that I was going to get married to him and that she must be the one to marry us.

My guru was taken aback. 'What are you saying?' she exclaimed. 'What sort of a sudden decision is this?'

'Amma, we thought about this long and hard and only then did we make this decision. It is not as if he'll tie a thali while the entire town comes to watch and participate in the marriage. We're going to exchange garlands and announce that we're married. He's called a few people on his side and they should soon be here. As for me, it is you who understands me. Not my parents or anyone else in this world. Please come with us to the temple and get us married.'

'That's all fine. But we need a Brahmin, a thali, an altar for the holy fire… where can I find these things at such short notice? Without them how does one perform a marriage?'

'He doesn't believe in circling the fire or tying a thali. Offer a simple worship at the temple with flowers and a coconut, and give us the garlands. We'll exchange those and be married.'

'What is this marriage without a thali?' my guru asked.

'If you insist on a thali, he says there must be two. He'll tie one around my neck and I have to do the same for him. So let's not have any thalis. All I want you to do is be my guru and conduct this wedding.'

My guru agreed. When my gurubais heard the news they looked at us in astonishment. 'Lucky Revathi,' I heard them say, 'first she got a job in an office, and now she's got herself a nice husband.'

My guru bought the things needed for the worship, and I bought the garlands. He and his friends went and got some sweets, and brought along a camera as well. Then we all went to the temple, and the exchange of garlands took place. By then, everyone in the neighbourhood had arrived at the temple to witness our marriage. An aravani getting married? They were stupefied.

After he had garlanded me inside the temple he held my hand tight and we walked out hand in hand. I felt teary-eyed with happiness when he did that. I was convinced that a man who held me thus would never abandon me.

We stood outside the temple and took photographs and distributed sweets. Though we had not got married in full view of the world, so to speak, we were happy to see those who had come even without being invited. Some aravanis and some women who stood watching asked us if we were going to stop with sweets, or if there would be a party. We promised them that we'd have a party and invite them.

Hand in hand, we approached the hamam. My gurubai was waiting with a plate of auspicious coloured water to do the aarthi. She did the aarthi and then asked us to drop some money into the aarthi plate. He looked at me with a smile and asked, 'So how much should I give?'

'Fifty or hundred,' I muttered.

He took a hundred rupee note and dropped it into the plate. We were then invited inside. Those who had come for the wedding greeted us and left. We too returned home.

We took off our garlands and after giving the film roll for developing, we went straight to the office. From there he called his many friends and told them that he had married Revathi. He handed me the phone and asked me to speak to his friends. They all spoke in English. I understood they were greeting us and thanked them. He had called his friends all over the country and he asked me to inform my friends and companions.

My gurubais were my friends and they were there at the hamam. Besides them I didn't know very many people, except my colleagues. My parents would not understand and if I were to tell my brothers, they'd say, 'What's this, two men getting married?' So I didn't want to tell any of them. Yet I wanted someone in my family to know, and so I called my sister and told her that I'd got married. She was happy on my account and wished me well. I requested her to keep it a secret.

I called some of the women I knew in the women's groups in Bangalore. I told them I had married the man I loved. Some refused to believe it. I handed the phone to him and only then did they accept what I'd told them. Many, in fact, did not believe that he had married me. Only after they came to the office and met us did they accept that we were married.

The office staff, the various sexual minorities who come to the office, people working in different NGOs, men and women, came to the office with flowers and greeted us. He gave them sweets and they, too, asked if this was going to be all or there'd be a party.

I must say I too was shocked when he called his friends and informed them about our marriage. I thought that only the aravanis of my house would know of the wedding. I was moved by what he did, and very happy.

That night, when we were alone, he said that he too was happy. He added that we ought to register our marriage and then apply for a ration card and so on. 'We must give a party to our friends and others like us. I am afraid that I cannot tell my parents about us. They won't accept it in any case. After they understand what's happening, we'll tell them.'

This made me happier, if that's possible. I was indeed lucky—no one else could possibly have a husband like mine.

Our life began.

twenty-eight

On one of my visits to my village, I took our wedding photo to show my sister. My mother later had spotted it while rummaging through my bag, but did not ask me about it. A few days after I reached Bangalore, she called me. Weeping on the phone, she said she was afraid that my husband would cheat me and lay claims to my property.

I was very upset by her words. 'You're only worried about the property, right? I'll come home tomorrow and write a document bequeathing it to you.'

Somehow that comforted her. Firmly I told her, 'I know how to run my life. I know very well what sort of a man I've married, and how much he respects and loves me. He's certainly not married me for my property. I'm ready to give up my property, but I can't live without him.'

My family members didn't dare say anything after my conversation with my mother. In fact, they invited us both home for festivals many times. But we never did go to my village. Poor man, he had no time to make personal trips.

I WAS HAPPY that my family and society at large had accepted our marriage. However, that happiness did not last long. He never got around to informing his parents about our marriage. As far as they were concerned, we were co-workers and roommates. He had dared take on the world for the cause of sexual minorities, but was unable to tell his own parents about us. Though he did think we needed a bigger house in case his parents came to stay with us and wanted to move out of the house I had leased.

'Why? This is not a bad house, and it's not far from our place of work. It's also somewhat close to where my guru and gurubais are. The rent is not much, and it's going to be hard to find another house like this. Why can't we continue to stay here?' I asked.

All he had to say was, 'My parents have consented to stay with me. We need a bigger place.'

Happy that I would be living with my parents-in-law I agreed and informed our house-owner. We found a larger place outside the city and both of us chipped in to pay the advance and the rent. While we were getting the new house ready, his parents came to Bangalore on a visit. When we went to see it with his parents, his mother wondered, 'Why do you two need such a big house? Won't the old one do? Also, why live in a house so far from the city?'

'Amma,' I replied, 'he said that you'd come and live with him. That's why we decided to take a larger house.'

'Us coming and staying in this house? Why would we? We have a house in the village—we don't want to leave that and come here. If my son gets married, then we might come and stay with him. But even then we won't stay with him permanently.'

His parents stayed with us for a while and during that period we slept separately. His mother was glad he had a companion at home, but kept entreating him to get married. She sometimes asked me to advise him to get married. I suffered, having to hear this, and not being able to tell her that I was married to him.

After his parents had left, I asked him, 'Your mother says that she wouldn't want to stay here. Do we really need such a large house?'

He did not answer my question and managed to get past the topic somehow. What was I to do? I decided that my place was with my husband and so put up with the shift. The rent for the house was four thousand rupees. I put in one thousand five hundred rupees and he wrote a cheque each month for the rest. To share other household expenses, each of us would put a thousand rupees into a box. We used that money to buy things for the house, pay the electricity bill, cable television charges, water bill and so on.

The new house was part of a layout that comprised individual houses. So people did not really speak with each other, let alone visit each other. The house was large and comfortable, but I felt exceedingly lonely there. On most days, he would return home only around midnight. Since the house was far away from the city I could not visit my guru and gurubais. I also could not meet Famila that often, for she had quit her job.

The office opened at half-past nine in the morning and since I was the office assistant, I had to open it. Some days I went with him on his bike, but most of the time I had to take the bus. In the mornings, he would most often work from home on the computer. But I could not afford to be late and so I would leave at half-past eight in the morning. In the evenings it was almost seven when I came home, usually by bus. After that I would cook, finish whatever housework there was to be done and by then it would be nine. Since there was no time for anything, we never went any place else, neither to the cinema nor other fun places. We did not have any time to talk about what we felt.

Even if he came home early some days, he spent time on the computer, writing and sometimes playing games. I had to do all the chores and make sure the bills were paid, that the household help was paid, etc. He did not have any time to do things around the house. Even if I were to accept all that work as my responsibility, there was his behaviour at night. He was less romantic and he did not speak as affectionately as before. I expected what all women expected from their husbands, but suffered because I could not bring myself to ask for it. I gave him all my love, and expected him to reciprocate at least to an extent. But once he sat at the computer, he tended to forget the whole world. I would let him be, excusing him because he dealt with so much tension in the office. I kept my desires locked inside myself, while I hurt all the while.

But how long could one live like this? Alone, on boiled

rice and within four walls, as they say. I decided that I must speak my mind to him. I explained my situation to him. It was as if I had to extract love and romance from my husband. But the thing is, he got angry when I asked to be loved.

'I can be romantic only when I feel like it. If you ask me to feel romantic, it as if I have no freedom of choice here.'

I felt confused by his response. Soon I began to get depressed. He advised me to see a counsellor, or speak to his friend. I spoke to this friend, and he suggested that we both see a counsellor. When we were with the friend, he agreed to make an effort, but as soon as we came home, he said, 'I am all right. It's you who has a problem. You go see a counsellor.' Since he was an educated man, he could say what he wanted, and he had this knack of countering everything I said, word for word. Often he made it impossible for me to speak. I would remain silent, like an uneducated village girl.

He stopped relating to me sexually. Gradually and slowly, he stopped making love to me. He even gave up hugging me as we slept. Sometimes, when I begged him to hug me, he would get angry, throw a sheet over my face and then hug me. I felt great anger and shock when he did this. I don't know what went on in my husband's heart, but he seemed to have lost all desire for me.

Is it wrong to ask one's husband to be affectionate? To tell him about my small desires? He thought it was wrong. He once accused me of loving only his body and not him. When he said this, I almost died. He accused me of trying to sexually assault him, and that broke my heart. His words made me feel it was better to be dead than lead the life I did.

Things reached such a pass that I could not bring myself

to speak with people at work or anywhere else. I hated everything. But he seemed unaffected and went about his work. We shared the rent, food, bought things for the house together, but he failed to share his love with me. He did not like it when his friends advised him. He claimed that he was greatly fond of Revathi and argued that it does not mean, therefore, that he should hug Revathi or be romantic to express his love. Whenever he argued so, quoting one example after another, it seemed as if he was right, but it caused me a great deal of anguish.

I did not understand what was going on. Nor did I know what to do. I sometimes thought that perhaps I was rooming with him, as a fellow staffer. I even wondered what sort of a relationship I had with him. He knew of my expectations, but did not want to acknowledge them. I asked myself if it was wrong of me to state what I wanted, openly and without any pretence. I loved him, was fond of him, and desired him beyond measure. I felt hurt that he seemed oblivious to the problems between us.

Whenever he felt desire, he would be romantic. If he felt like it, he would hug me. It might be that he wanted to eat out and so he would suggest we go out to a restaurant. Likewise, if he wished to see a movie, we would go to the cinema. Living by his whims and desires, I felt my own retreat till there was nothing left. If I asked for anything, he was quick to fend me off by saying he was not interested or had no time. In despair I would ask, 'When will you feel desire? When will the time come?' and then he would say all those things that hurt. He knew what my weakness was and used that as a reason to move away from me. If I were to say, 'Don't I go to the cinema when you want me to? Don't I put aside time for you when you ask for it? Why don't you do the same when I ask you to do something?' He was quick to retort, 'You could have said, "I won't go" when I asked you to go out.'

'What are you saying? We live in the same house, we share food and bed. We live as man and wife, we are good friends, and we work together. Should we not put time aside for each other, be willing to give up things for each other?'

'I've lost my freedom because of you. Because of you I've lost my peace of mind.' He said this often. Or, 'I made a mistake by marrying you. In fact, it is one of the biggest mistakes of my life…'

Though we both lived in that house, I was not sure when he'd leave me and go away. He only had to say that he was going out on work and I felt as if lightning had struck me. I had waited for days, months, hoping he would take me places, talk to me affectionately, but all I earned in return was a broken heart. On office trips, I would yearn to sit next to him on the bus, but he made sure that even such a paltry wish was not fulfilled.

IT WAS THE year the World Social Forum convened in Mumbai, and I was called to present my testimony. Around three thousand people were present in the special seminar hall set aside for this purpose and they all heard me speak. I spoke of what I endured in my parents' home, at the hands of the police and rowdies, about how the law was not in our favour, and about the pain that I was currently experiencing in my marriage.

The next morning he said to me, 'You've killed me by talking the way you did. Why did you speak like that?'

'I spoke of how the world treated me. You constantly encourage people to speak of what they've gone through. But when it comes to speaking about you, you claim that I've killed you. Do you realize that you've murdered me, not once, but several times? I have spoken to the papers, on television, in public forums, about my problems, my family, the police, about the abuse my community routinely encounters. Does that mean that I have no love for my parents, or that I don't respect the police? This is my testimony, that's all.'

'From now we have nothing to do with each other.' Saying this, he got up.

'Well, you wanted to talk. Why go away like this?' I gripped his hand and tried to stop him from leaving. He threw the bag he had in his hand at me furiously and went out. The way he hit me with the bag, the manner in which he left and the fury I witnessed in his eyes upset me. I screamed and wept, afraid that he would leave me, hate me and not have anything to do with me. Two of my colleagues stayed with me till we reached Bangalore. They never let me be alone as they were scared I would harm myself.

God knows who said what, or who cast the evil eye on us, a year after we got married, our relationship ended.

FRIENDS WHO SAW me suffer, tried to console me by saying they could arrange for me to get a monthly maintenance from him. All I could say to their offer was, 'I loved him. I wanted to live with him, not with his money. I don't need his money. Some day he'll understand and come back to me. I'll live in that hope. Let him do what he wants. But I want to make one thing clear. He married me, but failed to fulfill his duties.

How is he different from the average man? I wouldn't have been so sad if that sort of a man had cheated me and abandoned me.

'He decided to leave me, but is it right that he just walks away? You know how difficult it is for someone like me to find a house? I lived in that house for three months, all by myself. He did not even stay for the time it took me to get the advance back from the house-owner and find another house. This is the man who would say, in fact he would say this all the time, that women suffer a lot, husbands do not do housework, do not take responsibility, do not grant equal rights to women. He has said all this in public meetings, and now he irresponsibly leaves a woman. Let's not forget that he lent his voice to our claim that aravanis ought to be respected as women. This is what makes me heavy-hearted. Really, what's the difference between him and the man on the street? I don't think I can work with him in the office anymore.'

By this time, I had found rooms for myself in the same area. I said to the house-owner that my husband was going abroad on work and that we had decided to send our things back to the village. My guru and gurubais came to know of my plight and felt saddened. Some of them said that perhaps I was in the wrong. My guru would have none of it. She said that if he had been a real man, she wouldn't have minded falling at his feet to get him back together with me. But since he had left me, there was nothing to be done. 'Let him go. You'll be happier now that you're separated from him.'

But I could not bear to be parted from him. I did not find it easy to talk to anyone. I tried to get used to being alone. But I raved and ranted to myself inside that room. I cried out aloud. I did not sleep or eat properly. I was assailed by memories of him. My health began to steadily deteriorate. I began to drink a lot. Seeing my state, some of Sangama's board members called me and said that I need not give up my job. They suggested that I need not come to the office, but could go and meet my people, interview them and write a book. They assigned a year's project to me.

I, too, thought that if I were to stay on in Bangalore, thoughts of him would literally kill me. People would then say that I died for his sake. I felt I needed to live again, and experience a change of heart. So I agreed to work on the project, hoping it would help me forget and heal the wounds in my heart. I chose Tamil Nadu as the site for my project. I got money for Sangama for my travel, accommodation, to buy a tape recorder and so on. I also learnt from my friends how to conduct an interview and how narrate it on paper.

AS I WAS preparing to leave, something devastating happened. I felt like I had been struck by a thunderbolt from the sky. My chela, Famila, had killed herself. When I heard the news I did not believe it. Whenever I entertained thoughts of suicide, it was Famila who dissuaded me and advised me against it. I could not bear it that she who did this for me had killed herself. Her death affected me deeply. I ended doing for her what she as a chela should have done for me, her guru, after my time—I had to do her final rites.

Aravanis who had come for the funeral cried their hearts out, beat their breasts and keened loudly, saying, 'Revathi, it was wrong of you to leave your chela alone. Could you not have told her to live with us, her community? If she had lived as other chelas do, with restraint and discipline, this would have never happened!'

Famila. Our biggest struggle had been to bring about change in the lives of aravanis, sexual minorities. Unlike some gurus and chelas, we did not want our relationship to be one of bonded slavery. Though we did not meet often, Famila and I spoke on the phone quite frequently. Just a few days before her death, she had called me to ask for the recipe for radish chutney. I think that was the last time we spoke. Her last request continues to ring in my ears, 'Amma, how do you make radish chutney?'

That she died before I could know what was in her heart made me blame myself for her death. She considered me her mother, and would often say that she had earned good karma to have a guru like me. I considered it my good luck that she was my chela. I loved her as my daughter. She was educated, but she would say that she only knew a handful of things. As I've always said, I learnt a great deal from her.

I wished I could tell her, 'Daughter, I had hoped that you would be the one to throw a handful of mud over my grave, instead God has inverted the order of what should be. Is he especially angry with me that he has made my sorrow endless?'

I felt a huge sense of loss and I wondered if I should continue to live. It was my guru and gurubais who offered me consolation. Convinced that I ought to go away, and not be alone, I left for Tamil Nadu to carry out the research on aravanis for my book. I was not sure though how I was going to meet with other aravanis and interview them, considering how restless, sad, confused, pained and exhausted I felt. But my work turned out to be the healing balm that I needed.

twenty-nine

I met aravanis in Namakkal, Theni, Vellore, Chennai and Erode. My accounts turned out to be more than a record of interview sessions—they expanded to include my experience of living with the aravanis, eating with them, sharing their troubles, listening to them, and heeding their feelings and thoughts. A few of them wondered what use a book of this kind would be. Some asked me who had paid me to do this work, and if they would get some money. Once they understood my intent, they agreed to be interviewed. I met thirty people over a period of six months. They shared with me their life experiences and their sorrows and joys.

I still shudder, recalling the way the aravanis I spoke to sobbed and screamed when they recounted stories of their mothers, lovers, husbands… I who had asked if I had been singled out for sorrow found out through these interviews that many others were subject to enormous pain despite which they presented a smiling face to the world. My difficulties were nothing compared to some of the things I heard.

I WAS IN Theni district interviewing some aravanis and spent the night at the office of an NGO called Arogya Agam. At night, around half-past eleven, I received a phone call from Bangalore. The news that I heard from the other end filled me with dread and disbelief—some rowdies had stabbed and killed my guru and her body was in the hospital. I was thoroughly shaken. God, I screamed, what fresh horror is this? Who would want to murder my guru and why? I left that very night for Madurai and from there took a bus to Salem. From Salem I boarded a bus to Bangalore. Throughout the journey back to Bangalore, I was on the phone. People kept calling me, and I kept trying to get in touch with people. I could hear over the phone the wailing and keening of the aravanis gathered at the hospital.

The post mortem had been carried out and my guru's body was on the way to the hamam by the time I got off at Bangalore. As soon as they saw me, the aravanis who were there rushed to hug me and cry. I heard from them what had happened. That night there had been only three people at the hamam. One of them had been working inside the hamam and another was out to fetch water from the tap close to the hamam, while the third had gone to a phone booth to make a call. A gang of five had come to demand money from my guru and she had refused to yield. When they persisted, brandishing a knife at her, she had picked up a stick and yelled at them to get lost. The gang took to their heels, and my guru had thrown her stick at them and then followed them. Meanwhile, one of them had whipped his knife out at my gurubai, who was near the tap, and she took to her heels. The gang ran with my guru in pursuit and stopped when they were in a dark alley. There, the cowards that they were, they stabbed her repeatedly.

When I heard that they had stabbed her in her stomach six times, I beat my breast and started crying. I hit my head several times and continued to weep, 'Didn't the police get those chandalas? Did not anyone try to intervene when they chased her and cut her up? Were you all standing by and watching?'

The stabbing had occurred at 10 o'clock on the night of 26 December 2004 when a disaster of catastrophic proportions had swept the coasts of India earlier that day. Thousands had died in the tsunami and people had been tuned into the news on television. So they did not hear my guru's pleas for help, nor could they identify the killers.

The murder happened at a spot that was less than half a kilometre from the hamam, at the entrance to the Amman temple. My guru had fallen forward and literally bled to death. They found her in a pool of her own blood. I ran to the temple and went down on my knees at the spot where her blood had congealed on the ground and wept, cursing the temple deity for accepting my guru's offerings and bestowing nothing in return but cruel indifference.

At the hamam, I wept again, looking at my guru's scratched up face. 'Aiyo! Amma! You've left us! Who'll stand by us now?' It was my guru who had taken care of us all this while.

Whenever a rowdy or a policeman came to the hamam, it was she who would speak to them. At that time, we could live in that neighbourhood only if we paid off the rowdies. But that day, neither the police nor those rowdies could protect her. Those who murdered my guru were probably from another neighbourhood.

My guru's gurubai, that is, my kaalaguru, had not been well and was in the village during the murder. She too finally arrived. She looked dead, my kaalaguru. My guru had helped her out in many ways, stood by her and done her good on many occasions. My kaalaguru literally could not bear this loss, which froze into a permanent pain in her heart.

Meanwhile all the customary rites were carried out. The funeral procession was large and it filled the streets. I had buried my chela, and now I was consigning my guru to dust. I had truly become an orphan. I wailed, 'God, why should I suffer so? Is there no limit to what I am to endure? Why are you taking away all my loved ones from me? Today I have become an aravani without her guru or her chela. I don't have the strength to bear the blow upon blow that keeps falling on me. I feel my heart will surely break into two.'

WE RETURNED TO the hamam, washed our hands and feet, and sat down to decide about the various rituals that had to be done by chelas for a guru. In aravani society, it is the guru who looks after her chelas, in good times as well as bad. When a guru dies, the chelas become widowed, and are meant to observe widowhood. This is our custom and practice.

My guru had three chelas and I was the eldest of them all. My kaalaguru decked us with bangles and flowers, and applied pottu on the forehead. Then aravanis from the Chaukan house—who did the final rites—came and broke our bangles, wiped the pottu off the forehead, stripped the flowers from our hair, and declared that henceforth we were widows. We were made to sit in a corner of the house. We had to remain widows for forty days and wear only white during that period.

All those who had come for the funeral from the different parivars and the aravanis of the Chaukan house consoled us. They made tea for us and bought us buns to eat. They left once it was decided when the rites would happen. As widows, we were not supposed to step outside the house. But since this was a case of murder I had to go out to the police station and also to my office.

The police suspected the aravanis themselves of this crime. When they went to question aravanis, I went along to make sure that they were not beaten or tortured. The police argued that if they could not beat people, the latter were unlikely to speak the truth! They brought to the police station all those who were with my guru around the time of the murder and kept them there from eight in the morning until midnight and sometimes even later. They were convinced that the aravanis probably knew who had committed the murder and if they gave a few clues, the murderers could be caught. So they forced out information such as who usually receives payment, which rowdy rules which territory, and so on.

What could the aravanis do? Who could they tell on? They were afraid to say anything at all, for violence would their fate if they actually told on one of these men. It was only my gurubai who had caught a glimpse of the murderers when they threatened her while she was at the tap. The police interrogated her several times. But she could not really tell them who had done it. I was present at all these enquiry sessions, accompanying the aravanis to the police station.

THE MONTH ENDED and with it the year came to a close. Everyone got ready to greet the new year. They wore new clothes and went to the temple. But not us—our situation was different. We were still in mourning; sorrow, dread and anger threatening to overwhelm us. I had to go to work. But on the other hand, I felt that the aravani world would not approve if I did not do what I was expected to do. I could not ignore aravani culture, or worse, abandon my duty to my guru. In the end, I could not give up practices that generations had observed. We waited for the fortieth day, our hearts sorrowing.

The last rites took place in a mandapam. The Hindu rites were performed in the morning—we tended the holy fire, we called a Brahmin priest to pray for my guru's soul, and we fed the poor. Aravanis of all the houses took part in this ceremony. The naik of our house did not come, and this made us all sad.

The concluding rite that aravanis do is known as *roundap* and that is done the Muslim way. Those who do the roundap are meant to give us widowed aravanis coloured saris.

That afternoon, a senior aravani from the Chaukan house handed over to us three widows the saris that other aravanis had brought for us, and also some money. She gave us the saris in our hands, and dropped the money on our laps. The first sari, always a white sari, was given to us in the name of our naik. After that, each time a sari was given, it was done so in the name of the person who gave it, the name of her parivar, her house and the tradition she belonged to.

After this part of the roundap got over, our kaalaguru stood up to signify that she was our guru now, that she would stand by us, give us courage and console us. She helped us wear our nose-rings, anklets, lajja, toe-rings and bangles, saying that henceforth she would be our guru. Despite the ornaments, a widow remains what she is. One may henceforth consider oneself a *sumangali* or a widow, but that is based on one's choice. If we were to go to certain aravani functions, all dressed up and adorned, there would be some who would deride and reproach us, 'Look at how the widow comes, all dressed up, though her guru is dead.' In memory of my guru, I have stopped wearing toe-rings and glass bangles.

DESPITE THE LOSSES I had suffered, I somehow managed to finish writing my book, *Unarvum Uruvamum*. I decided to go away and live with my parents, leaving behind aravanis, my activist work and Sangama. Back at home, I had no money. I had no desire to live off the income of my ageing father. I asked around in local NGOs for work, but was saddened to find that someone like me—a fighter interested in public good—could not get a job. I could not even earn a couple of rupees.

Suddenly, one day, my mother who had blood pressure and diabetes fainted. I admitted her in the local hospital and we learnt that both her kidneys had failed. The doctor advised me to take her to Vinayaga Mission Hospital in Salem as he could not help her.

At Salem, they kept my mother in the intensive care unit for three days and then told me that she would be able to live only if she underwent regular dialysis. I was with my mother in the hospital for twenty days. To enable her to undergo dialysis they had to carry out certain operations. First they put a tube to her neck to clean and regulate the blood flow. Then they did surgery on her hand and said that we had to look after her carefully till that incision healed. Until that happened, the blood could be cleansed only through the tube attached to the neck.

For the next three months, I took care of my mother—from helping her bathe to cleaning her after she had used the toilet. Though my father and brothers visited my mother in hospital, I was the one who stayed with her and looked after her. Initially, she underwent dialysis once a week, and then it became twice a week. My mother was not in good shape. She'd had two lakh rupees in her name, which helped with the initial expenses, but the money situation was beginning to look very bad. Each dialysis session cost a thousand rupees and it cost another thousand to hire a car to take her to the hospital. If she showed signs of being able to walk, we would take a bus. And there was no one to help me with the expenses, not even two rupees could be had from anywhere.

Around that time, I got a job offer from an AIDS prevention group in Karnataka. They offered me work for fifteen days a month. I requested my eldest brother and his wife to look after my mother, and moved back to Bangalore. I started going for the training workshops organized by the group. I had to go to whatever town in Karnataka they sent me to, to do my work. But after they put me through all their training sessions, they failed to find work for me for the promised fifteen days. I had work only for one day in a month. For a day's work, their budget comprised a *per diem* amount, research percentage (due to me as a consultant) and fees. If they could have found work for me for at least ten days a month that would have helped me meet my house rent, food and travel expenses. But with a single day's income I could not afford to live in Bangalore.

I was pushed back into poverty. I did not have the heart to go from shop to shop begging. I decided to go back to doing sex work and so returned to the hamam. Even if my gurubais were willing to look after me, and make sure I got food to eat, how long could I depend on them? I needed work of my own. I did not want to live off the labour of others, and I did not expect them to take care of me forever. So, there I was, with colour on my lips, waiting for clients.

Getting back into sex work hurt me a lot, but I did not talk about this to anyone. It was difficult to do sex work, along with my guru's chelas and naathis. I could not really earn the sort of income I did before—clients would call me 'aunty' and they preferred younger women. Sometimes there were fights over clients and additionally I experienced anxiety over my mother. These problems made me feel terrible, especially when I thought of the work I had done all these years for the rights of sexual minorities.

After my guru's death, my guru's gurubai was very supportive. She tried to instill courage in me and gave me whatever money she could. That was of great help, but I did not like taking money from her. But she would have none of that, 'How much you've earned for me! It's not as if you have ten chelas of your own or your own hamam. You've left your job, you have no income. Initially you looked after me, earned for me. Now you have nothing. I am only giving you a bit of whatever little I earn from the hamam. Please don't say no to this. You have a right to this money, just as it is my duty to give it to you.'

How long could she thus support me, though? I could not bring myself to take her money. It would help me pay my rent, but I would be unable to do much for my parents or my brother's family. An aravani could help another aravani, but could not be expected to bear her family responsibilities.

Unable to make a living, I wondered if I should end my life. Interested as I was in social struggles and working for social change, I did not have the heart to continue doing sex work. Even if I had left my activism behind, it refused to leave me! But then there is no money in activism. In aravani society, you're respected if you have twenty chelas of your own and run two hamams. None of my chelas respected me, not one of them was in touch with me. In any case, even when my three chelas were around, I did not depend on them. I had lived on my own, as a single woman. But in thinking about others, I had forgotten to think about myself.

The future reared its head in the form of a gigantic question mark. I began to wonder if at the end of it all, I would be left doing sex work for the rest of my life. But as I grew older, I would not be able to do that either. What would I do then? Unlike others, I could no longer fully inhabit aravani culture. Besides, at a time when many of my contemporaries were bosses in their own right, I would have to remain a worker.

Though I'd had my chances, I had not chosen to become a boss—I had chosen to remain alone, alienated from the community.

Finally, I went back to work at Sangama.